WITH HONOURS

GCSE (9-1)

ITALIAN

Practice Questions with Detailed Solutions

D0879670

WITH HONOURS

Website: withhonours.co.uk
Email: contact@withhonours.co.uk

First edition 2018

ISBN: 978-1-9999452-1-3

Cover design by Alessandro Migliorato, Milano

Interior design by Danijela Mijailovic

Proofread by Maddalena Alvi, PhD student at the University of Cambridge

Notices

CONTENTS

Preface

The aim of this book is to equip you with the knowledge and skills necessary to excel in GCSE Italian. Each chapter has been carefully designed in order to help you practise and perfect your comprehension of the Italian language, with 340 practice questions in total. The GCSE Italian examination tests your reading, listening, writing, and speaking skills. Of the four skills formally assessed in the GCSE, our focus will be on reading, writing, and speaking, although the book's strong emphasis on building a solid vocabulary base will also help to equip you for the listening component of the exam.

This book has been rigorously developed to ensure comprehensive and equal coverage of the different topics, vocabulary and grammar assessed in the AQA and Edexcel GCSE (9-1) Italian syllabuses respectively, from education and technology to tourism and the world of work. Each question in this book is accompanied by an 'Extra Challenge', which serves to develop your speaking, writing and translation skills, through the application of topic-specific vocabulary. Where pertinent, 'Exam Tips' are also seamlessly integrated into each chapter, providing you with tailored advice on how to navigate the various types of questions that you will encounter in the exam, as well as key strategies to improve your written and spoken Italian. For clarity and ease of use, the first 11 chapters will follow the same format: 20 multiple choice questions (MCQs) on a given topic. The final 4 chapters will then each consist of 30 MCQs, designed to test your understanding and application of key concepts in Italian grammar. Detailed and informative solutions to these questions are provided at the end of each chapter, in order to help you constructively engage with the material in a methodical and systematic manner and outline the rationale between correct and incorrect responses. To make the most out of this book, we highly recommend that you read the detailed solutions carefully.

The practice questions provided can be completed as a series of mock exams (for which we would advise a 40-minute time frame per chapter) or attempted sequentially to help consolidate your learning. You may find that you score very highly in one topic, for example education, but poorly in another, such as global issues. If this is the case, you can take advantage of the self-contained nature of each chapter and target your revision by referring to the index at the back of the book. Along these lines, there is no need to work through the chapters chronologically; you are free to start with subject areas in which you are particularly confident, before moving on to weaker areas and vice versa.

In keeping with the division of GCSE Italian into Foundation and Higher tier, a difficulty rating of Easy (E), Moderate (M) or Hard (H) has been assigned to each question. Easy and moderate questions are aimed at Foundation tier candidates, while hard questions are geared towards those sitting the Higher tier paper. Higher tier candidates are expected to complete all of the questions in this book, while Foundation tier students need only complete the questions marked as easy or moderate. That being said, we would encourage the most ambitious Foundation tier students to attempt some of the hard questions. We have purposefully ordered these questions of varying difficulty throughout each chapter. For chapters 1-11 there are 20 questions: 6 easy (E), 6 moderate (M), and 8 hard (H), and for chapters 12-15 there are 30 questions: 10 easy (E), 10 moderate (M), and 10 hard (H). The following tables provide a useful indicator of performance for chapters 1-11 and 12-15 respectively:

Chapters 1-11

Foundation Tier (Easy and Moderate Questions) (/12)

Score for each Chapter	Descriptor	Grade
<4	Further revision needed	1-2
4-6	Good performance – keep practising!	3
7-9	Very strong performance – consolidate knowledge and understanding	4
10+	Fantastic! Move on to the Higher tier questions	5

Higher Tier (All Questions) (/20)

Score for each Chapter	Descriptor	Grade
<5	Further revision needed	1
5-7	Satisfactory performance – review areas of weakness	2-3
8-11	Good performance – keep practising!	4-5
12-15	Very strong performance – consolidate knowledge and understanding	6-7
16+	Fantastic! Your comprehension and knowledge of the Italian language is very strong	8-9

Chapters 12-15

Foundation Tier (Easy and Moderate Questions) (/20)

Score for each Chapter	Descriptor	Grade
<5	Further revison needed	1
5-7	Satisfactory performance – review areas of weakness	2
8-11	Good performance – keep practising!	3
12-15	Very strong performance – consolidate your knowledge and understanding of Italian grammar	4
16+	Fantastic! Move on to the Higher tier questions	5

Higher Tier (All Questions) (/30)

Score for each Chapter	Descriptor	Grade
<8	Further revision needed	1-2
8-15	A good grammar base, now focus on the grammatical skills you find most challenging	3-4
16-19	Good performance – keep practising!	5
20-23	Very strong performance – consolidate your knowledge and understanding of Italian grammar	6-7
24+	Fantastic! Your comprehension and knowledge of Italian grammar is very strong	8-9

We wish you every success in your GCSE Italian examination and your future language learning – buona fortuna!

The **With Honours** Team

CHAPTER 1

People and Relationships

The difficulty rating for each question (Easy [E], Moderate [M] or Hard [H]) can be found in parenthesis next to each question.

1.1. Read the text below about Sara and her family. How many mistakes can you spot in the text? (M)

Mi chiamo Sara e abita a Rimini con la mia famiglia. Sono abbastanza alta e porto gli occhiali. Ho un fratello che si chiama Lorenzo e due sorella che si chiama Simona e Roberta.

   A) Two
   B) Three
   C) Four
   D) Five

Extra Challenge: Transform the details of the text above to talk about yourself and your family. (Speaking)

1.2. The questions below about personal details are each missing a word. Fill in the gaps in the appropriate order. (E)

- Come ti .... ? Mi chiamo Fred.
- ...... abiti? Abito a Durham.
- Quando sei .... ? Sono nato il 23 marzo 2002.
- Qual è la tua .... ? Sono inglese.

   A) chiamo, quando, nata, compleanno
   B) chiami, chi, nata, nazionale
   C) chiamo, dove, morto, paese
   D) chiami, dove, nato, nazionalità

Extra Challenge: Answer the questions above giving information about yourself. (Speaking)

1.3. Which of the following sentences is the correct Italian translation of the text below? (E)

I am very tall and quite thin. I have short, black hair and green eyes. I do not wear glasses.

A)   Sono molto grande e abbastanza grasso. Ho i capelli corti e castani e gli occhi azzurri. Non porto occhiali.
B)   Sono abbastanza alto e molto magro. I capelli sono neri e gli occhi sono verdi. Non porto occhiali.
C)   Sono molto alto e abbastanza magro. Ho i capelli corti e neri e gli occhi verdi. Non porto gli occhiali.
D)   Io molto alto e magro. Io i capelli corti e neri e gli occhi azzurri. Porto gli occhiali.

Extra Challenge: Change the information in the text above to write about yourself. (Writing)

1.4.   Which pair of words in the list below is **not** associated with the family? (H)

Masculine	Feminine
il padre	la madre
il figlio	la figlia
il fratello	la sorella
il fratellastro	la sorellastra
il patrigno	la matrigna
il cugino	la cugina
il nipote	la nipote
il parrucchiere	la parrucchiera
il nonno	la nonna
il bisnonno	la bisnonna
il suocero	la suocera

A)   il suocero & la suocera
B)   lo zio & la zia
C)   il figlio & la figlia
D)   il parrucchiere & la parrucchiera

Extra Challenge: Create three separate sentences using any of the family members mentioned above. (Speaking)

1.5. Below are five definitions of family members in Italian with their relevant terms. Two of the pairings are incorrect. Can you identify which two pairings are **incorrect**? (E)

- È la sorella di mio padre ⇒ mio zio
- È la figlia di mia sorella ⇒ mia nipote
- Sono i genitori di mio nonno ⇒ i miei bisnonni
- Sono i figli dei miei zii ⇒ i miei cugini
- È il nuovo marito di mia madre ⇒ il mio fratellastro

A) mio zio & mia nipote
B) i miei bisnonni & i miei cugini
C) i miei bisnonni & mia nipote
D) mio zio & il mio fratellastro

Extra Challenge: Produce three definitions for family members not included above. (Speaking)

1.6. The following table shows different adjectives that can be used to describe physical attributes and personality traits. Two words have been put in the **incorrect** column. Can you identify which **two**? (M)

Physical Attributes	Personality Traits
alto	simpatico
basso	calvo
pigro	furbo
magro	attento
i capelli castani	sincero
i baffi	ordinato
la barba	gentile
giovane	antipatico
vecchio	egoista

A) vecchio & furbo
B) pigro & calvo
C) pigro & furbo
D) magro & calvo

Extra Challenge: Describe a family member or a friend using at least 5 items of vocabulary in the table above. (Speaking)

1.7. Read the text below where Alessandro describes himself and his family members. He has made **two** mistakes with adjectival agreements – can you identify them? (M)

Sono una persona sempre felice. Vado d'accordo con mia mamma perché è molto rilassato e gentile. Al contrario mio papà può essere stressato e un po' sensibile. Di solito, non litigo con i miei fratelli dato che sono divertenti ed attivi, come me. Infine, c'è mio nonno che è una persona proprio serio.

A) felice & sensibile
B) gentile & divertenti
C) stressato & attivi
D) rilassato & serio

Extra Challenge: Turn the positive sentences above into negative ones, and the negative sentences into positive ones. (Writing)

1.8. Read through the text below about Laura's family. (E)

Ci sono ………. persone nella mia famiglia. Mia madre si chiama Elvira e mio padre si chiama Roberto. I miei genitori sono …………., e mio padre si è risposato, perciò ho anche una …………. che si chiama Silvia. Ho due fratelli che si ……….. Davide e Marco. Davide ha diciannove anni e abita a Londra. Vado ………… con mio padre perché è davvero gentile, ma litigo con mia mamma a causa …… compiti.

Which of the following group of words makes the most sense in the gaps (in chronological order)?

A) sei, divorziati, matrigna, chiamano, d'accordo, dei
B) cinque, divorziato, patrigno, chiama, bene, dell'
C) quattro, sposata, fratellastro, chiamo, male, di
D) sette, separato, sorella, chiamiamo, delle

Extra Challenge: Using the text above as a guide, write a short paragraph about your family. (Writing)

1.9. Read the following text where Antonio describes his relationship with his family. (H)

Vado sempre d'accordo con la mia famiglia perché mi fido di loro e possiamo parlare di tutto. I miei fratelli sono comprensivi e mia sorella è davvero generosa. I miei genitori mi hanno insegnato l'importanza del rispetto e del lavoro. Per esempio, faccio i lavori di casa ma lo faccio con piacere perché mi fa apprezzare quello che ricevo. La cosa più importante è che tutti nella mia famiglia mi aiutino molto e mi accettino per quello che sono.

Which of the following best describes Antonio's views of his family?

A) both positive and negative
B) only positive
C) only negative
D) neither positive nor negative

Extra Challenge: Re-write the text above to describe your relationships with different family members. (Writing)

1.10. Which of the following reasons does Luca **not** give for his difficult relationship with his parents? (H)

Mia madre si arrabbia quando sto al telefono con i miei amici invece di fare i compiti. Ma lo faccio solo perché non mi permette di uscire con loro durante la settimana. Litigo spesso con il mio patrigno perché è troppo esigente e non mi lascia mai guardare la tivù per rilassarmi un po'.

A) His mum thinks he should do homework instead of talking to friends.
B) His step-father is too demanding.
C) His mum will not let him go out in the week.
D) His parents think that he relaxes in front of the television too much.

Extra Challenge: Translate the text above into English. (Translation)

1.11. Read the text below in which Giorgia talks about her best friend, Michela. (H)

La mia migliore amica si chiama Michela e ha quindici anni. A lei piacciono tanto i film ma a me non piacciono. Preferisco mangiare fuori o andare ad un concerto. Michela ha i capelli neri e gli occhi azzurri – è bellissima! Di carattere, è molto simpatica e divertente, ma può essere un po' pigra!

Which of the following facts about Michela is **false**?

A) She is 15 years old.
B) She prefers eating out to watching films.
C) She has black hair.
D) She is very kind but can be lazy.

Extra Challenge: Write a short paragraph about your best friend. (Writing)

1.12. In the text below, Alexandra is talking about what she plans to do with her friends this evening. (H)

Stasera vado in spiaggia per una festa con i miei amici. Nel mio zaino porterò il mio cellulare, un asciugamano, perché forse andremo a nuotare, e una palla per giocare a calcio.

Which of the following items does Alexandra **not** mention?

A) a ball
B) a towel
C) a phone
D) a water bottle

Extra Challenge: Translate the text above into English. (Translation)

1.13. Read Emma's opinion about her group of friends below. (E)

I miei amici sono divertenti, ma un po' troppo chiacchieroni! Abbiamo lo stesso senso dell'umorismo e ci piace fare sport insieme. A parte questo, non siamo molto simili perché io preferisco leggere mentre i miei amici preferiscono andare al cinema.

Which of the following statements is **false**?

A) Her friends are too chatty.
B) They have the same sense of humour.
C) None of them like doing sport.
D) Emma prefers to read.

Extra Challenge: How do you view your friends? Write a short paragraph about some of them. (Writing)

1.14. Which of the following descriptions would you **not** expect to see about an ideal friend? (M)

Un amico ideale….

A) ….mi criticherebbe sempre.
B) ….sarebbe sincero.
C) ….sarebbe qualcuno di cui ci si può fidare.
D) ….mi farebbe ridere.

Extra Challenge: What would an ideal friend be like for you? Give a response using the conditional tense. (Speaking)

1.15. Matteo is talking about a disagreement with a friend. (H)

La settimana scorsa io ed uno dei miei amici abbiamo litigato a causa di una battuta. Di solito abbiamo lo stesso senso dell'umorismo ma la sua battuta non era divertente. Infatti è stata davvero scortese e mi ha offeso. Non mi ha fatto ridere. Dopo avergli spiegato perché non mi è piaciuta, lui ha capito e adesso siamo amici come prima.

Why did Matteo and his friend fall out?

A) His friend told a joke which he found offensive.
B) Matteo's joke was not funny.
C) His friend made fun of Matteo's clothing.
D) Matteo liked his friend's joke but did not fully understand it.

Extra Challenge: Translate the text above into English. (Translation)

1.16. Which of the following is the most accurate translation of the sentence below? (M)

Nowadays, young people and old people do not understand each other; there are generational differences because of money, employment and housing.

A) Attualmente, gli giovani e gli vecchi non si conoscono; ci sono divisioni generazionali grazie ai soldi, al lavoro o all'alloggio.

B) Domani, i giovani e i vecchi non capiranno l'un l'altro; ci sono differenze generazionali grazie ai soldi, all'impiego e alla casa.

C) Oggi, le persone giovani e le persone vecchie non vanno d'accordo; c'è una divisione tra le generazioni a causa dell'economia, dell'impiego e della casa.

D) Oggigiorno, i giovani ed i vecchi non si capiscono; ci sono differenze generazionali a causa dei soldi, dell'impiego e del settore abitativo.

Extra Challenge: What are the major similarities and differences between different generations in your opinion? Write a short paragraph in Italian. (Writing)

1.17. Read the text below where Stefano gives his opinions about marriage. (H)

Sto insieme alla mia ragazza da quattro anni e, per dire la verità, non abbiamo intenzione di sposarci. La nostra vita assieme è felice e non posso immaginarmi un'esistenza senza di lei. In realtà, non so se il matrimonio sia una cosa positiva o negativa. Vorrei avere figli ma non penso che sia necessario sposarsi per essere un buon genitore.

Which of the following statements is **true**?

A) Stefano and his girlfriend have been together for five years.
B) They hope to get married.
C) He is unhappy in the relationship.
D) He would like to have children.

Extra Challenge: Translate the text above into English. (Translation)

1.18. Read Martina's account of her cousin's wedding below. (E)

La settimana scorsa sono andata al matrimonio di mia cugina. È stato un giorno perfetto perché tutta la famiglia era presente e il vestito di mia cugina era bellissimo. Dopo aver mangiato un'ottima cena, abbiamo ballato tutta la notte. La mattina seguente gli sposini sono partiti per la Spagna per il viaggio di nozze.

Which aspect of the wedding was **not** mentioned?

A) the honeymoon
B) the cake
C) the dress
D) the family

Extra Challenge: Translate the text above into English. (Translation)

1.19. Read Chiara's statement about having children below. (H)

Nonostante allevare bambini sia difficile, non ho alcuno dubbio che mi piacerebbe averne almeno tre.

Which of the following statements is **true**?

A) Chiara would like to have children.
B) Chiara would not like to have children.
C) Chiara is not sure if she would like to have children.
D) Raising children is too difficult.

Extra Challenge: Would you like to have children in the future? Give at least two reasons why/why not. (Speaking)

1.20. Which of the following is the most accurate translation of the sentence below? (M)

Celebrities are not always the best role models for teenagers.

A) Le celebrità sono sempre i migliori esempi per gli adolescenti.
B) Le persone famose non spesso le migliore modelli per gli adolescenti.
C) Le persone famose non sono spesso le migliori modelli per gli adolescenti.
D) Le celebrità non sono sempre i migliori esempi per gli adolescenti.

Extra Challenge: Write a short paragraph about what makes a good role model. (Writing)

CHAPTER 1

People and Relationships

Answers and
Detailed Solutions

1.1. B

There are three mistakes in the text, highlighted in **bold** below:

*Mi chiamo Sara e **abita** a Rimini con la mia famiglia. Sono abbastanza alta e porto gli occhiali. Ho un fratello che si chiama Lorenzo e due **sorella** che si **chiama** Simona e Roberta.*

The first mistake is *abita* (he/she lives), which should be *abito* (I live) because Sara is talking about herself. The second mistake is *sorella* (sister), which should be the plural (*sorelle*), because Sara has two sisters (*due sorelle*). The final mistake is *si chiama* (he/she is called) which should also be plural as it refers to Sara's two sisters: *si chiamano* (they are called). The text translates into English as follows: My name is Sara and I live in Rimini with my family. I am quite tall and I wear glasses. I have a brother called Lorenzo and two sisters called Simona and Roberta (*Mi chiamo Sara e **abito** a Rimini con la mia famiglia. Sono abbastanza alta e porto gli occhiali. Ho un fratello che si chiama Lorenzo e due **sorelle** che si **chiamano** Simona e Roberta*).

Exam Tip: When checking for mistakes in your own work, make sure you read it through at least twice.

1.2. D

The first question asks: 'what is your name?' (*come ti chiami?*) using the reflexive verb *chiamarsi* (to call oneself). The second question asks: 'where do you live?' (*dove abiti?*); we know this as the response is *abito a Durham* (I live in Durham). The third question uses the perfect tense and asks: 'when were you born?' (*quando sei nato?*). The question must be addressing a male, because in the response we see *sono nato* (I was born) rather than *nata*, which would be used for females. The final question is enquiring about nationality (*nazionalità*). We know this from the response *sono inglese* (I am English).

1.3. C

The correct translation is: *Sono molto alto e abbastanza magro. Ho i capelli corti e neri e gli occhi verdi. Non porto gli occhiali.* Translation A is incorrect because it uses the adjectives big (*grande*), fat (*grosso*), and brown (*castani*) to describe hair colour, and blue (*azzurri*) to describe eye colour. Translation B is incorrect because the adverbs 'very' (*molto*) and 'quite' (*abbastanza*) are in the wrong place and it does not use the verb *ho* (I have) to talk about eyes and hair. Translation D is incorrect because it does not use the verbs *sono* (I am) and *ho* (I have), nor does it use the negative (*non*) to talk about not wearing glasses.

1.4. D

The only pair of words that do not describe family members are *il parrucchiere* and *la parrucchiera*, which mean male and female hairdresser respectively. The meanings of the family vocabulary are listed in the table below.

Masculine	Feminine
il padre (father)	la madre (mother)
il figlio (son)	la figlia (daughter)
il fratello (brother)	la sorella (sister)
il fratellastro (step-brother)	la sorellastra (step-sister)
il patrigno (step-father)	la matrigna (step-mother)
il cugino (male cousin)	la cugina (female cousin)
il nipote (nephew)	la nipote (niece)
il nonno (grandfather)	la nonna (grandmother)
il bisnonno (great- grandfather)	la bisnonna (great- grandmother)
il suocero (father-in-law)	la suocera (mother-in-law)

1.5. D

There are two family members that do not match the definition assigned to them. Firstly, *la sorella di mio padre* (my dad's sister) is *mia zia* (my aunt) rather than *mio zio* (my uncle). Secondly, *il nuovo marito di mia madre* (my mother's new husband) is *il mio patrigno* (my step-dad) rather than *il mio fratellastro* (my step-brother). Notice also how the definite article (*il/lo/la* etc.) precedes the possessive adjective (*mio/mia/miei* etc.) before certain family members and not others. When the family member is singular you do not need the article e.g. *mio padre, mia sorella*, unless you are talking about 'their' family member, in which case you do use the article, e.g. *il loro padre*. If, however, a shortened or lengthened name is given for the family name, the article is needed, e.g. *il mio fratellino* (my little brother). For further practice with possessive adjectives, refer to question 14.10. and 14.11. in chapter 14.

1.6. B

Pigro (lazy) should go in the personality column, while *calvo* (bald) should go into the physical description category. The other options – *vecchio* (old), *furbo* (cunning), and *magro* (slim) – are all in the correct column. Translations of the other terms can be found in the table below:

Physical Attributes	Personality Traits
alto (tall)	simpatico (kind)
basso (short)	pigro (lazy)
magro (slim)	furbo (cunning)
i capelli castani (brown hair)	attento (attentive)
i baffi (moustache)	sincero (honest)
calvo (bald)	ordinato (tidy)
la barba (beard)	gentile (kind)
giovane (young)	antipatico (mean)
vecchio (old)	egoista (selfish)

1.7. D

The two adjectives that have not been correctly agreed with the noun are *rilassato* and *serio*. Firstly, *rilassato* (relaxed) is used to describe Alessandro's mum and should therefore be feminine - *rilassata*. Secondly, although he is describing his grandfather, he says *una persona*, which is feminine, therefore for the adjective to agree it should be *seria* (serious), rather than *serio*. The other adjectives in the text correctly agree with the nouns they describe and translate into English as follows: *felice* (happy), *gentile* (kind), *stressato* (stressed), *sensibile* (sensitive), *divertenti* (fun), and *attivi* (active). Refer to chapter 14 (Adjectives and Adverbs) for further information about adjectival agreement.

1.8. A

The first gap requires a number so any of the options could be possible. However, if we count the number of family members Laura mentions (Elvira, Roberto, Silvia, Davide, Marco and herself) we can see that there are six (*sei*). The second gap requires a plural adjective because she is describing her parents, therefore *divorziati* (divorced) is the only option. Thirdly, we need a feminine family member which discounts *patrigno* (step-father) and *fratellastro* (step-brother). *Sorella* is unlikely as Laura has just mentioned that her parents are divorced and her father has remarried so the most logical answer is *matrigna* (step-mother). Fourthly, a verb conjugated in the third-person plural is required as she is describing her brothers, therefore *si chiamano* (they are called) is needed. Finally, we need the correct form of the partitive article to say 'because **of** homework'. As *compiti* is masculine plural, the only option is *dei*.

1.9. B

There are a few clues which point us to the positive tone of the text. Firstly, the use of adverbs such as *sempre* (always) and *davvero* (really) suggest a strong connection to the adjectives used, whether positive or negative. When we look at the two adjectives we see that they are positive: *comprensivi* (understanding) and *generosa* (generous). More convincingly still, if we look at the verbs, we can see that they have positive connotations: *mi **fido** di loro* (I **trust** them), ***possiamo** parlare di tutto* (we **can** talk about anything), *i miei genitori mi hanno **insegnato*** (my parents have **taught** me), *mi fa **apprezzare*** (they make me **appreciate**), *mi **aiutino*** (they **help** me), and *mi **accettino*** (they **accept** me). Finally, the phrase *faccio i lavori di casa* (I help around the house) could be viewed as slightly negative, but it is a positive for Antonio because 'it makes me appreciate what I receive' (*mi fa apprezzare quello che ricevo*).

1.10. D

The reason that Luca does **not** mention for not getting along with his parents is D, that his parents think he relaxes in front of the television too much. He mentions that his step-father never lets him watch television to relax (*non mi lascia mai guardare la tivù per rilassarmi*). He does, however, give the following reasons: my mum 'gets angry when I am on the telephone with my friends instead of doing homework' (*si arrabbia quando sto al telefono con i miei amici invece di fare i compiti*), 'she does not allow me to go out with them during the week' (*lei non mi permette di uscire con loro durante la settimana*), and 'my step-father is too demanding' (*il mio patrigno è troppo esigente*). Notice that when talking about family members in the singular an article is often not needed, e.g. *mia madre*. However, when family members are discussed either in the plural or with a diminutive (an altered word e.g. *padre* ⇒ *padrino* [godfather]) the article is needed, e.g. *i miei cugini, il mio padrino*.

1.11. B

We know from the text that Giorgia's best friend, Michela, is 15 years old (*ha quindici anni*), has black hair (*ha i capelli neri*), and is very kind and funny but can be a little lazy (*è molto simpatica e divertente ma può essere un po' pigra*). However, while Michela really likes films (*a lei piacciono tanto i film*), it is Giorgia (the speaker) who prefers eating out and going to concerts (*preferisco mangiare fuori o andare ad un concerto*).

Exam Tip: When completing comprehension tasks, it is important to be mindful of false leads, negative constructions, and the identity of the speaker.

1.12. D

Alexandra is going to the beach this evening for a party with friends (*stasera vado in spiaggia per una festa con i miei amici*). In her bag she is taking her phone (*il mio cellulare*), a towel (*un asciugamano*), and a ball (*una palla*). She does not mention a water bottle (*una bottiglia d'acqua*). There were other clues that may have pointed you to the correct answer. For example, *perché forse andremo a nuotare* means 'because perhaps we'll go swimming', suggesting the need for a towel, even if you did not know the word for towel (*asciugamano*). Equally, *affinché possiamo giocare a calcio* means 'so that we can play football' which suggests the need for a ball.

1.13. C

Emma says that her friends are fun (*i miei amici sono divertenti*), but a little too chatty (*un po' troppo chiacchieroni*). She also says that they have the same sense of humour (*abbiamo lo stesso senso dell'umorismo*) and they like to do sport together (*ci piace fare sport insieme*). Therefore, the false statement is that 'none of them like doing sport' as she says they do. Finally, she says that they are not that similar because she prefers to read while her friends prefer to go to the cinema (*preferisco leggere mentre i miei amici preferiscono andare al cinema*).

1.14. A

It is perfectly reasonable that an ideal friend would be honest (*sarebbe sincero*), someone that you could trust (*sarebbe qualcuno di cui ci si può fidare*), and someone that would make you laugh (*mi farebbe ridere*). In this vein, the only description you would not expect to see about an ideal friend would be *mi criticherebbe sempre* (would always criticise me). For further information about how to conjugate the conditional tense in Italian, refer to question 13.25. in chapter 13.

1.15. A

Matteo argued with his friend because of a joke (*a causa di una battuta*). Matteo says that normally he and his friend have the same sense of humour (*di solito abbiamo lo stesso senso dell'umorismo*) but this particular joke was not funny (*non era divertente*). Instead it was rude (*scortese*), offended him (*mi ha offeso*), and did not make him laugh (*non mi ha fatto ridere*). However, after he explained why he did not like the joke to his friend (*dopo avergli spiegato perché non mi è piaciuto*), his friend understood (*lui ha capito*) and the two of them are now friends again (*siamo amici come prima*).

1.16. D

The most accurate translation of the English sentence is option D. Although the task of translation can be regarded as subjective, as there is often more than one way to translate particular words or phrases, the alternatives suggested as answers in this question are either grammatically or semantically incorrect or just unsuitable in this context. For example, the word 'nowadays' is closest to *oggigiorno* in Italian even though *attualmente* (currently), and *oggi* (today) would also make sense. *Domani* (tomorrow) would not be appropriate, which automatically discounts translation B. 'Young people' and 'old people' can be translated as *i giovani* and *i vecchi* (as *le persone giovani* is a more literal translation). *Capirsi* is the verb 'to understand each other', therefore the best translation of 'they do not understand each other' is *non si capiscono*. Notice that *conoscere*, in translation A, means 'to know'. The most appropriate translation of 'there are generational differences' is *ci sono differenze generazionali*, while 'because of' is *a causa di* (*grazie a* means 'thanks to', and is generally used in a more positive context). Finally, although other options are suggested for 'money, employment and housing', the sentence refers to these concepts very generally rather than specifically. As such, *dei soldi, dell'impiego e del settore abitativo* is the most suitable translation.

1.17. D

Stefano's comments about marriage are fairly neutral: *non so se il matrimonio sia una cosa positiva o negativa* (I am not sure whether marriage is a positive or negative thing). He says that he and his girlfriend have been together for four years (*sto insieme alla mia ragazza da quattro anni*), but they have no plans to get married (*non abbiamo intenzione di sposarci*). Nevertheless, he says that their life together is happy and that he could not imagine his life without her (*la nostra vita assieme è felice e non posso immaginarmi un'esistenza senza di lei*). He says that he would like to have children (*vorrei avere figli*) but that you do not necessarily have to be married to be a good parent (*non penso che sia necessario sposarsi per essere un buon genitore*).

1.18. B

The only part of the wedding that was not specifically mentioned is the cake (*la torta*), although Martina does mention an excellent dinner (*un'ottima cena*). The aspects of the wedding that were in the text include the fact that all the family were there (*tutta la famiglia era presente*), her cousin's dress was beautiful (*il vestito di mia cugina era bellissimo*), and the newlyweds went to Spain for their honeymoon (*i sposini sono partiti per la Spagna per il viaggio di nozze*). The other detail included was that they danced all night (*abbiamo ballato tutta la notte*).

Exam Tip: The construction *dopo aver* + past participle (after having…) can give further variety to your writing and speaking.

1.19. A

Chiara says that although raising children is difficult, there is no doubt that she would like to have them; *nonostante allevare bambini sia difficile, non ho alcuno dubbio che mi piacerebbe averne.* She also says that she would like to have at least three of them (*averne almeno tre*). Notice the use of *ne*, which can be used to replace a noun that is introduced by a number or expression of quantity, e.g. *quanti dolci hai?* ***Ne** ho quattro* (How many sweets do you have? I have four **of them**). For further practice of *ne* refer to question 12.28. in chapter 12.

1.20. D

The most accurate translation is D for a number of reasons. Although 'celebrities' could be translated as *le persone famose* or *le celebrità*, 'are not always' needs to be translated as *non sono sempre*. Remember that negation (turning sentences from the affirmative to the negative) entails the use of *non* before the verb and often another word after the verb, such as *mai* (never), *niente* (nothing), *nessuno* (no-one), etc. Refer to questions 15.15., 15.16., and 15.17. in chapter 15 for further questions and explanation about negatives. Next, 'the best role models for teenagers' would be translated *i migliori esempi per gli adolescenti*, as *esempi* and *adolescenti* are both masculine plural nouns.

Exam Tip: When translating, ensure that you have included all the key details from the original while remembering that the word order may be different in the new language.

CHAPTER 2

Home

The difficulty rating for each question (Easy [E], Moderate [M] or Hard [H]) can be found in parenthesis next to each question.

2.1. The following adjectives could be used to describe a house. They are in pairs of opposites. (M)

How many pairs of opposites are **incorrect**?

bello/a ⇔ brutto/a
antico/a ⇔ moderno/a
sporco/a ⇔ stretto/a
ordinato/a ⇔ disordinato/a
piccolo/a ⇔ grande
spazioso/a ⇔ pulito/a
pericoloso/a ⇔ sicuro/a

    A) One
    B) Two
    C) Three
    D) Four

Extra Challenge: Translate each pair of adjectives into English and come up with three more pairings. (Translation)

2.2. Read the description below about Gabriele's house. (M)

La mia casa è estremamente grande. Al pianterreno ci sono una sala da pranzo, una cucina, un ingresso e due bagni. Al primo piano ci sono quattro camere da letto, uno studio ed un altro bagno. Inoltre c'è un sottotetto.

Which of the following rooms are **not** mentioned in the text?

    A) attic
    B) dining room
    C) living room
    D) entrance hall

Extra Challenge: Change the information above to talk about where you live, adding at least three different adjectives. (Speaking)

2.3. Read the description about where rooms of the house are located. (M)

Si salgono le scale ed il bagno è a destra. Accanto al bagno c'è una camera da letto. In fondo al corridoio c'è un piccolo salotto. A sinistra c'è un'altra camera da letto. Non c'è uno studio.

According to the description, which of the following statements is **false?**

A) The bathroom is on the right when you go up the stairs.
B) The bathroom is next to the study.
C) There is a small living room at the end of the corridor.
D) There are two bedrooms.

Extra Challenge: Describe the location of a particular room in your house using similar directions. (Speaking)

2.4. The following table contains vocabulary associated with a bedroom (*una camera da letto*) and a kitchen (*una cucina*). Two of the words have been placed into the wrong column – can you identify which **two**? (M)

Camera da letto	Cucina
una libreria	un forno
un letto	un frigorifero
un lavandino	un armadio
una scrivania	un microonde

A) un letto & un forno
B) una libreria & un microonde
C) un lavandino & un armadio
D) una scrivania & un frigorifero

Extra Challenge: Describe what is in your bedroom. (Writing)

2.5. Read the four sentences below and decide in what order the vocabulary should be added. (E)

- C'è un bell'…….. nel giardino.
- Devo pulire la casa – dov'è l'………?
- Qual è il …………. nella tua zona?
- Sono cresciuto in una ………

A) albero, aspirapolvere, codice postale, fattoria
B) aspirapolvere, fattoria, albero, codice postale
C) codice postale, fattoria, aspirapolvere, albero
D) fattoria, aspirapolvere, albero, codice postale

Extra Challenge: Translate the phrases above into English. (Translation)

2.6. The following sentences describe different places to live. Which one is **illogical**? (H)

A) Il mio paesino è molto piccolo; tutti si conoscono.
B) La città in cui abito è storica; ci sono edifici antichi dappertutto.
C) Abito in una località costiera; il mare è proprio lontano.
D) Abitare nella mia zona è caro; tutto costa tantissimo.

Extra Challenge: Write a paragraph about your local area. (Writing)

2.7. Which of the following sentence pairings is **illogical**? (H)

A) La città si trova sul mare ⇔ Si può ammirare il bellissimo panorama.
B) Ci sono molti locali notturni ⇔ Si può ballare per tutta la notte.
C) Non ci sono negozi nel mio borgo ⇔ Si possono fare acquisti.
D) Il mio villaggio è un luogo placido ⇔ Ci si può godere la tranquillità.

Extra Challenge: Say five things that you can do in your village, town, or city. (Speaking)

2.8. Read the text below and decide in which order the four missing words should be added. (E)

Se cerchi un buon libro, puoi andare in .... mentre se vuoi guardare una partita di calcio ti consiglierei di andare allo .... Se ti sentissi molto male, dovresti andare subito all' .... Se, invece, volessi nuotare, potresti andare in ....

A) ospedale, biblioteca, stadio, piscina
B) ospedale, piscina, biblioteca, stadio
C) biblioteca, piscina, ospedale, stadio
D) biblioteca, stadio, ospedale, piscina

Extra Challenge: Give three similar examples (as above) of places and why you would go there. (Speaking)

2.9. Which of the words from the following list is **not** associated with food shopping? (E)

la pasticceria, la macelleria, l'edicola, la panetteria, il fruttivendolo, il pescivendolo

A) la macelleria
B) la pasticceria
C) l'edicola
D) il pescivendolo

Extra Challenge: Which shops do you go to most frequently? Write a short paragraph about where you go shopping. (Writing)

2.10. Decide which nouns should be placed in the **two** gaps in the following sentence. (E)

Ho deciso di lasciare .... ed abitare in un piccolo .... in campagna.

A) la capitale & paesino
B) il semaforo & parcheggio
C) la coda & ponte
D) l'autostrada & stazione

Extra Challenge: Substitute the nouns in the gaps for different options (three each). (Speaking)

2.11. Liliana is talking about where she lives in the text below. (H)

Mi piace esplorare la mia città. Ogni tanto vado nel centro storico per vedere i palazzi antichi e le belle chiese – gli studenti entrano gratuitamente e per tutti gli altri ci sono sconti. Inoltre a volte andiamo alla galleria d'arte vicino a casa nostra anche se può essere un po' costoso. Più di tutto, amo passare il mio tempo nelle grandi piazze.

Which of the following statements is **true**?

A) Liliana avoids going to the historic centre.
B) There is an art gallery near her house.
C) The city is very expensive.
D) Above all she enjoys eating pizza.

Extra Challenge: Translate the above text into English. (Translation)

2.12. Read the following text about where Lucia lives. (H)

Vivo da tutta la vita in un paesino vicino a Milano con i miei genitori. Abitiamo in una casa a schiera con due piccoli giardini. Non è una casa spaziosa ma è molto comoda. Anche i miei nonni abitano nella casa accanto!

Which of the following statements is **true**?

A) She lives in Milan.
B) She lives in a detached house.
C) She lives with her grandparents.
D) She has lived there her whole life.

Extra Challenge: Change the details in the text above to talk about where you live. (Speaking)

2.13. Read the text below about Agnese's cousins. (E)

I miei cugini abitano in un grattacielo a Bergamo. Per fortuna c'è un ascensore perché loro abitano all'ultimo piano. Non hanno un giardino però hanno una vista splendida sulla città.

Which of the following statements is **false**?

A) They live in a skyscraper.
B) They live on the top floor.
C) They do not have a garden.
D) There is no lift.

Extra Challenge: Write a similar paragraph about where some of your family members or friends live. (Writing)

2.14. Marisa is talking about living in the city in the text below. (M)

Abitare in città ha tanti vantaggi perché c'è sempre qualcosa da fare. Per esempio si può andare al cinema o a teatro facilmente, e non bisogna mai andare lontano per divertirsi. Inoltre, c'è più tolleranza, diversità e rispetto per gli altri. Il problema è che c'è troppo inquinamento ed a volte la città può essere troppo faticosa, rumorosa o affollata.

Which of the following does Marisa mention regarding **both** the advantages and disadvantages of living in the city?

A) You can watch sport but it is too noisy.
B) There is always something to do but too much pollution.
C) She can see her friends easily but it is very tiring.
D) There is more tolerance and diversity but she misses the countryside.

Extra Challenge: Translate the above text into English and say in Italian whether you agree with Marisa and why (I agree – *sono d'accordo*/I do not agree – *non sono d'accordo*…). (Speaking)

2.15. Which of the following sentences is **positive** about life in the city? (H)

A) Ogni sera c'è un ingorgo all'ora di punta.
B) Ogni giorno le strade sono sovraffollate.
C) I furti sono troppo comuni.
D) Di solito il trasporto pubblico è affidabile.

Extra Challenge: Write a list of other disadvantages of living in the city. (Writing)

2.16. Which of the following is a **disadvantage** of living in the countryside? (E)

A) È tranquillo.
B) Non c'è troppo traffico.
C) Si respira aria pulita.
D) Non ci sono abbastanza mezzi pubblici.

Extra Challenge: Write a short paragraph about whether you would prefer to live in the countryside or the city. (Writing)

2.17. Read the following text in which Lorenzo describes the town where he used to live. (H)

Benché adesso io abiti a Roma, fino a due anni fa abitavo in un piccolo borgo in Umbria. Non c'erano tante strutture ricreative ma quello che mi piaceva particolarmente era il senso di comunità, dal momento che non l'avevo mai sentito in città. Ogni sera giocavo nella strada dove abitavamo con i vicini e d'estate andavo a nuotare in piscina. Il mio paese mi manca un sacco!

Which of the following statements is **false** according to the text?

A) Lorenzo used to live in Rome.
B) There were not many leisure facilities where he used to live.
C) He used to play in the street with the neighbours.
D) He used to swim in the summer.

Extra Challenge: Talk about whether you have ever moved house in Italian. (Speaking)

2.18. Which of the following is the most accurate translation of the sentence below? (M)

You must take the first street on the left and then the second street on the right. Then you must go straight on at the roundabout. After you must cross the square.

A) Devi prendere prima strada a destra e la seconda strada a sinistra. Poi si deve andare sempre diritto all'incrocio. Dopo devi attraversare la ponte.

B) Devi prendere la prima strada a sinistra e la seconda strada a diritto. Poi devi andare sempre destra all'incrocio. Poi devi attraversare la piazza.

C) Devi prendere la prima strada a sinistra e poi la seconda strada a destra. Poi devi andare sempre diritto fino alla rotonda. Dopo devi attraversare la piazza.

D) Devi prendere la seconda strada a sinistra e la prima strada a destra. Poi si deve andare sempre diritto alla rotonda. Devi attraversare la ponte.

Extra Challenge: Give directions to your favourite place from a different location in Italian. (Speaking)

2.19. In the text below, Ludo is talking about where he will live next year. (H)

L'anno prossimo inizierò un nuovo lavoro, quindi dovrò trasferirmi. Cerco una villetta in campagna dove potrò fare passeggiate ogni sera d'estate e dove spero di conoscere tutti i miei vicini. Ho una grande famiglia, perciò avrò bisogno di spazio quando verranno a trovarmi a Natale.

Which of the following are **most** important to Ludo when considering where he will live?

A) Small house, hot weather and room for family.
B) Proximity to the countryside, good relationship with his neighbours and room for family.
C) Somewhere to work, far from everyone and with a big garden.
D) In the countryside, close to work and somewhere cosy for Christmas.

Extra Challenge: What are your priorities when looking for somewhere to live? Give three examples and use the future tense. (Speaking)

2.20. Luisa has written a blog post about her ideal place to live. (H)

Se potessi, abiterei in un villaggio in compagna, ma non troppo lontano dalla città perché mi piacerebbe avere accesso a servizi pubblici come le scuole e gli ospedali. Se potessi, comprerei una casa con un bosco ed un lago vicino per poter fare le passeggiate quando voglio. Sarebbe perfetto avere una casa con una piscina e un campo da tennis. Sarebbe la casa dei miei sogni!

Where would Luisa like to live?

A) in the countryside but not too far from amenities in the city
B) far away from everything
C) far away from forests and lakes
D) in a house with a cinema

Extra Challenge: Where would you like to live if you could live anywhere? (Writing)

CHAPTER 2

Home

Answers and Detailed Solutions

2.1. B

There are two mistakes in the pairs of adjectives: *stretto/a* means 'narrow' or 'tight' and should be opposite *spazioso/a* (spacious), while *pulito/a* means 'clean' and should go opposite *sporco/a* (dirty). Using a range of varied adjectives in your writing and speaking enriches your descriptions and shows creative flare. For further information about adjectives see chapter 14 (Adjectives and Adverbs). The meanings of the adjectives in question 2.1. can be found below.

bello/a (beautiful) ⟺ brutto/a (ugly)
antico/a (old) ⟺ moderno/a (modern)
sporco/a (dirty) ⟺ pulito/a (clean)
ordinato/a (tidy) ⟺ disordinato/a (messy)
piccolo/a (small) ⟺ grande (big)
spazioso/a (spacious) ⟺ stretto/a (narrow)
pericoloso/a (dangerous) ⟺ sicuro/a (safe)

Exam Tip: Understanding and using synonyms (similar words) and antonyms (opposite words) greatly improves both your language comprehension and your language production.

2.2. C

The only room not mentioned is a living room (*un salotto/un soggiorno*). The text mentions a dining room (*una sala da pranzo*), a kitchen (*una cucina*), an entrance hall (*un ingresso*), two bathrooms (*due bagni*), four bedrooms (*quattro camere da letto*), a study (*uno studio*), and an attic (*un sottotetto*). Another way of saying 'attic' is *una mansarda*. Notice the use of 'on the ground floor' (*al pianterreno*) and 'on the first floor' (*al primo piano*).

2.3. B

The false statement is B: the bathroom is next to the study. This must be false as there is no study (*non c'è uno studio*). The other statements are true. Firstly, the bathroom is on the right when you go up the stairs (*si salgono le scale ed il bagno è a destra*). Secondly, there is a small living room at the end of the corridor (*in fondo al corridoio c'è un piccolo salotto*). Thirdly, two bedrooms are mentioned (*c'è una camera da letto* and *c'è un'altra camera da letto*).

2.4. C

The words in the incorrect column are *un lavandino* (a sink) and *un armadio* (a wardrobe). The vocabulary related to a bedroom includes: *un letto* (a bed), *una libreria* (a bookshelf), and *una scrivania* (a desk). The vocabulary related to a kitchen includes: *un forno* (an oven), *un frigorifero* (a fridge), and *un microonde* (a microwave).

2.5. A

The first gap needs to be filled with *albero* (tree), making the sentence: *c'è un bell'albero nel giardino* (there is a nice tree in the garden). Secondly, *aspirapolvere* (hoover) should go in the next gap: *devo pulire la casa – dov'è l'aspirapolvere?* (I have to clean the house – where is the hoover?). Thirdly, *codice postale* means 'post code': *qual è il codice postale nella tua zona?* (what is the post code in your area?). Finally, the fourth gap should be filled by *fattoria* (farm): *sono cresciuto in una fattoria* (I grew up on a farm). For further practice with how nouns work in Italian, refer to chapter 12 (Articles, Nouns and Pronouns).

2.6. C

The illogical sentence is *abito in una località costiera; il mare è proprio lontano* because the first half means 'I live in a coastal town' whereas the second half means 'it is really far from the sea'. The other sentences are logical. Firstly, *il mio paesino è molto piccolo* (my village is very small) corresponds with the fact that *tutti si conoscono* (everyone knows each other). Secondly, *la città dove abito è storica* (the city where I live is historical) matches with *ci sono edifici antichi dappertutto* (there are old buildings everywhere). Finally, *abitare nella mia zona è caro* (living in my area is expensive) dovetails with *tutto costa tantissimo* (everything costs so much).

2.7. C

The illogical pairing is *non ci sono negozi nel mio borgo - Si possono fare acquisti*, because if there were no shops in the village, you would not be able to go shopping. The other pairings do make sense. For example, *la città si trova sul mare* (the city is by the sea) matches with *si può ammirare il bellissimo panorama* (one can admire the beautiful view). Notice here that *panorama* is masculine, despite ending in –a. Equally, *ci sono molti locali notturni* (there are lots of nightclubs) is in line with the fact that *si può ballare per tutta la notte* (one can dance all night). Finally, pairing D is logical because 'my village is a peaceful place' (*il mio villaggio è un luogo placido*) corresponds with 'one can enjoy the tranquility (*ci si può godere la tranquillità*).

2.8. D

The first gap requires somewhere where you can find a good book (*un buon libro*) therefore it should be a library (*una biblioteca*). Secondly, if you wanted to watch a football match (*se vuoi guardare una partita di calcio*) you should go to the stadium (*allo stadio*). Thirdly, *sentirsi male* means 'to feel ill', therefore the most appropriate place would be the hospital (*all'ospedale*). Finally, if you want to swim (*se vuoi nuotare*), you can go to the swimming pool (*in piscina*). The second two examples involve the following construction: *se* (if) + imperfect subjective (e.g. *volessi*) + conditional tense (*potresti*).

2.9. C

The only shop from the list that is not associated with food shopping is *l'edicola* (kiosk/newsstand). The other terms translate into English as follows: *la pasticceria* (cake shop), *la macelleria* (butcher's), *la panetteria* (bakery), *il fruttivendolo* (fruit shop), and *il pescivendolo* (fishmonger).

2.10. A

The only nouns that make sense in the context of the sentence are *la capitale* (the capital) and *paesino* (village): *ho deciso di lasciare la capitale ed abitare in un piccolo paesino in campagna* (I decided to leave the capital and live in a small village in the countryside). The other options would not be appropriate because of the meaning of the nouns: *semaforo* (traffic lights), *parcheggio* (parking), *coda* (queue/tail), *ponte* (bridge), *autostrada* (motorway), and *stazione*.

2.11. B

The first answer - Liliana avoids going to the historic centre – is incorrect as she says that she **sometimes** goes there (*ogni tanto vado al centro storico*). The third statement - the city is very expensive - is also false because, although the art gallery can be a little expensive (*può essere un po' costoso*), visiting the ancient buildings and churches is free for students (*gli studenti entrano gratuitamente*) and there are discounts for everyone else (*per tutti gli altri ci sono sconti*). The fourth statement confuses *piazza* (squares) with *pizza*, which leaves answer B as the only true statement. We know that the art gallery is near Liliana's house from the phrase *vicino a casa nostra* (near our house).

2.12. D

Statement A is false because she has lived in a village near Milan for her whole life, rather than in Milan itself (*Vivo da tutta la vita in un paesino vicino a Milano con i miei genitori*). Statement B is false because instead of living in a detached house (*una casa indipendente*), Lucia lives in a terraced house (*una casa a schiera*). Statement C is false because she lives next door to her grandparents (*i miei nonni abitano nella casa accanto*). Statement D is therefore the only true statement because she says that she has lived in the village for her whole life (*da tutta la vita*).

2.13. D

Agnese's cousins live in a skyscraper (*un grattacielo*) on the top floor (*all'ultimo piano*), and do not have a garden (*non hanno un giardino*). There is a lift (*c'è un ascensore*), which means that statement D must be the only one that is false.

Exam Tip: When reading paragraphs such as the one in question 2.13., be alert to negative constructions, which are sometimes red-herrings.

2.14. B

Many of the answers given were mentioned by Marisa but only B (always something to do but too much pollution) were **both** mentioned. She says there is always something to do (*c'è sempre qualcosa da fare*) and gives the examples of going to the cinema or theatre easily (*andare al cinema o a teatro facilmente*), saying that you never have to go far to have fun (*non bisogna mai andare lontano per divertirsi*). Another advantage is that there is more tolerance, diversity and respect for others (*c'è più tolleranza, diversità e rispetto per gli altri*). With regards to the disadvantages, Marisa says there is too much pollution (*c'è troppo inquinamento*) and that the city can sometimes be too tiring, noisy and busy (*a volte la città può essere troppo faticosa, rumorosa o affollata*).

Exam Tip: Sometimes underlining the key words in a text can facilitate reading comprehension tasks.

2.15. D

The only positive sentence is *di solito il trasporto pubblico è affidabile* (usually public transport is reliable). By contrast, the other statements have negative connotations: *ogni sera c'è un ingorgo all'ora di punta* (every evening there is a traffic jam at rush hour), *ogni giorno le strade sono sovraffollate* (every day the streets are overcrowded), and *i furti sono troppo comuni* (thefts are too common).

2.16. D

The only phrase that is a **disadvantage** of living in the countryside is *non ci sono abbastanza mezzi pubblici* (there are not enough public services). *I mezzi* by itself can also mean 'public transport', along with *i mezzi pubblici di trasporto*. The other phrases describe the benefits of living in the countryside, including: it is calm (*è tranquillo*), there is not too much traffic (*non c'è troppo traffico*), and one breathes clean air (*si respira aria pulita*).

2.17. A

Although Lorenzo lives in Rome now (*benché adesso io abiti a Roma*), he used to live in a small village in Umbria (*abitavo in un piccolo borgo in Umbria*). Notice that the first use of the verb *abitare* is in the subjunctive as it is followed by *benché* (although). For more information about the subjunctive, refer to question 13.29. in chapter 13. The other facts are true: there were not many leisure facilities (*non c'erano tante strutture ricreative*), Lorenzo used to play in the street with the neighbours (*giocavo nella strada dove abitavamo con i vicini*), and he used to swim in the summer (*d'estate andavo a nuotare in piscina*). He also mentions how he liked the feeling of community in the village (*quello che mi piaceva era il senso di comunità*), and that he misses his village a lot (*il mio villaggio mi manca un sacco*).

Exam Tip: Look carefully at punctuation in a text for clues about the structure and possible content.

2.18. C

The most accurate translation is C because the first street on the left is *la prima strada a sinistra* and the second street on the right is *la seconda strada a destra*. Remember that *sempre diritto* means 'straight on' and *rotonda* means 'roundabout'. *All'incrocio*, by contrast, means 'at the crossroads'. Finally, *attraversare* means 'to cross' and *piazza* means 'square', not to be confused with *ponte* (bridge).

Exam Tip: Modal verbs like *dovere* (to have to), *potere* (to be able to), and *volere* (to want) are often followed by the infinitive.

2.19. B

Ludo will start a new job next year (*l'anno prossimo inizierò un nuovo lavoro*) and therefore will have to move house (*quindi dovrò trasferirmi*). He mentions three things that are very important to him: proximity to the countryside so that he can go on walks (*in campagna dove potrò fare passeggiate*), knowing his neighbours (*spero di conoscere tutti i miei vicini*), and having space for his family when they come to visit him at Christmas (*ho una grande famiglia, perciò avrò bisogno di spazio quando verranno a trovarmi a Natale*). Notice how the text is in the future tense. For further practice of the future tense, refer to questions 13.22., 13.23., and 13.24. in chapter 13.

2.20. A

Luisa says that if she could, she would live in a village in the countryside (*un villaggio in compagna*), although she would not want to be too far from amenities in the city (*non troppo lontano dalla città perché mi piacerebbe avere accesso a servizi pubblici*). She then says that she would like a house near a forest and a lake (*con un bosco ed un lago vicino*) and that it would be great to have a house with a swimming pool and a tennis court (*sarebbe perfetto avere una casa con una piscina e un campo da tennis*). She describes this as the house of her dreams (*la casa dei miei sogni*). As it talks about hypothetical situations, this text uses the conditional tense. For further practice using the conditional tense refer to question 13.25. in chapter 13.

Exam Tip: Think carefully about the type of text you are reading – it could be a blog, letter, brochure, newspaper article, or something else. This could hold clues to the purpose and content of the text.

CHAPTER 3

Education

The difficulty rating for each question (Easy [E], Moderate [M] or Hard [H]) can be found in parenthesis next to each question.

3.1. The following words are school subjects in Italian. Which four are spelt **incorrectly**? (E)

storia, matimatica, informatica, musica, spanolo, francese, lingue stranieri, geografia, disegno, inglese, tedesco, biologia, chemica, fisica, sport

A) matimatica, spanolo, lingue stranieri, chemica
B) informatica, geografia, disegno, tedesco
C) storia, matimatica, spanolo, tedesco
D) musica, lingue stranieri, disegno, fisica

Extra Challenge: Which school subjects are missing and how do you say them in Italian?

3.2. In the text below, Patrizia is giving her opinion about different school subjects. (M)

Per fortuna mi piace la scuola. Mi piace leggere e ho già letto più di duecento romanzi polizieschi. Anche se le mie materie preferite sono le lingue straniere e la letteratura, le scienze sono le materie più importanti, la chimica e la biologia in particolare. Il corpo umano mi affascina e per questo voglio trovare un lavoro nella ricerca scientifica.

Based on Patrizia's text, which of the following facts is **true**?

A) For Patrizia, literature is the most important subject.
B) She has read over 50 books.
C) She dislikes foreign languages.
D) The human body fascinates her.

Extra Challenge: Write a paragraph about your favourite and least favourite school subjects. (Writing)

3.3.   Read the text below about how Simone's subject preferences have changed. (E)

Quando ero piccolo, mia madre mi portava al centro sportivo per praticare diversi sport, quindi a scuola preferivo l'educazione fisica come materia. Mi piacevano anche la storia - perché la trovavo interessante - e l'arte perché mi consideravo una persona molto creativa. Invece adesso l'informatica mi interessa più di tutto perché vorrei lavorare per una grande società tecnologica.

What is Simone's current favourite subject and why?

A)   Physical education (PE) – he loves a variety of sports
B)   Information and Communication Technology (ICT) – he would like to work in the technology industry
C)   History – the past is fascinating
D)   Art – he is a creative person

Extra Challenge: What subjects did you used to like when you were younger/at primary school? (Speaking)

3.4.   Tina is talking about getting to school. (M)

Quando andavo alle elementari, prendevo sempre la bicicletta perché era facile e veloce. Non ci andavo mai in macchina perché i miei genitori andavano a lavoro presto la mattina. Ora vado al liceo a piedi perché posso andare con le mie amiche e abbiamo tempo di chiacchierare. Ogni tanto, se piove, prendiamo l'autobus.

How does Tina normally travel to school?

A)   by car
B)   by bus
C)   by bike
D)   on foot

Extra Challenge: How do you get to school? (Speaking)

3.5. The table below contains vocabulary related to people (*persone*) and places (*luoghi*) in school. (H)

Two words have been put into the wrong category. Can you identify these **two** words?

Persone	Luoghi
l'insegnante	l'aula
il/la maestro/a	l'allievo
il/la professore/essa	il laboratorio
il bidello	l'entrata
la direttrice	la biblioteca
il direttore	la palestra
la mensa	il corridoio
l'alunno	la sala dei professori
il compagno di classe	il campo sportivo
l'infermiera scolastica	il cortile
il supplente	gli spogliatoi

A) l'insegnante & il cortile
B) il bidello & la palestra
C) la mensa & l'allievo
D) l'alunno & l'aula

Extra Challenge: What do the above items of vocabulary mean in English? (Translation)

3.6. Massimo is talking about his school in the text below. (E)

Frequento una scuola media nel centro della mia città. Ci sono circa mille alunni nella mia scuola e le lezioni cominciano alle otto meno un quarto e finiscono all'una. Trovo le materie stimolanti e gradevoli ma secondo me l'orario è troppo pesante, dato che abbiamo sei lezioni ogni giorno e solo mezz'ora di ricreazione.

Which of the following statements is **false**?

A) There are around 1000 students at Massimo's school.
B) The school day starts at 7.45.
C) Massimo enjoys the lessons.
D) He has seven lessons a day.

Extra Challenge: What is your school day like? (Writing)

3.7. Natalia is talking about school uniform. (H)

Se avessi la scelta, non indosserei una divisa scolastica perché secondo me, tutti si assomigliano e nessuno ha individualità. Dato che la divisa scolastica è brutta, costa tanto, e non è così comoda come i nostri vestiti, penso che la nostra scuola dovrebbe vietarla. Tuttavia vedo che è davvero pratica, causa forse meno discriminazione e fornisce un senso di identità agli studenti.

Are Natalia's views of school uniform:

A) more positive than negative
B) more negative than positive
C) equally positive and negative
D) neutral

Extra Challenge: Translate the text above into English. (Translation)

3.8. Which of the following is **not** a qualification related to formal education in Italy? (M)

A) laurea universitaria
B) diploma di maturità
C) patente di guida
D) licenza media

Extra Challenge: What are the equivalents of the above qualifications in your country? (Speaking)

3.9. Below is a piece of school equipment with the subject in which it could be used. Which pairing does **not** make sense? (M)

A) un atlante – geografia
B) una calcolatrice – matematica
C) una provetta – chimica
D) un temperamatite – educazione fisica

Extra Challenge: What equipment do you need for different lessons? (Speaking)

3.10. The following phrases are activities done in class. Which one does **not** make sense? (E)

A) Durante le lezioni di francese si usa un dizionario per le traduzioni.
B) Si scrivono gli appunti sia su un quaderno sia sulla lavagna interattiva.
C) Si ascolta l'orario per sapere dove andare.
D) Si correggono gli sbagli o a matita o a penna.

Extra Challenge: Correct and write out the incorrect phrase above. (Writing)

3.11. Stefania is talking about one of her teachers. (M)

Il mio professore di matematica è spesso di cattivo umore e parla sempre di cose irrilevanti. Quando parla di matematica, non spiega bene i termini usati nell'algebra ed io non capisco niente.

Which reason does Stefania **not** mention for disliking her maths teacher?

A) He does not give feedback.
B) He is often in a bad mood.
C) He always goes off topic.
D) He does not explain the terms well.

Extra Challenge: Describe one of your teachers. (Writing)

3.12. Which of the following is **not** an attribute of an ideal teacher? (E)

Un insegnante ideale….

A)   …avrebbe pazienza quando non capiamo.
B)   …ci urlerebbe raramente.
C)   …farebbe molte domande rilevanti.
D)   …sarebbe sempre di fretta.

Extra Challenge: Describe your ideal teacher using the conditional tense. (Speaking)

3.13. Read Orlando's opinions about homework below. (H)

So che i compiti possono essere molto pertinenti ed utili per consolidare ciò che abbiamo imparato nelle lezioni, ma non c'è dubbio che i nostri professori ce ne danno troppi. A dire il vero, li faccio ogni sera senza distrazione, ma trovo che ci sia troppo da leggere e gli argomenti siano interminabili.

What reason does Orlando give for finding homework so difficult?

A)   not enough time
B)   too much material to cover
C)   it is not related to the lessons
D)   too many distractions

Extra Challenge: Write a short paragraph about the advantages and disadvantages of homework. (Writing)

3.14. Read the text below about Mauro's school trip. (M)

La mia ultima gita scolastica è stata un vero e proprio disastro. La mia classe di francese ed io siamo andati in Francia per un corso linguistico. Benché fosse un piacere incontrare il mio amico di penna, Clément, non capivo niente durante le nostre lezioni, quindi ho deciso di saltarle. Quando il mio professore di francese si è reso conto, mi ha dato due settimane di punizione – e più compiti di francese!

Which of the following statements is **false**?

A)   Mauro's most recent school trip was with his chemistry class.
B)   Clément was Mauro's penfriend.
C)   Mauro decided to skip lessons.
D)   He was given detentions and extra homework.

Extra Challenge: Write a short paragraph in Italian about a school trip you have been on. (Writing)

3.15.   Read Marcella's description of her primary school. (H)

La mia scuola elementare era rinomata nella zona e non è difficile capire perché: era ben attrezzata e moderna con un'atmosfera che favoriva l'apprendimento. I professori erano non solo competenti ma anche molto incoraggianti e giusti. Ogni aula era ben fornita e c'era una grande gamma di attività extrascolastiche. Ciò nonostante non era perfetta; mi sarebbe piaciuto che ci fossero una biblioteca più grande e più scelta nella mensa.

Are Marcella's opinions:

A)   only positive
B)   only negative
C)   more positive than negative
D)   more negative than positive

Extra Challenge: What was your primary school like? Write a description using the perfect and imperfect tenses. (Writing)

3.16.   Luisa is talking about what her ideal school would be like. (H)

Nella mia scuola ideale, ci sarebbero più .... tecnologiche, soprattutto tablet in modo che tutti gli alunni possano fare .... su internet. Oggigiorno i posti di .... richiedono conoscenze tecnologiche, quindi le scuole dovrebbero .... a questa nuova realtà. Inoltre, la mia scuola ideale avrebbe più lezioni e corsi che ci preparano al lavoro, e l'atmosfera sarebbe più ....

Fill in the blanks with the correct vocabulary in the correct order.

A) attrezzatura, apprendimento, gioco, insegnare, concentrato
B) cosa, cultura, occupazione, frequentare, risoluti
C) risorse, ricerche, lavoro, adattarsi, concentrata
D) spazio, lavoro, disoccupazione, ripetere, risolute

Extra Challenge: What would your ideal school be like? Use the conditional tense in your answer. (Speaking)

3.17. Read the following text in which Marco describes exam preparations at his school. (H)

Gli esami cominciano fra una settimana e sono preoccupato! La sola cosa buona è che sono ben preparato. Infatti ho già ripassato tanto. Anche mia sorella gemella si è impegnata molto, il che è raro! Il mio migliore amico invece mi preoccupa un po' perché non ha fatto niente: detesta ripassare e non ha tempo di studiare. La nostra classe invece ha lavorato sodo per almeno tre settimane per prepararsi agli esami.

According to the text who has **not** revised for their exams?

A) Marco
B) his best friend
C) his twin sister
D) his class

Extra Challenge: Translate the text above into English. (Translation)

3.18. Four people are talking about their gap years. Which of the following is the only **negative** opinion given? (H)

A) Il mio anno sabbatico è stato noioso; non vedo l'ora di andare all'università.
B) Il mio anno sabbatico è stato un'esperienza affascinante.
C) Ho incontrato giovani di culture diverse e quindi è stata un'esperienza molto interessante.
D) Durante l'anno sabbatico, ho fatto esperienze lavorative; è stato molto utile perché ho risparmiato.

Extra Challenge: What are the advantages and disadvantages of a gap year? (Speaking)

3.19. Read Giuseppe's opinion about university. (H)

Sento una grande pressione perché i miei genitori si aspettano che io lavori per la ditta di famiglia dopo aver finito il liceo, nonostante andare all'università sia il mio sogno.

Does Giuseppe want to go to university?

A) Yes – but he is concerned about his family's expectations for him to work
B) Yes – but he would rather work first
C) No – he would prefer to work for the family business
D) No – when he finishes high school he would like to take a gap year

Extra Challenge: Would you like to go to university when you finish school? (Writing)

3.20. Which of the following is **not** an advantage of studying abroad? (E)

Studiare all'estero…

A) …ti permette di incontrare gli altri
B) …ti dà l'opportunità di imparare una lingua
C) …ti mostra una cultura diversa
D) …ti lascia senza soldi

Extra Challenge: Would you like to study abroad? Answer in Italian using the conditional tense. (Speaking)

CHAPTER 3

Education

Answers and Detailed Solutions

3.1. A

The correct spellings of the school subjects are: mat**e**matica (maths), spa**g**nolo (Spanish), lingue stranier**e** (foreign languages), and chimica (chemistry). Most of the school subjects on the list are cognates, with the exception of: *storia* (history), *tedesco* (German), *inglese* (English), and *fisica* (physics). Other school subjects that were not on the list include: *religione, latino, teatro* (drama), and, of course, *italiano*!

3.2. D

According to Patrizia's opinions, only one of the statements given is true: she is fascinated by the human body (*il corpo umano mi affascina*). As a result of this, she would like to find a job in scientific research (*voglio trovare un lavoro nella ricerca scientifica*). Her favourite subjects are foreign languages (*le lingue straniere*) and literature (*la letteratura*), and she has read more than 200 (not 50) crime novels (*ho già letto più di duecento romanzi polizieschi*). She does, however, say that the most important subject for her is science, particularly chemistry and biology (*le scienze sono le matterie più importanti, la chimica e la biologia in particolare*).

3.3. B

In the past Simone used to prefer physical education (PE) as a subject (*preferivo l'educazione fisica come materia*) because his mum took him to a sports centre where he did a variety of sports (*mia madre mi portava al centro sportivo per praticare diversi sport*). He also liked history because he found it interesting (*la storia - perché la trovavo interessante*) and art because he considered himself to be a creative person (*l'arte perché mi consideravo una persona molto creativa*). However, now he prefers Information and Communication Technology (ICT) above all else (*adesso l'informatica mi interessa più di tutto*) because he would like to work for a big technology company (*vorrei lavorare per una grande società tecnologica*).

Exam Tip: Make sure that you pay close attention to the tenses used in texts and the tense used in the question. For more practice with the imperfect tense refer to questions 13.19., 13.20., and 13.21. in chapter 13.

3.4. D

All four ways of getting to school (by car, by bus, by bike, and on foot) are mentioned in the text therefore we need to read it carefully to find the answer. Tina used to go to primary school by bike because it was easy and quick (*prendevo sempre la bicicletta perché era facile e veloce*). She never went by car because her parents went to work very early (*non ci andavo mai in macchina perché i miei genitori andavano a lavoro presto la mattina*). At the end of the text, she says she takes the bus occasionally if it rains (*ogni tanto, se piove, prendiamo l'autobus*). The answer, however, is that she normally goes to school on foot because she can go with her friends and they have time to chat (*vado al liceo a piedi perché posso andare con le mie amiche e abbiamo tempo di chiacchierare*).

Exam Tip: Notice the use of *ci* (there) throughout the text to avoid repetition of *la scuola*, e.g. *ci vado* (I go there).

3.5. C

The two items of vocabulary that are not in the correct place are: *la mensa* (cafeteria/dining hall) and *l'allievo* (pupil). The other words are in the correct categories for people and places, as outlined in the translations below:

Persone	Luoghi
l'insegnante (teacher)	l'aula (classroom)
il/la maestro/a (primary teacher)	il laboratorio (laboratory)
il/la professore/essa (teacher)	l'entrata (entrance)
il bidello (caretaker)	la biblioteca (library)
la direttrice (head teacher – f)	la palestra (gym)
il direttore (head teacher – m)	il corridoio (corridor)
l'alunno (student)	la sala dei professori (staff room)
il compagno di classe (classmate)	il campo sportivo (sports field)
l'infermiera scolastica (school nurse)	il cortile (courtyard/playground)
il supplente (supply teacher)	gli spogliatoi (changing rooms)

3.6. D

Massimo has six (*sei*), not seven (*sette*), lessons a day (*abbiamo sei lezioni ogni giorni*). His school is in the centre of town (*nel centro della mia città*), has around 1000 students (*ci sono circa mille alunni*), starts at 7.45 (*le lezioni cominciano alle otto meno un quarto*), and finishes at 1pm (*finiscono all'una*). Massimo finds the lessons stimulating (*stimolanti*) and enjoyable (*gradevoli*) but thinks the timetable is too full (*l'orario è troppo pesante*), especially as there is only half an hour for break (*solo mezz'ora di ricreazione*).

3.7. B

Natalia's opinions about school uniform are more negative than positive. In fact, she gives five reasons why it should be banned: no-one is individual (*nessuno ha individualità*), everyone looks the same (*tutti si assomigliano*), it is ugly (*è brutta*), it costs a lot (*costa tanto*), and it is not as comfortable as our own clothes (*non è così comoda come i nostri vestiti*). She also says that she believes the school should ban it (*penso che la nostra scuola dovrebbe vietarla*). However, Natalia gives three reasons why a school uniform might be important: it is very practical (*è davvero pratica*), perhaps causes less discrimination (*causa forse meno discriminazione*), and provides a sense of identity among students (*fornisce un senso di identità agli studenti*).

Exam Tip: When giving your opinions, try to provide the other side of the argument, even if you then discredit it.

3.8. C

The only qualification not linked to formal education in Italy is C, as a *patente di guida* is a 'driving licence'. A *laurea universitaria* is a university degree, while a *diploma di maturità* is the equivalent of an A-Level and is taken at the end of *scuola superiore* (sixth form). The *esame di licenza media* is taken at the end of *scuola media* (high school/secondary school) in Italy.

3.9. D

The illogical pairing is D; *un temperamatite* means 'a pencil sharpener' and so is less likely to be needed in Physical Education (*educazione fisica*). On the other hand, a test tube (*una provetta*) is likely to be used in chemistry (*chimica*), a calculator (*una calcolatrice*) in maths (*matematica*), and an atlas (*un atlante*) or a globe (*un globo*) in geography (*geografia*).

Exam Tip: Notice how many of the words related to school equipment are cognates.

3.10. C

The phrase that does not make sense is C, because *si ascolta* means 'one listens', which does not fit with the rest of the sentence, *l'orario per sapere dove andare* (the timetable to know where to go). Instead *si guarda* (one looks at) would have been more appropriate. The other sentences are more logical and translate as follows: *durante le lezioni di francese si usa un dizionario per le traduzioni* (in French lessons, one uses a dictionary for translations), *si scrivono gli appunti sia su un quaderno sia sulla lavagna interattiva* (one writes notes either in an exercise book or on the interactive board), and *si correggono gli sbagli o a matita o a penna* (one corrects errors either by pencil or by pen). Notice the use of both *sia....sia* and *o...o*, which mean 'either...or'.

3.11. A

Stefania does not mention whether her maths teacher gives feedback (*commenti*) or not. Instead she says that he is often in a bad mood (*è spesso di cattivo umore*), talks about irrelevant things (*parla sempre di cose irrilevanti*), and does not explain the terms used in algebra well (*lui non spiega bene i termini usati nell'algebra*). As a result, she says that she does not understand anything (*non capisco niente*).

3.12. D

An ideal teacher would have patience when we do not understand (*avrebbe pazienza quando non capiamo*), would rarely shout at us (*ci urlerebbe raramente*), and would ask lots of relevant questions (*farebbe molte domande rilevanti*). They would not, however, always be in a rush (*sarebbe sempre di fretta*). For further examples of the conditional tense refer to questions 3.15., 13.25., and 13.26. in chapters 3 and 13 respectively.

3.13. B

Orlando believes his teachers give too much homework (*i nostri professori ce ne danno troppi*), there is too much to read (*ci sia troppo da leggere*), and the topics are unending (*gli argomenti siano interminabili*). Notice the subjunctive is the last two phrases (*ci sia* and *siano*); this is used because they are preceded by *trovo che* (I find that). He says that he does the homework every evening without distractions (*li faccio ogni sera senza distrazione*) and considers it to be useful for consolidating what he learns in lessons (*utili per consolidare ciò che abbiamo imparato nelle lezioni*).

Exam Tip: Notice how two of the possible answers are mentioned, and could therefore be seen as red herrings.

3.14. A

Mauro describes his recent school trip as a complete disaster (*La mia ultima gita scolastica è stata un vero e proprio disastro*). Although he enjoyed seeing his penfriend (*benché fosse un piacere incontrare il mio amico di penna*), who was called Clement, he didn't understand any of the lessons (*non capivo niente durante le nostre lezioni*). As a result, he decided to skip lessons (*quindi ho deciso di saltarle*). Unfortunately, his French teacher realised this and gave him two weeks of detention and more French homework (*quando il mio professore di francese si è reso conto mi ha dato due settimane di punizione – e più compiti di francese*). Therefore, the only statement that is false is A, as Mauro did not go with his chemistry class (*la mia classe di chimica*) but with his French class (*la mia classe di francese*).

3.15. C

Marcella describes many advantages to her primary school, including the fact that it was renowned in the area (*era rinomata nella zona*), well-equipped (*ben attrezzata*), and modern with an atmosphere that facilitated learning (*moderna con un'atmosfera che favoriva l'apprendimento*). Furthermore, she says that the teachers were not only competent, but also very encouraging and fair (*erano non solo competenti ma anche molto incoraggianti e giusti*), and that the classrooms were well resourced and there was a big range of extracurricular activities (*ogni aula era ben fornita e c'era una grande gamma di attività extrascolastiche*). However, she said the school was not perfect (*non era perfetta*). She would have liked it if there was a bigger library and more choice in the cantine (*mi avrebbe piaciuto che ci fossero una biblioteca più grade e più scelta nella mensa*). On balance, as we can see, her views are far more positive than negative.

3.16. C

The first gap should be filled with *risorse*, partly because we know a feminine plural noun is needed (because of the adjective *tecnologiche*) and partly because the sentence continues: above all tablets (*soprattutto tablet*). *Attrezzatura* (equipment) and *cosa* (thing) are both in the singular here, so would not work grammatically, whereas *spazio* (space) does not fit with the context and is a masculine noun. *Fare ricerche* (to do research) is the only logical answer for the second gap. We need 'places of work' (*i posti di lavoro*) for the third gap because 'game' (*gioco*), 'employment' (*occupazione*) and 'unemployment' (*disoccupazione*) are not suitable; the sentence means 'nowadays jobs require technological knowledge'. In the fourth gap a verb is needed. Luisa is saying that schools should adapt to the new reality of the workplace therefore the answer is *adattarsi*; again, *insegnare* (to teach), *frequentare* (to attend), and *ripetere* (to repeat) are not appropriate in the context of the sentence. Finally, we need a feminine singular adjective to describe the atmosphere, therefore the only option is *concentrata* (focused).

3.17. B

Marco is worried (*preoccupato*) about the forthcoming exams but is well prepared (*sono ben preparato*) and has already done a fair amount of revision (*ho già ripassato tanto*). He also mentions that his twin sister has worked hard (*mia sorella gemella si è impegnata molto*). His class have also studied hard for at least three weeks (*la nostra classe ha lavorato sodo per almeno tre settimane*). This leaves his best friend as the only person who has not revised for the exams; Marco is worried because his friend has not done anything (*non ha fatto niente*), hates revision (*detesta ripassare*), and does not have time to study (*non ha tempo di studiare*).

3.18. A

The only negative opinion about a gap year is A, because the year is described as 'boring' (*noioso*) and the person cannot wait to go to university (*non vedo l'ora di andare all'università*). The other experiences were far more positive. Person B says it was a fascinating experience (*un'esperienza affascinante*), person C met young people from different countries (*giovani di culture diverse*) which was a very interesting experience (*è stata un'esperienza molto interessante*), and person D got work experience (*ho ottenuto esperienza lavorativa*) and saved some money (*ho risparmiato*).

3.19. A

It is Giuseppe's dream to go to university (*andare all'unversità sia il mio sogno*) but he feels a great pressure and expectation to work for the family business when he finishes high school (*sento una grande pressione perché i miei genitori si aspettano che io lavori per la ditta di famiglia dopo aver finito il liceo*). He does not mention a gap year (*un anno sabbatico*) nor that he wishes to work before going to university (*preferirei lavorare prima di andare all'università*).

3.20. D

The one statement which is not an advantage of studying abroad is statement D: *studiare all'estero ti lascia senza soldi* (studying abroad leaves you without any money). By contrast, the other statements are positive: *...ti permette di incontrare gli altri* (allows you to meet others), *...ti dà l'opportunità di imparare una lingua* (gives you the opportunity to learn a language), and *...ti mostra una cultura diversa* (shows you a new culture).

CHAPTER 4

Leisure

The difficulty rating for each question (Easy [E], Moderate [M] or Hard [H]) can be found in parenthesis next to each question.

4.1. From the list below, which of the following is **not** a sport in Italian? (E)

la pallacanestro, il tennis, il calcio, il nuoto, il ciclismo, il figlio, il canottaggio, il footing, il pugilato, la ginnastica

A) il calcio
B) il figlio
C) il canottaggio
D) il pugilato

Extra Challenge: Translate the list of sports above into English. (Translation)

4.2. The following verbs are often used in association with sports. Fill in the blanks with the correct word in the correct order. ['…' means that no word is needed.] (M)

- Gioco ___ tennis.
- Faccio ___ jogging.
- Pratico ___ sci.

A) a, di, il
B) al, lo, …
C) a, … , lo
D) … , il, del

Extra Challenge: Create your own examples with each of the three verbs used above. (Speaking)

4.3. Read Rosa's opinions about sport. (H)

Amo il canottaggio per diverse ragioni. Innanzitutto mi dà la possibilità di stare in compagnia. Inoltre, mi piace passare il mio tempo libero all'aria fresca e le gare sono sempre emozionanti.

What reason does Rosa **not** give for enjoying rowing?

A) spending time in the fresh air
B) the races are always exciting
C) it allows her to be social
D) the training can be emotional

Extra Challenge: Translate the above text into English. (Translation)

4.4. Which of the following opinions is **negative**? (H)

A) I giochi di squadra mi danno fastidio.
B) Lo sport mi dà la possibilità di socializzare.
C) Mi aiuta a mantenermi in forma.
D) Imparo il lavoro di squadra quando pratico lo sport.

Extra Challenge: What are the advantages and disadvantages of playing a sport? Write a list in Italian. (Writing)

4.5. The following table contains sports vocabulary related to people (*persone*), places (*luoghi*), and sports (*gli sport*). There are three words that have been put in the **incorrect** column – can you identify all **three**? (E)

Le persone	I luoghi	Gli sport
allenatore	campo da tennis	pallamano
giocatore	arbitro	tiro con l'arco
equitazione	piscina	palestra
atleta	pista da corsa	pallavolo
tifoso	campo da calcio	sci

A) allenatore, pista da corsa, pallamano
B) equitazione, arbitro, palestra
C) atleta, piscina, pallavolo
D) tifoso, campo da calcio, tiro con l'arco

Extra Challenge: Write a sentence in Italian about a sport you do including one example from each category above [sport, person, and place]. (Writing)

4.6. Which of the following is the most accurate translation of the sentence below? (M)

I watch a soap at 5.30 every Friday but last Friday I watched a documentary.

A) Vedo un sapone a sei e mezza ogni venerdì, però venerdì prossimo ho visto un documentario.

B) Vedo una telenovela alle cinque e quarto ogni giovedì, ma il giovedì scorso ho veduto un documentario.

C) Guardo una telenovela alle cinque e mezza ogni venerdì, ma venerdì scorso ho guardato un documentario.

D) Guardo un sapone alle sei e mezza ogni venerdì, però il venerdì prossimo ho veduto un documentario.

Extra Challenge: Say a similar sentence in Italian about your weekly viewing habits. (Speaking)

4.7. Which of the following lists does **not** exclusively contain types of television programme? (M)

A) il documentario, il programma di sport, il gioco.

B) il cartone animato, la telenovela, le serie.

C) il telegiornale, le previsioni meteo, il poliziesco.

D) il programma di musica, la pubblicità, il romanzo.

Extra Challenge: Which types of television programme do you like and why? (Speaking)

4.8. Which of the following phrases offers a **positive** opinion about television? (E)

A) È una perdita di tempo.

B) Rende l'informazione accessibile.

C) Contiene molta violenza.

D) È nociva per la salute.

Extra Challenge: Using the opinions above and your own examples, write a short paragraph about the advantages and disadvantages of television. (Writing)

4.9. Read the text below where Matteo talks about his television habits in the past. Fill in the blanks with the correct words in the correct order. (H)

Prima guardavo spesso i .... di musica però adesso li trovo troppo moderni – ho sempre .... la musica tradizionale. Quando ero bambino, guardavo sempre i cartoni animati ma .... preferisco i documentari perché sono più seri.

A) programmi, preferito, ora
B) programme, preferita, domani
C) programme, piaciuto, mai
D) programmi, piaciuta, dopo

Extra Challenge: Translate Matteo's text into English. (Translation)

4.10. Read the text below about Roberto's film preferences. (E)

Mi piacciono molto i film di fantascienza. Di fatto vado al cinema quasi ogni settimana per vedere gli ultimi film di questo genere. Invece non mi piacciono tanto i film di guerra perché possono essere un po' noiosi e detesto i film romantici.

Which of the following film genres is **not** mentioned by Roberto?

A) westerns
B) romantic films
C) science-fiction
D) war films

Extra Challenge: Say two sentences about the types of film that you like and dislike. (Speaking)

4.11. Which of the following sentences is **illogical**? (H)

A) I film romantici mi fanno piangere: sono molto tristi.
B) Il personaggio principale di un film è il protagonista.
C) I film comici non fanno ridere: sono molto seri!
D) La colonna sonora è la musica del film.

Extra Challenge: How could you correct the illogical description above? (Speaking)

4.12. Martina is talking about a film she recently saw. (H)

L'ultima volta che sono andata al cinema ho visto un film d'azione. A dire la verità è stato un po' deludente. Il film era troppo commerciale e non mi sono piaciuti né gli attori né gli effetti speciali. Quello che mi è piaciuto di più è stata la fine perché non me l'aspettavo!

Which of the following did Martina like about the film?

A) the special effects
B) the actors
C) the advertising
D) the end

Extra Challenge: Translate the above text into English. (Translation)

4.13. Which of the following phrases does **not** refer to reading? (M)

A) Per tenermi al corrente, compro un giornale ogni mattina.
B) Il mio passatempo preferito è giocare a carte.
C) Preferisco i romanzi perché posso fuggire dalla vita quotidiana.
D) Mi piacciono le riviste perché lavoro nella moda.

Extra Challenge: Put the phrases above into the conditional tense. (Writing)

4.14. Read the following text about young people's music preferences. (H)

Un recente sondaggio tra i giovani ha indicato che la digitalizzazione della musica è diffusa in Italia. Gli studenti non hanno più una collezione di CD ma ascoltano la musica su internet o su cellulare. La maggior parte dei giovani scarica la sua musica da internet e molti ora non sanno nemmeno che cosa sia un CD.

Which of the following statements is **false**, according to the text?

A) Digitalization of music is widespread in Italy.
B) Students no longer have CD collections.
C) They listen to music online or on their phones.
D) About half of young people download their music.

Extra Challenge: What type of music do you prefer and how do you listen to music? Write a short paragraph. (Writing)

4.15. Which of the following verb + noun constructions do **not** make sense? (E)

A) cantare una canzone
B) pubblicare ad un concerto
C) suonare uno strumento
D) formare un gruppo

Extra Challenge: Say whether you play a musical instrument or not, and why. (Speaking)

4.16. The table below contains vocabulary related to music, sport and other hobbies (*altro*). Three words have been put into the **wrong** category. Can you identify all **three**? (E)

Musica	Sport	Altro
il clarinetto	la partita	cantare
il concerto	la squadra	la fotografia
il campo	la corsa	leggere fumetti
il pianoforte	lo sci	viaggiare
la chitarra	il giardinaggio	fare volontariato
il flauto	il giocatore	gioco da tavolo

A) la chitarra, la squadra, leggere fumetti
B) il pianoforte, il giocatore, viaggiare
C) il flauto, la partita, la fotografia
D) il campo, il giardinaggio, cantare

Extra Challenge: Write a short paragraph about what you like to do in your free time. (Writing)

4.17. Which of the following pairs of translations is **incorrect**? (M)

A) Stasera vado a correre ⇔ This evening I am going for a run
B) Domani faremo una passeggiata ⇔ Tomorrow we will go sailing
C) Se avessi più tempo libero farei un giro in bici ⇔ If I had more free time I would go for a bike ride
D) In futuro non giocherò a scacchi ⇔ In the future I will not play chess

Extra Challenge: Say what you will do next weekend, using the future tense. (Speaking)

4.18. Read the text below describing Sara's free time. (M)

Sara cerca sempre di fare molte attività diverse. Per esempio, le piace leggere libri e ascoltare la musica. Non le interessa più andare a mangiare fuori perché preferisce stare a casa.

Which activity does Sara **not** enjoy?

    A)   staying at home
    B)   listening to music
    C)   reading a book
    D)   eating out

Extra Challenge: Think of a friend or family member and describe what they like and do not like to do in their free time. (Speaking)

4.19. Nino is talking about what he did last weekend. (H)

Lo scorso weekend sono stato molto occupato! Di sabato ho fatto trekking con i miei amici. Quando siamo tornati, siamo andati al ristorante per pranzo. La sera ho letto un romanzo. Di domenica ho giocato a calcio con la mia squadra e poi mia nonna è venuta a trovarmi. Di solito esco ogni giorno con il mio cane, Mario, ma questa domenica non avevo tempo quindi Mario era un po' irritato!

Which of the following statements is **true**?

    A)   He walked his dog on Sunday.
    B)   He went hiking with his family.
    C)   He played football with his team.
    D)   His grandfather visited him.

Extra Challenge: Write a short paragraph about what you did last weekend. (Writing)

4.20. Which of the following sentences is **illogical**? (H)

A) Se mio fratello vincesse alla lotteria, mi comprerebbe una nuova macchina.
B) Se ci fossero più strutture ricreative nella mia città, resterei a casa.
C) Se mio zio avesse più tempo, farebbe più esercizi.
D) Se i miei nonni fossero più giovani, viaggerebbero per il mondo.

Extra Challenge: Translate the sentences above into English. (Translation)

CHAPTER 4

Leisure

Answers and Detailed Solutions

4.1. B

The only word which is not a sport is *figlio*, which means 'son'. All the other words in the list are sports. The non-cognates include *pallacanestro* (basketball), *calcio* (football), *nuoto* (swimming), *canottaggio* (rowing), and *pugilato* (boxing).

4.2. C

It is important to learn which prepositions go with which verbs when talking and writing about sport. Firstly, *giocare* is always followed by the preposition *a* (e.g. *gioco a tennis, giochiamo a calcio, ho giocato a carte*). *Fare* is generally followed directly by the noun (e.g. *faccio jogging, fa nuoto*) but it can also be followed by the indefinite article (*uno/una/un'*) (e.g. *faccio una gara, abbiamo fatto una partita*). Finally, *praticare* is followed directly by the definite article (e.g. *pratico l'equitazione, pratichiamo il judo*). For more practice with definite and indefinite articles, refer to chapter 12 (Articles, Nouns and Pronouns).

4.3. D

The speaker gives several reasons for loving rowing including spending time in the fresh air (*mi piace passare il mio tempo libero all'aria fresca*), exciting races (*le gare sono sempre emozionanti*), and opportunities for socializing (*mi dà la possibilità di stare in compagnia*). Notice firstly that 'training' (*allenamento*) is not mentioned, and secondly that the false friend *emozionante* (exciting) is present; remember, *emotivo* means 'emotional'.

4.4. A

The negative opinion given is that *i giochi di squadra mi danno fastidio* (team sports annoy me). All the other opinions are positive. For example, *lo sport mi dà la possibilità di socializzare* means that 'sports give me an opportunity to socialise'. Furthermore, *mi aiuta a mantenermi in forma* means 'it helps me keep in shape', while *imparo il lavoro di squadra quando pratico lo sport* translates as 'I learn teamwork when I do sport'.

Exam Tip: Be confident in expressing the advantages and disadvantages of different topics, e.g. playing sport, technology, the environment, where to live, etc.

4.5. B

Equitazione means 'horse-riding' and should go in the 'sports' category, *arbitro* means 'referee' and should go in the 'people' category, and *palestra* means 'gym' so should go in the 'places' column (although it can also mean 'exercise' more generally). See the table below for the correct answers with their English translations.

Le persone	I luoghi	Gli sport
allenatore (coach) giocatore (player) atleta (athlete) tifoso (fan) arbitro (referee)	campo da tennis (tennis court) palestra (gym) piscina (swimming pool) pista da corsa (running track) campo da calcio (football pitch)	pallamano (handball) tiro con l'arco (archery) equitazione (horse-riding) pallavolo (volleyball) sci (skiing)

4.6. C

The first translation can be disregarded because it translates 'soap' as *sapone*, which is the type of soap one washes with, rather than a TV soap (*una telenovela*). The second translation can be disregarded because it says Thursday (*giovedì*) instead of Friday (*venerdì*). Finally, the fourth translation is incorrect because in the second clause it says next Friday (*venerdì prossimo*) rather than last Friday (*venerdì scorso*). Some of the translations also mix the verbs 'to watch' (*guardare*) and 'to see' (*vedere*). The correct translation should therefore be: *Guardo una telenovela alle cinque e mezza ogni venerdì, ma venerdì scorso ho guardato un documentario.*

4.7. D

Three of the lists only contain types of television programme. These programmes include: *il documentario, il programma di sport, il gioco* (a gameshow), *il cartone animato* (a cartoon), *la telenovela* (a soap), *le serie, il telegiornale* (the news), *le previsioni meteo* (the weather), and *il poliziesco* (a crime drama). List D contains one television programme (*il programma di musica*) along with the words for 'advert' (*la pubblicità*) and 'novel' (*il romanzo*). Notice that the word for 'programme' in Italian (*il programma*) is masculine, despite ending in –a, just like *panorama* and *clima* (refer to question 12.4. in chapter 12 for more information about masculine nouns).

4.8. B

The only positive opinion given about television was opinion B: *rende l'informazione accessibile* (it makes information accessible). The other opinions are more negative: *è una perdita di tempo* (it is a waste of time), *contiene molta violenza* (it contains a lot of violence), and *è nociva per la salute* (it is harmful to one's health).

4.9. A

The first blank needs to be *programmi* because it is masculine plural (remember that *programma* is masculine despite ending in –a). The second gap should be filled with *preferito*, firstly because a past participle does not agree when the auxiliary is *avere*, and secondly because *piaciuto* would need to be used as follows: *mi è piaciuta la musica tradizionale*. Thirdly, the time phrase needed must be one that relates to the present and is positive, so *ora* (now) is the only one that would fit. *Mai* (never), *domani* (tomorrow), and *dopo* (after) would not work in the context.

4.10. A

The only film type not mentioned in the paragraph were 'westerns' (*i film western*). Romantic films (*i film romantici*), science-fiction films (*i film di fantascienza*), and war films (*i film di guerra*) were all mentioned in the text. Remember that when describing films the third-person plural of the verb *piacere* is needed, e.g. *mi **piacciono** i film di azione*.

4.11. C

The sentence with an incorrect description is *i film comici non fanno ridere: sono molto seri!* (comedy films do not make you laugh: they are very serious!). To make the sentence logical you could remove the *non* and replace *seri* with *buffi* or *divertente* (funny). The other sentences make sense: *i film romantici mi fanno piangere: sono molto tristi* (romantic films make me cry; they are very sad), *il personaggio principale di un film è il protagonista* (the main character of a film is the protagonist), and *la colonna sonora è la musica del film* (the soundtrack is the music in the film).

4.12. D

Martina liked the end of the film because she was not expecting it (*mi è piaciuto è stata **la fine** perché non me l'aspettavo*). However, she also said that the film was disappointing (*deludente*), too commercial (*troppo commerciale*) and she did not like the actors (*gli attori*) nor the special effects (*gli effetti speciali*). For further practice of the perfect tense, refer to questions 13.14., 13.15., and 13.16. in chapter 13.

4.13. B

The second phrase is about playing cards, and does not relate to reading: *il mio passatempo preferito è giocare a carte* (my favourite hobby is playing cards). The other phrases all relate to reading different things: *per tenermi al corrente, compro un giornale ogni mattina* (to stay informed, I buy a newspaper every morning), *preferisco i romanzi perché posso fuggire dalla vita quotidiana* (I prefer novels because I can escape daily life), and *mi piacciono le riviste perché lavoro nella moda* (I like magazines because I work in fashion).

4.14. D

The statement that 'about half of young people download their music' is false because the text says *la maggior parte dei giovani scarica la sua musica da internet* (most young people download their music from the internet). The other statements are correct. The digitalization of music is widespread in Italy (*la digitalizzazione della musica è diffusa in Italia*). Students no longer have CD collections (*gli studenti non hanno più una collezione di CD*). They listen to music online or on their phones (*ascoltano la musica su internet o su cellulare*). Notice the use of the word *diffusa* (widespread), and the use of the negative construction *non...più* around the verb to mean 'no longer/any more'.

4.15. B

The phrase that makes little sense is *pubblicare ad un concerto* (to publish at a concert). It would be more logical to say *pubblicare un CD* (to release a CD) or *recitare ad un concerto* (to perform in a concert). The other phrases make more sense: *cantare una canzone* (to sing a song), *suonare uno strumento* (to play an instrument), and *formare un gruppo* (to form a band).

Exam Tip: Be sure to remember the difference between *suonare* (to play [an instrument]) and *giocare* (to play [a game/sport]).

4.16. D

The three words in list D (*il campo, il giardinaggio, cantare*) are not in the correct columns. *Il campo* means 'the pitch' and therefore belongs in the 'sport' column, *il giardinaggio* is 'gardening' and should be in the 'other' category, and *cantare* means 'to sing' so belongs in the 'music' section. See the table below for the meanings of all the vocabulary in the table.

Musica	Sport	Altro
il clarinetto (clarinet) il concerto (concert) il pianoforte (piano) la chitarra (guitar) il flauto (flute) **cantare (to sing)**	la partita (match) la squadra (team) la corsa (race) lo sci (skiing) il giocatore (player) **il campo (pitch)**	la fotografia (photography) leggere fumetti (to read comics) viaggiare (to travel) fare volontariato (to do volunteering) gioco da tavolo (board game) **il giardinaggio (gardening)**

4.17. B

Translation B is incorrect because *faremo una passeggiata* means 'we will go for a walk' (not 'we will go sailing'); remember that *la vela* is 'sailing'. The other translation pairings are correct. *Stasera farò footing* (this evening I am going for a run), *se avessi più tempo libero farei un giro in bici* (if I had more free time I would go for a bike ride), and *in futuro non giocherò a scacchi* (in the future I will not play chess).

Exam Tip: Notice how very often the time phrase in the sentence will indicate which tense should be used, e.g. *domani* – future tense.

4.18. D

Sara is no longer interested in eating out (*non le interessa più andare a mangiare fuori*). Instead she prefers to stay at home (*preferisce stare a casa*). We also find out that she likes reading books and listening to music (*le piace leggere libri e ascoltare la musica*).

Exam Tip: Remember to include information about other people (not just first-person perspectives) when you are writing and speaking.

4.19. C

The only true statement from the list is C; we know Nino played football with his team as he says *ho giocato a calcio con la mia squadra*. The other statements are false. Firstly, he did not walk his dog on Sunday because he did not have time (*non avevo tempo*). Secondly, he did go hiking but not with his family. Instead he went with his friends (*ho fatto trekking con i miei amici*). Finally, it was his grandmother – not his grandfather – who visited him (*mia **nonna** è venuta a trovarmi*).

4.20. B

The illogical sentence is B: *se ci fossero più strutture ricreative, resterei a casa*, because if there were more leisure facilities in the city, the speaker would be unlikely to stay at home. The other sentences are logical and translate as follows: *se mio fratello vincesse alla lotteria, mi comprerebbe una nuova macchina* (if my brother won the lottery, he would buy me a new car), *se mio zio avesse più tempo, farebbe più esercizi* (if my uncle had more time, he would do more exercise), and *se i miei nonni fossero più giovani, viaggerebbero per il* mondo (if my grandparents were younger they would travel around the world). All the phrases in question 4.20. use the construction *se* (if) + imperfect subjective (e.g. *vincesse*) + conditional tense (*comprerebbe*).

Exam Tip: Using a construction with *se* (if) can add variety to your sentences and uses two different tenses in quick succession.

CHAPTER 5

Technology

The difficulty rating for each question (Easy [E], Moderate [M] or Hard [H]) can be found in parenthesis next to each question.

5.1. Read the following newspaper headline. (M)

Gli esperti dicono che la tecnologia può diminuire la qualità del nostro sonno.

What can technology diminish according to the experts?

A) our work
B) our relationships
C) our exercise
D) our sleep

Extra Challenge: Repeat the newspaper headline using the other three options listed above. (Speaking)

5.2. Which of the following is **not** a piece of technological equipment? (H)

A) un lettore DVD
B) un mobile
C) un portatile
D) un tablet

Extra Challenge: What types of technology do you use? (Speaking)

5.3. Read the text below about how Gianna uses technology. (E)

Sin da bambina ho sempre amato la tecnologia. Quando ero più piccola, giocavo ai videogiochi ma adesso uso la tecnologia per prenotare gli alberghi, chattare con amici e comprare vestiti.

Which of the following does Gianna **not** use technology for any more?

A) to book hotels
B) to chat with friends
C) to buy clothes
D) to play videogames

Extra Challenge: How has the way in which you use technology changed over time? You may wish to use the text above to help structure your answer. (Writing)

5.4. Read the text below about Antonio's mother and technology. (E)

Recentemente mia mamma ha provato una .... senza tecnologia perché è dipendente. Il primo giorno .... andata in palestra invece di navigare su internet. Il secondo giorno ha fatto una .... nel parco con sua sorella invece di guardare la televisione.

Fill in the gaps with the correct list of words in the correct order.

A) settimana, è, passeggiata
B) mese, ha, bicicletta
C) giorno, hanno, pizza
D) anno, sono, judo

Extra Challenge: Answer the following question: *potresti sopravvivere un giorno senza tecnologia?* (Could you survive a day without technology?) (Speaking)

5.5. Below are four definitions with four terms related to technology. Two of the definitions, however, do not match their respective words. Which **two** terms should be switched over? (E)

Un blog – una pagina web dove le persone possono scrivere articoli o commentare su temi diversi
Gli internauti – un messaggio mandato col cellulare
La pubblicità – il mezzo per far conoscere alla gente un prodotto o informazione
Un SMS – le persone che utilizzano la rete

A) Un blog & la pubblicità
B) Un blog & un SMS
C) Un'internauta & la pubblicità
D) Un'internauta & un SMS

Extra Challenge: Use the four terms in four different sentences. (Speaking)

5.6. Susanna describes some of the disadvantages of technology below. (H)

Lo svantaggio principale della tecnologia è che i giovani non imparano nulla di pratico. Per esempio non sanno né cucinare né scrivere una lettera. Inoltre, nel passato i bambini potevano divertirsi in maniera semplice, invece, oggigiorno si annoiano rapidamente senza tecnologia.

Which of the following statements does Susanna **not** mention?

A) Young people do not learn life skills like cooking and letter writing.
B) In the past children entertained themselves.
C) Children today get bored quickly.
D) Technology causes tensions between different generations.

Extra Challenge: What are some of the advantages of technology? (Speaking)

5.7. Which of the following nouns does **not** relate to a computer? (H)

A) la tastiera
B) la stampante
C) il cellulare
D) lo schermo

Extra Challenge: Use each of the four words above in a sentence. (Speaking)

5.8. Which of the following phrases does **not** relate to an action you would do on a computer? (E)

A) scaricare un film
B) navigare su internet
C) caricare un video
D) apparecchiare la tavola

Extra Challenge: Write two sentences about how (and how often) you use technology. (Writing)

5.9. Which of the following words does **not** relate to the internet? (M)

A) la rete
B) l'aceto
C) in linea
D) la banda larga

Extra Challenge: Use the internet-related words above in three separate sentences. (Speaking)

5.10. Read the text below about Italians' use of the internet. (M)

Gli italiani usano la rete per mandare posta elettronica, cercare informazioni e guardare la televisione.

Which of the following uses is **not** mentioned?

A) sending emails
B) using social networks
C) looking up information
D) watching television

Extra Challenge: What do you use the internet for? (Speaking)

5.11. Which of the following is the only **good** habit associated with people using the internet? (M)

A) Passo troppe ore su internet.
B) Non riesco a vivere senza internet.
C) Non parlo mai con sconosciuti in linea.
D) La protezione dei dati personali non mi interessa.

Extra Challenge: Translate the four habits above into English. (Translation)

5.12. Read the following extract from a newspaper article. (H)

Secondo una recente indagine, la città italiana con la percentuale più alta di internauti è Milano, mentre a Roma gli uomini utilizzano internet più delle donne.

According to the extract, which of the following statements is **true**?

A) More people use the internet in Rome.
B) More women are internet users in Milan than Rome.
C) Milan is the Italian city with the highest percentage of internet users.
D) The percentage of men in Rome is lower than in Milan.

Extra Challenge: Translate the extract above into English. (Translation)

5.13. Read the text below in which Giulia warns about the dangers of the internet. (H)

Benché internet possa essere molto utile, è anche pericoloso. Non solo il furto d'identità e la frode sono diventati sempre più comuni in rete ma anche i nuovi giochi d'azzardo creano sempre più dipendenza tra gli utenti.

Which of the following dangers of the internet does Giulia **not** mention?

A) fake news
B) identity theft
C) fraud
D) gambling

Extra Challenge: Write a short paragraph about the dangers of the internet. (Writing)

5.14. Which of the following is the most accurate translation of the sentence below? (E)

My current email address is not working.

A) Il mio indirizzo email attuale non funziona.
B) Il mio attuale incinta email non funziona.
C) Il mio incinta attuale di email non lavora.
D) Il mio attuale indirizzo email non lavora.

Extra Challenge: Do you prefer to communicate online or face-to-face? (Speaking)

5.15. Read through the following text about the advantages and dangers of mobile phones. (H)

I cellulari rappresentano uno sviluppo tecnologico enorme. Nonostante tutto però gli esperti mettono in dubbio che questo progresso sia davvero positivo per la società. Se da un lato, possiamo stare in contatto con la nostra famiglia facilmente e forse ci sentiamo più sicuri con il cellulare a portata di mano, d'altra parte, questa tecnologia può distrarre gli studenti dal lavoro, danneggiare le amicizie e facilitare il cyberbullismo.

What reasons are given for the **positive** impact of mobile phones?

A) safety & a revision tool
B) contact with family & safety
C) contact with family & making new friends
D) a revision tool & making new friends

Extra Challenge: What other advantages are there to having a mobile phone? (Speaking)

5.16. Re-read the text in question 5.15. above. (H)

Which of the following is **not** given as a disadvantage of mobile phones?

A) They can ruin friendships.
B) They can be a distraction from work.
C) They can facilitate crime.
D) They can be a means for cyberbullying.

Extra Challenge: Write a short paragraph about if, when, and why you use a mobile phone. (Writing)

5.17. Franco is giving his opinion about mobile phones. (M)

Non c'è dubbio che i cellulari abbiano migliorato la nostra vita sociale, sviluppato la nostra conoscenza del mondo e semplificato il nostro lavoro.

Are Franco's opinions:

A)   only positive
B)   only negative
C)   both positive and negative
D)   neither positive nor negative

Extra Challenge: Translate Franco's text into English. (Translation)

5.18.   Read the following advice given to users of social networks. (M)

Quando usi i social network è importante che tu segua questi semplici consigli. Dovresti: 1) cambiare la password regolarmente, 2) verificare chi può vedere i tuoi posts e, 3) non postare mai niente che non diresti a tua nonna!

Which of the following pieces of advice is **not** mentioned above?

A)   change your password regularly
B)   only add people that you know
C)   check who can see your posts
D)   never post anything that you would not say to your grandma

Extra Challenge: Add three extra pieces of advice about social media use that have not been included above. (Speaking)

5.19.   Read the text below in which Oriana shares her story about social media. (H)

Non uso più i social network perché il mese scorso uno sconosciuto mi ha mandato dei messaggi sessisti ed offensivi sotto falso nome che mi hanno profondamente sconvolto. Secondo me, quando una persona si sente nell'anonimato su internet crede di poter dire quello che vuole senza alcuna conseguenza.

Why does Oriana no longer use social networks?

A) She feels anonymous.
B) She received unpleasant messages from a friend.
C) She received unpleasant messages from a stranger.
D) She received too many messages.

Extra Challenge: Translate the above text into English. (Translation)

5.20. Which of the following is a **disadvantage** of social networks? (E)

A) Ti confronti con altri.
B) Rimani in contatto coi vecchi amici.
C) Ti informi sulle ultime notizie.
D) Puoi condividere le foto.

Extra Challenge: Write a short paragraph about the advantages and disadvantages of social networks. (Writing)

CHAPTER 5

Technology

Answers and Detailed Solutions

5.1. D

The key word to help us identify the answer is *sonno*, which means 'sleep', therefore the sentence *oggigiorno gli esperti dicono che la tecnologia può diminuire la qualità del nostro sonno* translates as 'nowadays the experts say that technology can diminish the quality of our sleep'. The other three options would have been: *nostro lavoro* (our work), *nostri rapporti* (our relationships), and *nostro esercizio* (our exercise).

5.2. B

When talking about technology *un mobile* is a false friend as it means 'a piece of furniture' (or as an adjective *mobile* means 'moveable'). The other items in the list are pieces of technological equipment: *un lettore DVD* (a DVD player), *un portatile* (a laptop), and *un tablet* (a tablet).

Exam Tip: Watch out for false friends when completing reading and listening tasks.

5.3. D

Gianna used to play videogames (*giocavo ai videogiochi*) but now she uses technology for booking hotels (*prenotare gli alberghi*), chatting with friends (*chattare con amici*), and buying clothes (*comprare vestiti*). Notice the difference between the imperfect tense (*giocavo*) and the present tense (*uso*). There are also some time markers that help us to identify the correct answer: 'when I was younger' (*quando ero più piccola*) and 'but now' (*ma adesso*).

5.4. A

Antonio talks about how his mum tried to go a week without technology because she is a little addicted to it (*mia mamma ha provato una settimana senza tecnologia perché è dipendente*). *Settimana* must go in the first gap as it is the only time phrase mentioned that is feminine. *Mese* (month), *giorno* (day), and *anno* (year) are all masculine and so would be preceded by *un*. Secondly, *è* is needed as the verb *andare* (to go) takes *essere* as its auxiliary in the perfect tense therefore *ha* is not appropriate. *Hanno* and *sono* do not work either as they are in the third-person plural (*loro*). Finally, while *pizza* would have also made sense in the context, *passeggiata* (walk) was the most logical answer. Notice too the use of *invece di* (instead of) to make comparisons.

5.5. D

The definition of *gli internauti* (internet users) should be *le persone che utilizzano la rete* (people who use the web), while un SMS should be defined as *un messaggio mandato col cellulare* (a message sent with a mobile phone). The other two definitions are with their correct terms. *La pubblicità* means 'advertising' and as such is defined as *il mezzo per far conoscere alla gente un prodotto o informazione* (the way of making people aware of a product or information). Finally, *un blog* is defined as *una pagina web dove le persone possono scrivere articoli o commentare su temi diversi* (a web page where people can write articles or comment on different issues).

5.6. D

Susanna believes that the main disadvantage of technology (*lo svantaggio principale della tecnologia*) is that young people do not learn practical skills (*i giovani non imparano nulla di pratico*). She gives the examples of not knowing how to cook nor write letters (*non sanno né cucinare né scrivere una lettera*). She then gives a comparison with the past, saying that children used to be able to entertain themselves easily (*i bambini potevano divertirsi in maniera semplice*), while nowadays, without technology, they get bored quickly (*oggigiorno si annoiano rapidamente senza tecnologia*).

5.7. C

The noun that is not directly related to computers is *il cellulare* (mobile phone). The others are components or accessories of a computer: *la tastiera* (keyboard), *la stampante* (printer), and *lo schermo* (the screen). Unlike a lot of vocabulary linked to technology, these words are not cognates and therefore need to be learned independently.

5.8. D

The only phrase that does not relate to a computer-based action is *apparecchiare la tavola* (to lay the table). The other phrases are all actions that would generally be done online: *scaricare un film* (to download a film), *navigare su internet* (to surf the internet), and *caricare un video* (to upload a video). Notice how the prefix 's' before a verb (e.g. *scaricare*) is often used to create the opposite, e.g. *vantaggio* (advantage) ⇒ *svantaggio* (disadvantage), *fortuna* (luck) ⇒ *sfortuna* (misfortune).

5.9. B

The only word in the list that does not relate to the internet explicitly is *l'aceto* (vinegar). The other items of vocabulary are often used when referring to the internet: *la rete* (the net/web), *in linea* (online), and *la banda larga* (broadband).

5.10. B

Using social networks (*utilizzare i social network*) was the only use not mentioned in the sentence. The other uses of the internet include: *mandare posta elettronica* (sending emails), *cercare informazioni* (looking up information), and *guardare la televisione* (watching television).

5.11. C

The only possible good habit listed for people using the internet is *non parlo mai con sconosciuti in linea* (I never talk to strangers online). The other habits are likely to be negative: *passo troppe ore su internet* (I spend too many hours on the internet), *non riesco a vivere senza internet* (I cannot live without the internet), and *la protezione dei dati personali non mi interessa* (I am not interested in protecting personal data).

5.12. C

The true statement is that 'Milan is the Italian city with the highest percentage of internet users' (*la città italiana con la percentuale più alta di internauti è Milano*). The second part of the sentence informs us that in Rome more men use the internet than women (*a Roma gli uomini utilizzano internet più delle donne*).

5.13. A

Giulia starts by saying that although the internet can be very useful, it is also dangerous (*benché l'internet possa essere molto utile, è anche pericoloso*). She then mentions that identity theft (*il furto d'identità*) and fraud (*la frode*) are becoming more and more common online (*sono diventati sempre più comuni in rete*), and then says that users are becoming more and more addicted to new gambling games (*i nuovi giochi d'azzardo creano sempre più dipendenza tra gli utenti*). The danger that Giulia does not mention is therefore A, fake news.

5.14. A

The most appropriate translation for 'my current email address is not working' is *il mio indirizzo email attuale non funziona*. Firstly, 'email address' in Italian is *indirizzo email* not *incinta* (pregnant). Secondly, the adjective *attuale* (current) needs to go after the noun *(il mio indirizzo email)* as is typical in Italian – refer to questions 14.2. and 14.3. in chapter 14 for further practice with adjectival placement. Thirdly, the verb *funzionare* means 'to work' in the sense of functioning properly, whereas the verb *lavorare* means 'to work' in the sense of employment.

5.15. B

Contact with family (*stare in contatto con la nostra famiglia*) and feeling safe (*ci sentiamo più sicuri*) are cited as the primary reasons why having a mobile close to hand (*a portata di mano*) may be positive. Ensure you read through the text carefully for a second time before attempting the questions.

Exam Tip: When lots of adverbs and adjectives are used in a text (like in question 5.15.), attempt to understand the gist of the passage by picking out the verbs and nouns used before tackling the meaning of the whole text.

5.16. C

Three negative implications of mobile phones are set out in the text in question 5.15., these include the fact that they can distract students from work (*distrarre gli studenti dal lavoro*), damage friendships (*danneggiare le amicizie*), and facilitate cyberbullying (*facilitare il cyberbullismo*).

5.17. A

Franco's opinions are only positive and he gives three distinct reasons. Firstly, he says that mobile phones have improved our social lives (*i cellulari abbiano migliorato la nostra vita sociale*). Secondly, he says that they have developed our understanding of the world (*sviluppato la nostra conoscenza del mondo*). Thirdly, he says that they have simplified our work (*semplificato il nostro lavoro*).

5.18. B

The only piece of advice not mentioned in the text is B: only add people that you know. The text starts by saying: when you use social networks, it is important that you follow this simple advice (*quando usi i social network è importante che tu segua questi consigli semplici*). The advice is that you should (*dovresti*): change your password regularly (*cambiare la password regolarmente*), check who can see your posts (*verificare chi può vedere i tuoi posts*), and never post anything that you would not say to your grandma (*non postare mai niente che non diresti a tua nonna!*).

5.19. C

Oriana no longer uses social networks because of an incident last month (*il mese scorso*). She says that a stranger sent her sexist and offensive messages under a false name (*uno sconosciuto mi ha mandato i messaggi sessisti ed offensivi sotto falso nome*). As a result, she believes that when a person feels anonymous online they can say what they like without repercussions (*quando una persona si sente nell'anonimato su internet crede di poter dire quello che vuole senza alcuna conseguenza*).

5.20. A

The disadvantage mentioned with regard to social networks is that you compare yourself to others (*ti confronti con altri*). The advantages of social media mentioned in the other three answers include: you stay in touch with old friends (*rimani in contatto coi vecchi amici*), you keep up to date with the latest news (*ti informi sulle ultime notizie*), and you can share photos (*puoi condividere le foto*).

CHAPTER 6

The World of Work

The difficulty rating for each question (Easy [E], Moderate [M] or Hard [H]) can be found in parenthesis next to each question.

6.1. Look at the list of jobs in Italian. Which two words should **not** be in the list? (E)

diplomatico, commesso, cameriere, cassiere, tovagliolo, infermiera, calciatore, professore, dottore, direttore, specchio, giudice, interprete, cantante, pilota, dentista

    A)   commesso & cantante
    B)   cameriere & pilota
    C)   specchio & tovagliolo
    D)   cassiere & giudice

Extra Challenge: Translate the vocabulary above into English. (Translation)

6.2. Many job titles in Italian are the same in their masculine and feminine forms. Which of the following lists contains words that are the **same** for both males and females? (H)

    A)   avvocato, professore, direttore
    B)   camionista, giornalista, capo
    C)   cuoco, dottore, macellaio
    D)   scrittore, segretario, maestro

Extra Challenge: Write a list of other job titles in Italian which are the same in masculine and feminine forms. (Writing)

6.3. Which of the following do **not** relate to work and employment? (M)

guadagnare, lavorare, impiegare, licenziare, nascondere, andare in pensione, fare domanda, avere un colloquio

    A)   impiegare
    B)   nascondere
    C)   licenziare
    D)   fare domanda

Extra Challenge: Translate the verbs and verbal phrases above into English. (Translation)

6.4.   Which of the following verbs does **not** mean 'to send'? (E)

A)   andare
B)   mandare
C)   spedire
D)   inviare

Extra Challenge: Use each of the four verbs above in a different sentence. (Speaking)

6.5.   Read the five sentences below in which the speaker outlines what they would like to do for work and why. Two of the jobs do not match with the reason given. Which **two** jobs need to be swapped? (M)

- Vorrei lavorare come **veterinaria** perché mi piacciono molto gli animali.
- Voglio diventare **avvocatessa** perché conosco bene la mia città.
- Voglio diventare **contabile** perché le cifre mi affascinano.
- Mi piacerebbe lavorare come **giornalista** perché guardo sempre le notizie e mi piace scrivere.
- Vorrei essere una **guida turistica** perché la giustizia mi interessa.

A)   veterinaria & giornalista
B)   contabile & avvocatessa
C)   guida turistica & contabile
D)   avvocatessa & guida turistica

Extra Challenge: Write a similar sentence about what job you would like to do in the future and why. (Writing)

6.6.   The table below shows different jobs and their locations. Which **two** words should fill in the two blanks? (M)

Lavoro	Luogo
pompiere	caserma dei pompieri
traduttore	ufficio
	chiesa
fornaio	

A) prete & panetteria
B) barbiere & studio
C) camionista & azienda
D) attore & ospedale

Extra Challenge: Give three more examples of jobs and the places where the work is done. (Speaking)

6.7. The following words relate to the process of getting a job. Each word has a missing letter. Decide which letter is missing (in the correct order) from the options below. (E)

collo..uio, lau..eato, es..erienza, f..rie, sti..endio, colle..a, contra..to, c..po

A) r, s, s, a, p, t, c, u
B) q, r, p, e, p, g, t, a
C) p, r, t, e, r, m, t, i
D) t, r, p, o, p, f, c, e

Extra Challenge: Use all of the items of vocabulary above in three sentences. (Writing)

6.8. Which of the following terms does **not** match the definition below? (H)

Il periodo in cui si fanno esperienze di lavoro per capire come funziona una professione.

A) un colloquio
B) un curriculum
C) un contratto
D) uno stage

Extra Challenge: Provide definitions for the other three terms. (Speaking)

6.9. Which of the following professions does **not** match the task? (H)

A) Un idraulico guida un taxi.
B) Un giornalista scrive gli articoli.
C) Un pompiere estingue il fuoco.
D) Uno scienziato scopre le nuove cose.

Extra Challenge: Give four more examples of tasks unique to specific professions. (Speaking)

6.10. Which of the following is the **only** logical sentence? (E)

A) Bruno è professore; lavora in un negozio.
B) Marcella lavora come dottoressa in un ospedale.
C) Filippo ha un lavoro a tempo pieno; lavora solo lunedì e martedì.
D) Secondo Caterina, il suo lavoro è divertente perché lo stipendio è simpatico.

Extra Challenge: Re-write the **illogical** sentences above so that they make sense. (Writing)

6.11. Read the following description of someone's work experience. (M)

Ho fatto uno stage molto duro e un po' pericoloso. Ho lavorato in una fabbrica vicino casa mia. Purtroppo, il salario era bassissimo e non c'erano alcune ferie. È stato una perdita di tempo e non voglio più tornare a lavorarci.

Is the text:

A) negative
B) positive
C) both positive and negative
D) neither positive nor negative

Extra Challenge: Translate the text above into English. (Translation)

6.12. Luciano is talking about his working hours below. (H)

Vorrei lavorare a tempo pieno per poter guadagnare più ma attualmente ho un contratto part-time e lavoro dieci ore a settimana. Mia moglie invece è in pensione.

How often does Luciano work?

A) full-time
B) 10 hours/week
C) 12 hours/week
D) never

Extra Challenge: Translate the following sentence into Italian: 'I would like to work part-time so that I can see my family more'. (Translation)

6.13. Read the text below about a nurse's opinion of her job. (M)

Sono infermiera. Mi piace molto il mio lavoro perché è molto gratificante e fin da bambina ho sempre voluto aiutare gli altri. Inoltre le mie colleghe sono divertenti e lo stipendio è adeguato. L'unico svantaggio riguarda i turni; spesso devo lavorare di notte.

Are the opinions given:

A) all positive
B) all negative
C) more positive than negative
D) more negative than positive

Extra Challenge: Write a short paragraph about some of the challenges of working in the medical profession. (Writing)

6.14. Read the following passage about the world of work. (H)

Which list of words are most suitable in the gaps below?

Secondo me avere un orario flessibile è più importante che guadagnare ……..... . Il mio ……….. è sempre più prezioso dei soldi. Tre anni fa sono rimasto disoccupato per due mesi – è stato un periodo ………. stressante, mentre adesso ho un lavoro sicuro che mi permette di ………….. una varietà di persone.

A) molto, ragazzo, meno, cercare
B) bene, tempo, molto, incontrare
C) male, salario, più, trovare
D) abbastanza, stipendio, felicemente, parlare

Extra Challenge: Which alternative words could you use to fill in the blanks in the text above? (Speaking)

6.15. Read the text below about a part-time job. (E)

Lavoro in un ristorante francese nel mio quartiere. Di solito ci lavoro tre volte alla settimana. È faticoso però ricevo tante mance.

In what order is the information given?

A) advantage, how often, location of job, disadvantage
B) how often, location of job, advantage, disadvantage
C) disadvantage, location of job, advantage, how often
D) location of job, how often, disadvantage, advantage

Extra Challenge: Translate the above text into English. (Translation)

6.16. Read the text below about the job that Simone would like to do in the future. (H)

Siccome sono una persona attiva, in futuro vorrei fare un lavoro molto pratico, quindi un lavoro da avvocato o contabile non mi interesserebbe. Invece sono molto interessato a diventare calciatore. Perciò dovrò allenarmi almeno sei volte alla settimana e mangiare bene. Se non potessi diventare calciatore, mi piacerebbe essere allenatore o insegnante in una scuola; sebbene lavorare coi bambini sia impegnativo, può essere davvero gratificante.

Which of the following statements is **true**?

A) Simone would like to be a lawyer or accountant.
B) He will have to train at least 5 times a week.
C) If he does not become a footballer, he would like to be a coach.
D) He thinks working with children is easy.

Extra Challenge: Write a short paragraph about a job that you would **not** like to do in the future. (Writing)

6.17. Read the text below where Roberto talks about the importance of languages in the world of work. (H)

Parlare altre lingue straniere è molto importante nel mondo del lavoro. In primo luogo, si può comunicare con più persone in tutto il mondo. Secondo, le società internazionali preferiscono candidati con capacità linguistiche. Inoltre, si capiscono meglio altre culture e si impara a rispettare le prospettive degli altri.

Which of the following does Roberto **not** mention in relation to languages and work?

A) Global companies prefer employees who can speak other languages.
B) You can communicate with everyone.
C) With additional languages, you can understand other cultures more easily.
D) It helps you to appreciate different perspectives.

Extra Challenge: Translate the text above into English. (Translation)

6.18. Which of the following is the only **disadvantage** of a job? (E)

A) È un lavoro molto vario.
B) Non mi danno abbastanza responsabilità.
C) Non mi annoio mai.
D) Mi permette di viaggiare all'estero.

Extra Challenge: Name three other potential advantages of a job. (Speaking)

6.19. Which of the following is the only **advantage** of a job? (M)

A) Può essere pericoloso.
B) Si fanno le ore lunghe.
C) È veramente soddisfacente.
D) I miei colleghi sono scortesi.

Extra Challenge: Arrange the advantage and disadvantages above into a short paragraph, using conjunctions to connect them together and adding extra details. (Writing)

6.20. Read the following text about Nicola's dream job. Fill in the blanks with the correct verbs in the conditional tense. (H)

Essere dottore .... difficile ma molto gratificante. Se volessi studiare medicina all'università, ... studiare biologia e chimica a scuola. Aiutare la gente mi .... molto e se avessi il tempo, ... una clinica privata.

A) sarebbe, dovrei, interesserebbe, fonderei
B) troverei, dovrebbe, interesserebbero, inizieresti
C) penserei, dovere, interesserà, inizierebbe
D) sarebbero, dovrò, interesserei, fonderebbe

Extra Challenge: What would your dream job be? (Speaking)

CHAPTER 6

The World of Work

Answers and Detailed Solutions

6.1. C

Specchio (mirror) and *tovagliolo* (napkin) are the only items of vocabulary on the list that do not refer to jobs. The other words on the list mean the following in English: *diplomatico* (diplomat), *commesso* (shop assistant), *cameriere* (waiter/waitress), *cassiere* (cashier), *infermiera* (nurse), *calciatore* (footballer), *professore* (teacher), *dottore* (doctor), *direttore* (director), *giudice* (judge), *interprete* (interpreter), *cantante* (singer), *pilota* (pilot), and *dentista* (dentist).

6.2. B

Only the jobs in list B are the same in masculine and feminine forms: *camionista* (lorry driver), *giornalista* (journalist), and *capo* (boss). The other jobs change depending on whether the subject is male or female: *l'avvocato/l'avvocatessa* (lawyer), *il professore/la professoressa* (teacher), *il direttore/la direttrice* (director/headteacher), *il cuoco/la cuoca* (cook), *il dottore/la dottoressa*, *il macellaio/la macellaia* (butcher), *il scrittore/la scrittrice* (writer), *il segretario/la segretaria*, and *il maestro/la maestra* (primary school teacher).

6.3. B

Nascondere (to hide) is the only verb that does not directly relate to employment. The others all refer to work in some way: *guadagnare* (to earn), *lavorare* (to work), *impiegare* (to employ), *licenziare* (to fire), *andare in pensione* (to retire), *fare domanda* (to apply), and *avere un colloquio* (to have an interview).

6.4. A

Andare means 'to go' while *mandare*, *spedire*, and *inviare* all mean 'to send'. *Spedire*, along with *imbucare*, is more likely to be used in the context of sending something by post, while *inviare* and *mandare* could be used in the context of sending an email or a message.

Exam Tip: Remember that just as there are many synonyms in English, so too are there many words with similar meanings in Italian. Try to watch out for them in reading and listening tasks, and use them in your own writing and speaking.

6.5. D

The jobs in the incorrect place are *avvocatessa* (lawyer) and *guida turistica* (tour guide). Sentence 2 should be *guida turistica* because the justification is 'because I know my city well' (*perché conosco bene la mia città*). Whereas the sentence 5 should use *avocatessa*, as the justification is that 'justice interests me' (*la giustizia mi interessa*). The other jobs and justifications include: 'a vet because I really like animals' (*veterinaria perché mi piacciono molto gli animali*), 'an accountant because numbers fascinate me' (*contabile perché le cifre mi affascinano*), and 'a journalist because I always watch the news and I like to write' (*giornalista perché guardo sempre le notizie e mi piace scrivere*).

6.6. A

A priest (*prete*) works in a church (*chiesa*) while a baker (*fornaio*) works in a bakery (*panetteria*). The other jobs mentioned as possible answers would not have fitted appropriately in the space: *barbiere* (barber), *camionista* (lorry driver), and *attore* (actor). Equally, the following locations would not have been suitable: *studio*, *azienda* (agency), and *ospedale* (hospital). The completed table with translations can be found below.

Lavoro	Luogo
pompiere (firefighter)	caserma dei pompieri (fire station)
traduttore (translator)	ufficio (office)
prete (priest)	chiesa (church)
fornaio (baker)	panetteria (bakery)

6.7. B

The words in the list are spelt as follows: *colloquio* (interview), *laureato* (graduate), *esperienza* (experience), *ferie* (holidays), *stipendio* (salary), *collega* (colleague), *contratto* (contract), and *capo* (boss).

6.8. D

Il periodo in cui si fanno esperienze di lavoro per capire come funziona una professione (the period when one gains work experience to learn how a profession works) refers to *uno stage* (work experience). This could also be referred to as *un tirocinio* (an internship), *un apprendistato* (apprenticeship), and *formazione* (training). *Un colloquio* is a job interview, *un curriculum* refers to a CV, and *un contratto* is a contract.

6.9. A

The illogical sentence is A, *un idraulico guida un taxi*, because a plumber does not drive a taxi but rather repairs water systems. Conversely, the other sentences make logical sense: *un giornalista scrive gli articoli* (a journalist writes articles), *un pompiere estingue il fuoco* (a firefighter extinguishes fires), and *uno scienziato scopre le nuove cose* (a scientist discovers new things).

6.10. B

Sentence B is the only one that makes sense: *Marcella lavora come dottoressa in un ospedale* (Marcella works as a doctor in a hospital). Sentence A does not make sense because if Bruno is a teacher he would not work in a shop. Instead the sentence should be either *Bruno è professore; lavora in una scuola* or *Bruno è commesso; lavora in un negozio*. Sentence C is also illogical because if Filippo works full time he would work more than just on Mondays and Tuesdays. It should be either *Filippo ha un lavoro part-time; lavora solo lunedì e martedì* or *Filippo ha un lavoro a tempo pieno; lavora da lunedì a venerdì*. Sentence D is also illogical because Caterina's salary cannot be described as 'kind'. In Italian only a person can be described as *simpatico*. Instead the sentence should read as either *i colleghi sono simpatici* or *lo stipendio è buono*.

6.11. A

The work experience description is entirely negative. The first indication of this is the use of adjectives such as *duro* (hard) and *pericoloso* (dangerous). Secondly, the negative constructions used (e.g. *non…alcune*; *non…mai*) have negative connotations. Thirdly, the use of *purtroppo* (unfortunately) and *è stato una perdita di tempo* (it was a waste of time) generally suggests that a negative sentence will follow. Finally, the fact that the salary was *bassissimo* (very low), there were no holidays (*non c'erano alcune ferie*), and the speaker does not want to return (*non voglio più tornare*) lead us to conclude that the work experience was negative.

6.12. B

Luciano currently has a part-time contract (*attualmente ho un contratto part time*) and works for 10 hours a week (*lavoro dieci ore a settimana*). He mentions that he would like to work full time so that he can earn more money (*vorrei lavorare a tempo pieno per poter guadagnare più*), and that his wife is retired (*in pensione*).

Exam Tip: There are many examples of when an Italian word has been borrowed from the English language, e.g. part-time. Check the context of these cognates to ensure that they have the same meaning.

6.13. C

The speaker gives four reasons for liking her job, including: it is rewarding (*gratificante*), she has wanted to help others since childhood (*ho sempre voluto aiutare gli altri*), she has fun colleagues (*le mie colleghe sono divertenti*), and the pay is fine (*lo stipendio è adeguato*). She only mentions one disadvantage, which is working night shifts (*i turni di notte*).

Exam Tip: When faced with this type of question – whether in the listening or reading exam – look out for signposts such as *e* (and), *inoltre* (furthermore), and *comunque* (however) to decide whether the speaker's comments are likely to be positive or negative.

6.14. B

The first gap needs an adverb to describe the verb *guadagnare*. Although all of the options are adverbs, only *bene*, *molto* or *abbastanza* would work, given the context of the text, e.g. *secondo me avere un orario flessibile è più importante che guadagnare bene/molto/ abbastanza* (for me, having flexible working hours is more important than earning well/a lot/enough). *Male* (badly) would not make sense given the nature of the opinion expressed. The second sentence leads on from the first and so the only appropriate noun is *tempo* (time), e.g. *il mio tempo è molto più prezioso dei soldi* (my time is more precious than money). Although they would be grammatically correct, *salario/stipendio* (salary) do not make sense in the context, while *ragazzo* (boyfriend) could be a viable option. Another adverb is needed for the third gap to describe just how stressful the period of time was; only *molto* can be used in this context to describe the adjective *stressante*. Finally, an infinitive must follow *mi permitte di* (allows me to). *Trovare* (to find), *cercare* (to look for), and *parlare* (to speak) do not make sense in this context, therefore the correct answer must be *incontrare* (to meet).

6.15. D

Firstly, the speaker gives the location of the job: a French restaurant in my area (*un ristorante francese nel mio quartiere*). Secondly, we find out that he/she works there three times a week (*tre volte alla settimana*). Notice also the use of the pronoun *ci* (there) to avoid repeating *il ristorante*. Thirdly, a disadvantage is given: it is tiring (*è faticoso*). This is followed by the advantage that the speaker receives lots of tips (*ricevo tante mance*).

6.16. C

Simone describes himself as an active person (*una persona attiva*) and would like to do a practical job (*vorrei fare un lavoro molto pratico*). He therefore says that a job such as a lawyer or an accountant would not interest him (*un lavoro da avvocato o contabile non mi interesserebbe*). Instead he would like to be a footballer (*calciatore*), which would mean he will have to train at least six times a week (*dovrò allenarmi almeno sei volte alla settimana*). The true statement (C) is that if he does not become a footballer, he would like to be a coach or a teacher (*se non potessi diventare calciatore, mi piacerebbe essere allenatore o insegnante in una scuola*). Finally, statement D is also false because he says that although working with children is challenging, it can be rewarding (*sebbene lavorare coi bambini sia impegnativo, può essere davvero gratificante*). For further practice with the future tense, refer to questions 13.22 and 13.23. in chapter 13.

6.17. B

Roberto gives several reasons for why speaking foreign languages can enhance your career. He begins by saying that you can communicate with more people (*si può comunicare con più persone in tutto il mondo*). This was a red herring because *più persone in tutto il mondo* means **more** people around the world, not 'everyone'. Make sure that you read through the whole sentence before deciding which answer to choose. Other reasons that Roberto cites include: global companies preferring multilingual employees (*le società internazionali preferiscono candidati con capacità linguistiche*), the fact that languages help you to understand other cultures (*si capiscono meglio altre culture*), and respect different perspectives (*si impara a rispettare le prospettive degli altri*).

6.18. B

The only disadvantage in the list is *non mi danno abbastanza responsabilità* (they do not give me enough responsibility). The other options are all positive aspects of a job: *è un lavoro molto vario* (it is a very varied job), *non mi annoio mai* (I never get bored), and *mi permette di viaggiare all'estero* (it allows me to travel abroad).

6.19. C

The only advantage of a job given in the list is *è veramente soddisfacente* (it is really gratifying). The other options are all disadvantages: *può essere pericoloso* (it can be dangerous), *si fanno le ore lunghe* (there are long hours), and *i miei colleghi sono scortesi* (my colleagues are rude).

6.20. A

The conditional tense allows you to talk about what you **would** do either hypothetically or potentially in the future. Nicola talks about the fact that being a doctor **would be** hard but rewarding (***sarebbe** difficile ma molto gratificante*). Remember *sarebbe* comes from the verb *essere*, which has an irregular stem. *Dovere* also has an irregular stem, *dovr-*, in the future and conditional tenses. The second sentence therefore should say 'I **would have to/I should** study biology and chemistry at school' (***dovrei** studiare la biologia e la chimica a scuola*). Thirdly, Nicola says 'helping people **would interest me** a lot (*aiutare la gente **mi interesserebbe** molto*) and fourthly, 'I would set up a clinic' (***fonderei** una clinica privata*).

Exam Tip: Notice how in many cases the construction *se* (if) + imperfect goes in tandem with the conditional tense. For more information about how to form the conditional tense, refer to question 13.25. in chapter 13.

CHAPTER 7

Tourism

The difficulty rating for each question (Easy [E], Moderate [M] or Hard [H]) can be found in parenthesis next to each question.

7.1. Which of the following phrases would you **not** say to someone who is about to go on holiday? (E)

A) buon viaggio
B) buone vacanze
C) buon divertimento
D) buona notte

Extra Challenge: Translate the four phrases above into English. (Translation)

7.2. Identify the correct list (in the correct order) of the following modes of transport: by car, by bus, by airplane, by coach, by train. (E)

A) in aereo, in pullman, a cavallo, in aereo, in motocicletta
B) in motorino, in bicicletta, a piedi, in traghetto, in pullman
C) in pullman, in macchina, in aereo, in metropolitana, in treno
D) in macchina, in autobus, in aereo, in pullman, in treno

Extra Challenge: What are your preferred means of transport when going on holiday and why? (Speaking)

7.3. Which of the following words does **not** relate to travelling by plane? (M)

A) partenze
B) binario
C) bagagli
D) volo

Extra Challenge: Which other words would you associate with plane travel? Write a list. (Writing)

7.4. Which of the following two words would be most appropriate in the two gaps below? (E)

Si può .... le vacanze al lago in un campeggio francese o un agriturismo ...... nella campagna italiana.

A) passare & tranquillo
B) spendere & vario
C) viaggiare & possibile
D) fare & rumorosa

Extra Challenge: Write three other choices about where one can go on holiday, including location and where one would stay. (Writing)

7.5. Which of the following holiday problems has been resolved? (H)

A) L'aria condizionata nella camera era rotta ma l'hanno riparata.
B) Mi sono rotto il braccio però non avevo l'assicurazione di viaggio.
C) Il conto dell'albergo era troppo alto e non ho potuto pagarlo.
D) Io sono stata fermata alla dogana, perché ho perso i miei documenti.

Extra Challenge: Name three other potential problems faced by holidaymakers.

7.6. Which of the following sentences about holidays is **logical**? (H)

A) Preferisco organizzare tutto da sola, quindi andrò in un'agenzia viaggi.
B) Mi piace nuotare quindi passerò le mie vacanze in una pensione senza piscina.
C) Per me proteggere l'ambiente è essenziale. Per questo viaggio sempre in aereo o in macchina.
D) Voglio rilassarmi; di conseguenza ho intenzione di andare in spiaggia ogni giorno.

Extra Challenge: Correct and write out the illogical sentences above so that they make sense. (Writing)

7.7. Read the following extract and fill in the gaps with the most appropriate options in the correct order. (H)

I miei genitori sono ……… di andare in vacanze in altre ……… perché dicono che è sempre …….. stressante. Invece ……………. le vacanze in una località dove possono scappare dalle ……… affollate.

- A) stanchi, città, troppo, preferiscono, spiagge
- B) stanci, città, troppa, preferisce, spiaggie
- C) stanchi, citte, troppo, preferivano, spiaggia
- D) stanci, citte, troppa, preferiranno, spiaggi

Extra Challenge: Talk about what type of holidays you like. (Speaking)

7.8. The following phrases refer to the process of going on holiday. Place them in chronological order. (M)

- A) fare la valigia, partire per le vacanze, prenotare, tornare
- B) partire per le vacanze, tornare, fare la valigia, prenotare
- C) prenotare, fare la valigia, partire per le vacanze, tornare
- D) tornare, fare la valigia, prenotare, partire per le vacanze

Extra Challenge: Conjugate the four phrases above in the present, past and future tenses. (Speaking)

7.9. Which of the following is the most accurate translation of the sentence below? (E)

Usually, I go to the mountains on holiday with my sister.

- A) Vado sempre in vacanza alle montagne con la mia sorella.
- B) Qualche volta vado in vacanza con mio fratello.
- C) Non vado in vacanza in montagna.
- D) Di solito vado in vacanza in montagna con mia sorella.

Extra Challenge: Where do you usually go on holiday? (Speaking)

7.10. Gilberto is talking about his reasons for going on holiday in the text below. (M)

Capisco che per la maggioranza delle persone le vacanze sono un'occasione di riposarsi, non fare nulla e mangiare molto senza sensi colpa, ma per me lo scopo principale di una vacanza è scoprire una nuova cultura.

For Gilberto, what is the main reason for going on holiday?

A)   to relax
B)   to do nothing
C)   to eat a lot without feeling guilty
D)   to discover a new culture

Extra Challenge: Write a short paragraph about what the key components of a good holiday are for you. (Writing)

7.11. Which of the following are you **not** likely to do on holiday? (H)

A)   usare una piantina
B)   mandare una cartolina
C)   noleggiare una macchina
D)   sbrigarsi

Extra Challenge: Write a short paragraph about what you did during your last holiday. (Writing)

7.12. The following sentences describe different tourist attractions available on holiday. (E)

Which one is **illogical**?

A)   Per quelli che amano gli sport acquatici, ci sono tanti musei.
B)   i cattolici possono andare a Messa.
C)   Per le persone attive, c'è una grande varietà di attività.
D)   Per quelli che amano rilassarsi, ci sono una spiaggia ed un centro benessere.

Extra Challenge: Using the examples above as a template, describe the tourist attractions available in a holiday location of your choosing. (Speaking)

7.13. Which of the lists **only** contains vocabulary related to accommodation? (M)

A) campo estivo, contorno, compreso
B) albergo, alloggio, campeggio
C) crociera, disponibile, straniero
D) tenda, viaggio, località balneare

Extra Challenge: Write a list of other accommodation types in Italian. (Writing)

7.14. Read Carolina's short account of her most recent holiday. (H)

Due mesi fa sono andata in Francia in traghetto; la traversata è stata tremenda perché soffro di mal di mare! Quando siamo arrivati, abbiamo scoperto che l'albergo ci aveva dato una camera singola invece di una camera doppia e non c'era più spazio! Mio marito si è sentito male dopo aver mangiato del pesce marcio, e alla fine siamo stati costretti a rincasare tre giorni in anticipo.

Is Carolina's account:

A) only positive
B) only negative
C) both positive and negative
D) neither positive nor negative

Extra Challenge: Translate the text above into English. (Translation)

7.15. The following table contains different countries and nationalities. How many words are in the wrong column? (H)

Countries	Nationalities
Italia	inglese
Austriaco	francese
Grecia	spagnolo
Inghilterra	italiano
Tedesca	indiano
Stati Uniti	scozzese
Scozia	tedesco
Cina	russo
Australia	portogallo
Svizzera	giapponese
Irlanda	Americano
India	greco

A) One
B) Two
C) Three
D) Four

Extra Challenge: Add five countries and nationalities to the list above. (Writing)

7.16. Elena is talking about her dream holiday. (M)

La mia vacanza da sogno sarebbe in Giappone dato che la cultura giapponese mi ha sempre affascinata. Se avessi più soldi, ci andrei per vedere le loro innovazioni tecnologiche oltre all'architettura antica. Non resterei in albergo perché vorrei conoscere e capire meglio le loro tradizioni.

Which of the following does Elena **not** mention?

A) where she would go
B) with whom she would go
C) why she would go there
D) what she would do

Extra Challenge: Describe your ideal holiday using the conditional tense. (Speaking)

7.17. Serena is talking about her part-time job. (E)

Durante l'estate, ho lavorato come guida turistica nella mia città natale – Firenze! È un luogo perfetto per i turisti grazie ai suoi musei, ai bei giardini ed a vari concerti ed eventi culturali. È stato un lavoro molto bello perché sono fiera della mia città.

Which of the following statements is **false**?

A) Serena worked during the winter.
B) Serena is from Firenze.
C) The city is perfect for tourists.
D) Serena is proud of her city.

Extra Challenge: Write a short paragraph about the tourist attractions in your town. (Writing)

7.18. Read the text below about Marco's disastrous holiday. (H)

La mia ultima vacanza è stata un disastro! Sono andato in Spagna con mio fratello e appena siamo arrivati all'aeroporto, abbiamo perso i nostri bagagli. Poi il secondo giorno, quando eravamo in spiaggia, mio fratello si è scottato prendendo il sole. L'ultimo giorno, siamo andati al ristorante dove ho mangiato del cibo scaduto – dopo ho vomitato dappertutto! Almeno però ha fatto bel tempo!

Which **three** reasons does Marco cite for his holiday being a disaster?

A) a lost suitcase, sunburn, and stale food
B) a missed flight, weather at the beach, and bad food
C) a lost phone, an ugly beach, and rudeness at the restaurant
D) a missed train, a fight with his brother, and bad weather

Extra Challenge: Translate the text above into English. (Translation)

7.19.   Read the hotel review below. (H)

Ho soggiornato in un albergo che si chiama 'San Giovanni'. Si trova nel cuore della città vicino ai negozi e alle vecchie chiese. L'albergo aveva quattro stelle ma a mio avviso, ne meritava di più. La camera era pulitissima ed il personale era molto amichevole. C'era una vista meravigliosa sul lago dove facevamo la colazione e l'arredamento era molto elegante. Se avessi tempo, ci tornerei subito!

Is the hotel review:

A)   only positive
B)   only negative
C)   more positive than negative
D)   more negative than positive

Extra Challenge: Write a review of somewhere you have stayed recently. (Writing)

7.20.   Read the text below about Mattia's holiday plans for next year. (M)

L'anno prossimo andrò negli Stati Uniti e non vedo l'ora! Ci andrò con la mia migliore amica, che è molto divertente, e passeremo del tempo a New York ed a Washington DC. Non sarà molto rilassante ma credo che sarà un'esperienza indimenticabile perché non ci sono mai andato.

Which of the following adjectives does Mattia use to describe what he thinks the holiday will be like, and why?

A)   relaxed – more free time
B)   unforgettable – he has never been there
C)   inspirational – his favourite actor is from New York
D)   fun – it is a different experience

Extra Challenge: Describe your holiday plans for next year using the future tense. (Writing)

CHAPTER 7

Tourism

Answers and
Detailed Solutions

7.1. D

Buona notte means 'good night' and therefore does not relate to someone going on holiday. The other phrases could be used to wish someone a good trip: *buon viaggio* (have a good trip), *buone vacanze* (enjoy your holidays), and *buon divertimento* (have fun).

7.2. D

Notice that most modes of transport are preceded by *in*, meaning 'by'. Although 'by foot' and 'by horse' both use *a* (*a piedi/a cavallo*). Other vocabulary listed includes: *motocicletta* (motorbike), *motorino* (moped), *traghetto* (ferry), *metropolitana* (tube/underground), *bicicletta* (bike), *macchina* (car), *aereo* (aeroplane) *treno* (train), *autobus* (bus), and *pullman* (coach).

7.3. B

Binario means 'platform', and so would be associated with train travel rather than plane travel. The other three items of vocabulary all relate to plane travel: *partenze* (departures), *bagagli* (baggage) and *volo* (flight). Other associated words may include: *biglietto* (ticket), *aeroporto*, *passeggero* (passenger), *arrivi* (arrivals), and *ritardo* (delay).

7.4. A

The verb *passare* (to spend) makes the most sense in the context of the sentence, although *fare* can also be used. Note that the verb *spendere* means 'to spend' in terms of spending money. The adjectives are more interchangeable, however *tranquillo* is the most appropriate as an *agriturismo* is a farm in the countryside that is known for being quiet, peaceful and remote. As such, *rumorosa* (loud) would not be appropriate in the context, and in any case should be in the masculine (*rumoroso*) rather than the feminine. Accordingly, *tranquillo* is the most appropriate adjective.

7.5. A

Four holiday problems are stated but only one is resolved. Problem A is that the air conditioning in the room was broken (*l'aria condizionata nella camera era rotta*) but the solution is that they repaired it (*l'hanno riparata*). No solution was given for the other three holiday problems, which were: I broke my arm but I did not have any travel insurance (*mi sono rotto il braccio però non avevo l'assicurazione di viaggio*), the hotel bill was too high and I could not pay it (*il conto dell'albergo era troppo alto e non ho potuto pagarlo*), and I was stopped at customs because I lost my documents (*io sono stata fermata alla dogana perché ho perso i miei documenti*).

7.6. D

The only sentence that makes sense is D: *voglio rilassarmi; di conseguenza ho intenzione di andare in spiaggia ogni giorno* (I want to relax; as such, I intend to go to the beach every day). The first sentence is incorrect because the speaker prefers organizing everything alone yet will go to the travel agents (*preferisco organizzare tutto da sola, quindi andrò in un'agenzia viaggi*). The second sentence is also illogical as the speaker claims to like swimming but will go to a bed & breakfast without a pool (*mi piace nuotare quindi passerò le mie vacanze in una pensione senza piscina*). Finally, the third sentence is illogical as the speaker says that protecting the environment is essential yet only travels by plane or car (*per me proteggere l'ambiente è essenziale. Per questo viaggio sempre in aereo o in macchina*).

7.7. A

Stanchi is the first word needed; the parents (*i genitori*) are being described so a masculine, plural adjective is necessary. Notice how the 'h' is added to the adjective *stanchi* for pronunciation purposes. Secondly, the word *città* (city) does not change in the plural form e.g. *una città, due città*, therefore options C and D are incorrect. Thirdly, the speaker would like to say that 'it is always too stressful'. *Troppo* (too) does not change when it is used with an adjective e.g. *troppo stressante*. However, when it is used with a noun it changes according to the gender and number of the noun, e.g. *troppe persone* (too many people). The verb 'prefer' is being used to talk about the parents, therefore the third-person plural is needed in the present tense, e.g. *preferiscono*. Finally, the noun *spiaggia* (beach) loses the second 'i' in the plural form as the 'gi' sound is retained by the 'e', e.g. *spiagge*.

7.8. C

The most logical order for the four activities to take place is: *prenotare* (to book), *fare la valigia* (to pack), *partire per le vacanze* (to go on holiday), *tornare* (to return). Notice how the verb 'to pack' can be translated 'to make the suitcase' (*fare la valigia*) in Italian.

7.9. D

Di solito (usually) is a good way to start a sentence about your holidays, and is typically followed by the present tense. The time phrases used in answers A and B include: *qualche volta* (sometimes) and *sempre* (always). Translation A could not be correct because you do not need the article when referring to singular family members (e.g. *la mia sorella* ⇒ *mia sorella*). Equally 'to the mountains' moves from the plural in English to the singular in Italian (*in montagna*). Translation B uses the wrong time phrase, does not include the mountains, and uses 'brother' (*fratello*) rather than 'sister' (*sorella*). Finally, Translation C uses the negative (*non*) in front of the verb and fails to include the person with whom the speaker goes.

7.10. D

Gilberto says that the main aim of a holiday is to discover a new culture (*lo scopo principale di una vacanza è scoprire una nuova cultura*). However, he also admits that for most people (*per la maggioranza delle persone*) holidays are an opportunity to 1) relax (*riposarsi*), 2) do nothing (*non fare nulla*), and 3) eat a lot without feeling guilty (*mangiare molto senza sensi colpa*).

7.11. D

On holiday, it is quite likely that you will 'use a map' (*usare la piantina*), 'send a postcard' (*mandare una cartolina*), and 'hire a car' (*noleggiare una macchina*). It is less likely that you will 'hurry up' (*sbrigarsi*)!

7.12. A

The first sentence is illogical because 'those who like water sports' (*quelli che amano gli sport acquatici*) will not necessarily be looking to go to museums (*musei*). The other three options make logical sense: *i cattolici possono andare a Messa* (Catholics can go to Mass), *per le persone attive, c'è una grande varietà di sport* (for those who are active, there is a big variety of sports), and *per quelli che amano rilassarsi, ci sono una spiaggia ed un centro benessere* (for those who love to relax, there is a beach and a well-being centre).

7.13. B

List B contains only words related to holiday accommodation, although the other lists also contain some accommodation vocabulary, including: *albergo* (hotel), *alloggio* (accommodation), *campeggio* (camping), *tenda* (tent), and *crociera* (cruise). Additional accommodation vocabulary could include: *ostello della gioventù* (youth hostel), *caravan*, *appartamento*, and *una pensione* (inn). Other items in the lists include: *campo estivo* (summer camp), *contorno* (side dish), *compreso* (included), *disponibile* (available), *straniero* (foreign), *viaggio* (journey), and *località balneare* (seaside resort) – words that are associated with holidays more generally but are not specific types of accommodation.

7.14. B

Carolina's holiday was not at all successful and therefore the answer is B, only negative. Firstly, the ferry crossing was awful because she suffers from sea sickness (*la traversata è stata tremenda perché soffro di mal di mare*). Secondly, the hotel gave them a single rather than a double room (*l'albergo ci aveva dato una camera singola invece di una camera doppia*). Finally, her husband became ill after eating rotten fish (*il mio marito si è sentito male dopo aver mangiato del pesce marcio*), which meant that in the end they had to return home three days early (*alla fine siamo stati costretti a rincasare tre giorni in anticipo*).

7.15. C

There are three mistakes in the table: *austriaco* (means 'Austrian', not 'Austria'), *tedesca* (means 'German' (f) rather than 'Germany', which is *Germania*), and *Portogallo* (means 'Portugal', rather than 'Portuguese', which is *portoghese*). Only *svizzera* can go in both categories, meaning both 'Swiss' (f) and 'Switzerland'. The non-cognates in the table include: *Stati Uniti* (United States), *Inghliterra* (England), and *inglese* (English), and *giapponese* (Japanese).

Exam Tip: Remember that in Italian nationalities are generally written in lower case while countries tend to begin with a capital letter.

7.16. B

Elena mentions that her dream holiday would be in Japan (*la mia vacanza da sogno sarebbe in Giappone*) because Japanese culture has always fascinated her (*dato che la cultura giapponese mi ha sempre affascinata*). She would like to see both Japan's technological innovations (*per vedere le loro innovazioni tecnologiche*) and ancient architecture (*l'architettura antica*). She also says that she would not stay in a hotel because she would like to get to know and understand their traditions better (*non resterei in albergo perché vorrei conoscere e capire meglio le loro tradizioni*). However, she does not mention with whom she would go.

7.17. A

Serena worked as a tour guide during the summer (*durante l'estate, ho lavorato come guida turistica*) rather than the winter (*l'inverno*), therefore statement A is false. She mentions that she is from Firenze when she describes it as *la mia città natale*. She also says it is the perfect place for tourists (*è un luogo perfetto per i turisti*) thanks to its museums, beautiful gardens, concerts and cultural events (*grazie ai suoi musei, ai bei giardini ed a vari concerti ed eventi culturali*). Finally, Serena mentions that the job was very good because she is proud of her city (*sono fiera della mia città*).

7.18. A

After giving some details about his holiday such as where it was (*Spagna*) and who he went with (*mio fratello*), Marco outlines three reasons why it was so terrible. Firstly, he says that 'as soon as we arrived at the airport, we lost our suitcase' (*appena siamo arrivati all'aeroporto, abbiamo perso i nostri bagagli*). Secondly, when they were at the beach his brother got sunburnt (*mio fratello si è scottato prendendo il sole*). Finally, he ate stale food and vomited everywhere (*ho mangiato del cibo scaduto – dopo ho vomitato dappertutto*). He does add that at least the weather was good (*almeno però ha fatto bel tempo*), which serves as a red herring.

7.19. A

The review is entirely positive. The main advantages of the hotel are its proximity to shops and old churches (*vicino ai negozi e le vecchie chiese*), its very clean rooms (*la camera era pulitissima*), friendly staff (*il personale era molto amichevole*), marvelous view (*vista meravigliosa*), and elegant décor (*l'arredamento era molto elegante*). The reviewer even says that it deserved more than four stars (*l'albergo aveva quattro stelle e, a mio avviso, ne meritava di più*) and that, if they had time, they would return straight away (*se avessi tempo, ci tornerei subito*).

Exam Tip: Notice how the text uses a wide range of tenses and adjectives. Aim to emulate this range in your own writing.

7.20. B

Mattia thinks that the holiday to the United States will be *un'esperienza indimenticabile* (an unforgettable experience) because he says *non ci sono mai andato* (I have never been there). Although he does use the word 'fun' (*divertente*), he uses it to describe his friend rather than the holiday itself. He also says that the holiday will not be relaxing (*rilassante*).

CHAPTER 8

Identity, Culture and Festivals

The difficulty rating for each question (Easy [E], Moderate [M] or Hard [H]) can be found in parenthesis next to each question.

8.1. The list below contains vocabulary related to items of clothing in Italian. Each word is missing a letter. Following the order of the list, which letters need to be added? (E)

L'abbig..iamento, i cal..ini, la ca..icia, la ci..tura, la cra..atta, la gia..ca, la magli..tta, i pan..aloni, le s..arpe, il vest..to.

A) h, t, n, m, f, p, a, z, t, e
B) l, s, d, n, m, c, o, t, p, a
C) h, z, b, m, v, h, u, s, l, u
D) l, z, m, n, v, c, e, t, c, i

Extra Challenge: Translate the items of clothing above into English. (Translation)

8.2. Read the text below about what Daniela and Luigi are wearing. (E)

Daniela si mette un bel vestito blu perché va a una festa. Si mette anche le scarpe bianche e una giacca verde perché fa freddo. Luigi va alla stessa festa e si mette un paio di pantaloni neri e una camicia rossa.

Which of the following is **not** mentioned in the text?

A) blue dress
B) black trousers
C) red shoes
D) green jacket

Extra Challenge: Describe the clothing that you are wearing in Italian. (Speaking)

8.3. In the text below Francesco describes what he wears on different occasions. (M)

Quando vado a scuola mi metto la divisa scolastica e un cappotto invernale, mentre quando esco coi miei amici mi metto una felpa e un cappello di lana nero. Quando andiamo in chiesa devo essere più elegante quindi porto i pantaloni neri e una camicia bianca. Quando gioco a tennis invece sono meno formale e mi metto le scarpe da tennis e una maglietta sportiva.

According to the text, which pairing is **incorrect**?

A)   school ⇔ school uniform and a winter coat
B)   out with friends ⇔ a fleece and a woolly hat
C)   church ⇔ brown trousers and a green shirt
D)   playing tennis ⇔ trainers and a sports t-shirt

Extra Challenge: Write a short paragraph on the types of clothes that you wear on different occasions. (Writing)

8.4. Read the text below in which Sofia talks about fashion. (H)

Milano è la capitale mondiale della moda. Ci abito da sempre e la amo. Il mese scorso sono andata alla settimana della moda di Milano per la prima volta: è stata un'esperienza sbalorditiva. Ha avuto luogo a febbraio a Palazzo Reale e per un giorno ho potuto sedere proprio in prima fila a fianco della passerella. L'ultissima moda era in mostra e ho imparato tanto per il mio lavoro da stilista.

According to the text, which of the following statements is **false**?

A)   Milan is the fashion capital of the world.
B)   Sofia has lived there since last month.
C)   She went to Milan Fashion Week for the first time recently.
D)   She sat right next to the catwalk.

Extra Challenge: Translate the text above into English. (Translation)

8.5. Which of the following is the most appropriate translation of the sentence below? (E)

My sister and I surprised our mum with some flowers for Mother's Day.

A) Mia sorella ed io abbiamo sorprenduto nostra madre con il cioccolato per la festa della mamma.

B) Mia sorella ed io sorprendiamo nostra madre con dei fiori per il giorno della mamma.

C) Mia sorella ed io abbiamo sorpreso nostra madre con dei fiori per la festa della mamma.

D) La mia sorella e me abbiamo sorpreso la nostra madre con fiori per il giorno della mamma.

Extra Challenge: Write a sentence in Italian about a gift you have recently given to someone and what it was like. (Writing)

8.6. Four people are talking about their birthdays below. Which of the following is the only **logical** sentence? (H)

A) Il mio compleanno è d'estate: è il cinque luglio.

B) Quest'anno il mio compleanno è durante il weekend: è martedì 15 giugno.

C) Non festeggio il mio compleanno: ho una festa ogni anno.

D) Il mio compleanno è il giorno di Natale: il diciassette gennaio.

Extra Challenge: How do you normally celebrate your birthday? (Speaking)

8.7. Read the passage below in which Eva describes her birthday. (H)

Mercoledì scorso ho dato una festa per il mio diciottesimo compleanno; è stata bellissima! C'era musica e una torta enorme ed abbiamo ballato. Mi sono piaciuti tutti i regali che ho ricevuto ma la parte migliore è arrivata quando i miei genitori mi hanno sorpreso con i fuochi d'artificio alla fine della festa.

What was the best part of Eva's birthday?

A) the cake
B) the fireworks
C) the presents
D) the music

Extra Challenge: Write a short paragraph about what you will do for your next birthday. (Writing)

8.8. In the following text, Christina talks about gifts she bought last Christmas. (H)

Lo scorso natale ho comprato un sacco di regali per la mia famiglia e qualche amico. Per mia mamma ho trovato un vecchio romanzo firmato dal suo autore preferito. Poi, per mio papà ho organizzato una lezione di sci, perché ha sempre voluto provare a sciare. Per mia sorella, ho comprato un bel paio di orecchini verdi e a mio fratello ho regalato un videogioco. Per la mia migliore amica ho comprato una gonna rosa.

Which of the following gifts did Christina **not** buy?

A) a signed novel
B) green earrings
C) a pink dress
D) a ski lesson

Extra Challenge: Adapt the text above using the future tense. (Speaking)

8.9. Which of the following words do **not** describe a follower of a religion? (M)

A) un cristiano
B) un ebreo
C) un musulmano
D) un cielo

Extra Challenge: Translate each term into English. (Translation)

8.10. Which of the following terms is **not** associated with Christmas? (E)

A) la stella
B) la Natività
C) gli angeli
D) la ruota

Extra Challenge: Write a short paragraph about what you normally do during the Christmas holidays. (Writing)

8.11. Read the passage below about Christmas food. (M)

A Natale in Italia si mangia molto bene: per esempio di solito come antipasto si mangia il pesce. Poi, come primo piatto si mangia la carne - sia di pollo sia d'agnello. Ci sono anche tante verdure come patate e funghi. Come dolce gli italiani mangiano il panettone o il torrone – che pasto delizioso! Buon appetito!

According to the text, which of the following lists contains food that Italians eat at Christmas?

A) chicken, lamb, potatoes, mushrooms, panettone, nougat
B) chicken, duck, potatoes, peas, panettone, jelly
C) lamb, beef, potatoes, asparagus, panettone, chocolate cake
D) lamb, duck, potatoes, carrots, panettone, fruit cake

Extra Challenge: Does your family celebrate Christmas, and if so what do you eat? (Speaking)

8.12. Read the text below in which Roberta compares Christmas in Italy and in the United Kingdom (UK). (M)

Il Natale in Italia è abbastanza simile a quello nel Regno Unito anche se tradizionalmente noi Italiani non mangiamo la carne la Vigilia di Natale. Inoltre non mangiamo spesso il tacchino come nel Regno Unito. Nei due paesi i bambini aspettano Babbo Natale, ma in Italia si aspetta anche la Befana che arriva il sei gennaio e porta altri regali.

According to the text, which of the following statements is **true**?

A) Christmas is very different in Italy compared to the UK.
B) Traditionally Italians do not eat meat on Christmas Eve.
C) Italians generally eat turkey at Christmas time.
D) A witch delivers presents on boxing day.

Extra Challenge: Translate the text above into English. (Translation)

8.13. Read the following text about the Venice Carnival. (E)

Il Carnevale di Venezia è una delle feste più famose e più misteriose al mondo. Ha luogo ogni anno in febbraio nei dieci giorni che precedono i quaranta giorni della Quaresima. I cittadini di Venezia indossano le maschere per nascondere la propria identità e ci sono diverse sfilate di maschere ogni sera.

How often and for how long does the Venice Carnival take place?

A) every year for ten days
B) twice a year for three evenings
C) once every two years for forty days
D) once every four years for ten days

Extra Challenge: Write a short paragraph about a festival or celebration in your local area. (Writing)

8.14. Melania is talking about Easter in the text below. (H)

Sono cattolica e quest'anno per la prima volta andrò in Vaticano la Domenica di Pasqua. Sarà un onore vedere il Papa.

Which of the following does Melania **not** mention?

A) She will go to the Vatican for the first time.
B) She will go there on Easter Sunday.
C) It will be a privilege to see the Pope.
D) She has seen the Pope once before.

Extra Challenge: Translate the text above into English. (Translation)

8.15.   Read the text below about Naples. (E)

Simbolo dell'Italia, la pizza Margherita .... da Napoli e assomiglia alla .... italiana con il rosso del ...., il bianco della mozzarella ed il verde del basilico.

Which of the following lists of words would be most appropriate to fill in the blanks?

A)   arriva, inno, cavolo
B)   succede, identità, cipolla
C)   viene, bandiera, pomodoro
D)   apre, paese, carota

Extra Challenge: Write a short paragraph about speciality foods in your town, region or country. (Writing)

8.16.   What is the speaker excited about in the following text? (M)

Non vedo l'ora di vedere l'ultima tappa del Giro d'Italia il mese prossimo. È una corsa di ciclismo molto difficile. Secondo me, il Giro d'Italia è l'evento sportivo più importante in Italia – ancora più importante dei mondiali!

A)   Ferragosto
B)   the next hour
C)   the World cup
D)   a cycling race

Extra Challenge: What cultural events are happening near you this summer? (Speaking)

8.17.   Which of the following words makes the most sense in the blank space? (M)

Il .... segna la fine di un anno e l'inizio di un altro.

A)   Pasqua
B)   Capodanno
C)   giorno
D)   Epifania

Extra Challenge: Make a list of three new year's resolutions using the future tense. (Writing)

8.18. Read the description below of a church in Sicily. (H)

Il Duomo di Monreale in Sicilia è una delle più belle cattedrali non solo dell'Italia ma anche del mondo. Dato che è un luogo sacro, si consiglia ai visitatori di vestirsi appropriatamente.

Which of the following is mentioned?

A) clothing
B) cost of entry
C) guided tours
D) opening hours

Extra Challenge: Describe a tourist destination near where you live, including information about the four categories mentioned above. (Speaking)

8.19. Which of the following words would be most appropriate in the three blank spaces in the text below? (H)

Lo scopo della giornata internazionale della ...., festeggiata l'8 marzo in molti paesi nel ...., è di celebrare il ruolo della donna nella vita pubblica e di .... le disuguaglianze esistenti tra uomo e donna.

A) uomo, globo, riflettere
B) danza, pianeta, dimenticare
C) donna, mondo, sottolineare
D) musica, centro, ignorare

Extra Challenge: Write a short paragraph about inequality (*la disuguaglianza*). (Writing)

8.20. Read the text below about *La Festa della Repubblica*. (H)

La Festa della Repubblica è una delle feste nazionali più importanti d'Italia e viene festeggiata il 2 giugno. Si celebra la data in cui l'Italia è diventata una repubblica costituzionale. Ogni anno a Roma si tiene una parata militare, seguita dall'esibizione delle Frecce Tricolori.

What does *La Festa della Repubblica* commemorate and what does it entail?

A)   When Italy became a Republic / a military parade
B)   The start of the summer / art exhibitions
C)   Italy's place in the European Union (EU) / a carnival procession
D)   The end of the Republic / a film exhibition

Extra Challenge: Describe a recent commemorative event in your local area. (Speaking)

CHAPTER 8

Identity, Culture and Festivals

Answers and
Detailed Solutions

8.1. D

The items of vocabulary all relate to clothing. The words are accompanied by their English translations, as follows: *l'abbigliamento* (clothing), *i calzini* (socks), *la camicia* (shirt/blouse), *la cintura* (belt), *la cravatta* (tie), *la giacca* (jacket), *la maglietta* (t-shirt), *i pantaloni* (trousers), *le scarpe* (shoes), and *il vestito* (dress).

8.2. C

The only item of clothing not mentioned in the text are red shoes (*le scarpe rosse*). The items of clothing in the text include: *un bel vestito blu* (a nice blue dress), *una giacca verde* (a green jacket), *le scarpe bianche* (white shoes), *un paio di pantaloni neri* (a pair of black trousers), and *una camicia rossa* (a red shirt). Notice how the adjectives – in this case different colours – change according to the gender and number of the noun (e.g. masculine, feminine, singular, plural). For further practice with adjectives refer to questions in the first half of chapter 14.

8.3. C

The key word in this question is *quando* (when) as it acts as a marker for each answer. The incorrect pairing is that when he goes to church, Francesco does not wear brown trousers and a green shirt but rather black trousers and a white shirt (*i pantaloni neri e una camicia bianca*). By contrast, he does wear a school uniform and winter coat (*la divisa scolastica e un cappotto invernale*) at school, a fleece and black woolly hat (*una felpa e un cappello di lana nero*) when out with friends, and trainers and a sports t-shirt (*le scarpe da tennis e una maglietta sportiva*) when he plays tennis. For further practice with colours in Italian, see question 11.9. in chapter 11.

8.4. B

Three of the statements are true. Firstly, Sofia says that Milan is the fashion capital of the world (*Milano è la capitale mondiale della moda*). Secondly, she went to Milan Fashion Week for the first time last month (*il mese scorso sono andata alla settimana della moda di Milano per la prima volta*) and she described it as an amazing experience (*è stata un'esperienza sbalorditiva*). Thirdly, she says that one day she sat in the front row right next to the catwalk (*per un giorno ho potuto sedere proprio in prima fila a fianco della passerella*). As such, the false statement is that Sofia has lived in Milan since last month, in fact she has always lived there (*ci abito da sempre*).

8.5. C

The most appropriate translation is C: *Mia sorella ed io abbiamo sorpreso nostra madre con dei fiori per la festa della mamma*. Firstly, remember that for many singular family members the definite article is not needed before the possessive adjective e.g. *mia sorella, nostra madre*. For more on this see question 1.5. in chapter 1. Secondly, the verb *sorprendere* (to surprise) should be in the past tense and its past participle is irregular (*sorpreso*), therefore 'we surprised' should be translated as *abbiamo sorpreso*. Finally, 'Mother's Day' is translated in Italian as *la festa della Mamma*.

8.6. A

The only logical sentence is A: *il mio compleanno è d'estate: è il cinque luglio* (my birthday is in the summer: it is the 5th July). The other options are illogical: *quest'anno il mio compleanno è durante il weekend: è il martedì 15 giugno* does not make sense because if the speaker's birthday was on the weekend it would not be on a Tuesday (*martedì*). *Non festeggio il mio compleanno* (I do not celebrate my birthday) does not correspond with *ho una festa ogni anno* (I have a party every year). Finally, *il mio compleanno è il giorno di Natale* (my birthday is on Christmas day) cannot be true as it is *il diciassette gennaio* (17th January).

8.7. B

Eva talks about her 18th birthday party and mentions music (*la musica*), an enormous cake (*una torta enorme*) and dancing (*abbiamo ballato*). She also liked the presents she received (*mi sono piaciuti tutti i regali che ho ricevuto*). However, the best part was when her parents surprised her with fireworks at the end of the party (*i miei genitori mi hanno sorpreso con i fuochi d'artificio alla fine della festa*).

8.8. C

The gift Christina did not buy was a pink dress (*un vestito rosa*) – although she did buy a pink skirt for her best friend (*una gonna rosa*). For her mother, she bought a signed novel by her favourite author (*un vecchio romanzo firmato dal suo autore preferito*), for her father she organised a ski lesson (*una lezione di sci*), for her sister she bought a nice pair of green earrings (*un bel paio di orecchini verdi*), and for her brother she bought a videogame (*un videogioco*).

Exam Tip: When reading longer texts, look out for time phrases to help your understanding of how the narrative is developing.

8.9. D

The only word that does not describe a follower of a religion from the list is *cielo*, which means both 'sky' and 'heaven'. The followers of religions include: *un cristiano* (Christian), *un ebreo* (Jew), and *un musulmano* (Muslim).

8.10. D

The star (*la stella*), the nativity (*la Natività*), and the angels (*gli angeli*) are all related to Christmas, whereas *la ruota* means 'wheel'.

8.11. A

The following foods (among many others!) are eaten during Christmas time in Italy: *il pesce* (fish), *carne* (meat), *pollo* (chicken), *agnello* (lamb), *verdure* (vegetables), *patate* (potatoes), *funghi* (mushrooms), *panettone*, and *torrone* (nougat). Notice the reference to three courses (*antipasto* [starter], *primo piatto* [first course], and *dolce* [dessert]) as well as the use of the impersonal *si mangia* (one eats).

Exam Tip: The use of exclamations such as *che pasto delizioso!* and *Buon appetito!* can be an excellent way of making your writing and speaking stand out.

8.12. B

The only true statement, according to Roberta's text, is B: traditionally Italians do not eat meat on Christmas Eve (*tradizionalmente noi italiani non mangiamo la carne la Vigilia di Natale*). The other three statements do not correspond to the text. Firstly, Roberta says that Christmas is quite similar in Italy and the United Kingdom (*il Natale in Italia è abbastanza simile a quello nel Regno Unito*). Secondly, she says that Italians do not generally eat turkey like in the United Kingdom (*non mangiamo spesso il tacchino*). Thirdly, Roberta says that Father Christmas is traditional in both countries (*nei due paesi i bambini aspettano Babbo Natale*) and that a witch (*la Befana*) comes on the 6th January and brings other presents (*arriva il sei gennaio e porta altri regali*).

8.13. A

According to the text, the Venice Carnival takes place every year in February in the ten days that precede the forty days of Lent (*ha luogo ogni anno in febbraio nei dieci giorni che precedono i quaranta giorni della Quaresima*). The text also tells us that the Carnival is one of the most famous and mysterious festivals in the world (*è una delle feste più famose e più misteriose al mondo*). The citizens of Venice wear masks to hide their identity (*i cittadini di Venezia indossano le maschere per nascondere la propria identità*) and there are different parades every evening (*ci sono diverse sfilate di maschere ogni sera*).

8.14. D

Melania says she is going to the Vatican for the first time on Easter Sunday (*per la prima volta andrò in Vaticano la Domenica di Pasqua*). She also says that it will be an honour to see the Pope (*sarà un onore vedere il Papa*). The answer is therefore D, as she does not mention that she has seen the Pope before.

Exam Tip: Ensure that you read the question carefully – particularly when it contains a negative construction.

8.15. C

The most appropriate words with which to fill in the blanks would be *viene*, *bandiera*, and *pomodoro*. Firstly, the sentence says that the Margherita pizza **comes from** Naples (*la pizza Margherita **viene da** Napoli*) therefore the verbs *arriva* (arrives), *succede* (happens), and *apre* (opens) would not be suitable. A feminine noun starting with a consonant is needed in the second gap as it is preceded by *la*. As the sentence is saying that the pizza resembles the Italian flag (*assomiglia alla bandiera italiana*), the word needed is *bandiera*. *Inno* (anthem), *identità* (identity), and *paese* (country) do not have colours so would not work in the context. In the final space, it is the red of the tomato (*pomodoro*), not the *cavolo* (cabbage), *cipolla* (onion), or *carota* (carrot), that features in the pizza Margherita.

8.16. D

The speaker is excited about the Giro d'Italia, a famous cycling race in Italy. *Non vedo l'ora* means 'I cannot wait', although literally translates as 'I do not see the hour'. The speaker says that they consider the Giro d'Italia as the most important sporting event in Italy – even more important than the World Cup (*il Giro d'Italia è l'evento sportivo più importante in Italia – ancora più importante dei mondiali*), By contrast, *ferragosto* is a holiday in Italy in mid-August and is celebrated across the country.

8.17. B

The word missing from the sentence is *capodanno* (New Year), as the sentence translates as 'New Year marks the end of one year and the beginning of another' (*il capodanno segna la fine di un anno e l'inizio di un altro*). The other celebrations mentioned include *Pasqua* (Easter) and *Epifania* (Epiphany [6th January]).

8.18. A

The Monreale cathedral in Sicily is described as one of the most beautiful cathedrals not just in Italy but in the world (*il Duomo di Monreale in Sicilia è una delle più belle cattedrali non solo dell'Italia ma anche del mondo*). Information about the cost of entry, guided tours and opening hours is not provided. Instead, the text mentions clothing: *dato che è un luogo sacro, si consiglia ai visitatori di vestirsi appropriatamente* (given that it is a sacred place, visitors are advised to dress appropriately).

8.19. C

The text talks about International Women's Day (*la giornata internazionale della donna*) which is celebrated on the 8th March in many countries across the world (*festeggiata l'8 marzo in molti paesi nel mondo*). As such, the first two answers are *donna* and *mondo*; additional clues are provided with the preceding *della* (+ feminine noun) and *nel* (+ masculine noun). The third blank space needs to be filled with an infinitive. As the aim of International Women's Day is unlikely to be 'to forget' (*dimenticare*) or 'to ignore' (*ignorare*) inequality between men and women, the only two options are 'to highlight' (*sottolineare*) or 'to reflect' (*riflettere*). The latter cannot work as 'to reflect on' is *riflettere su*, therefore the answer must be *sottolineare*.

Exam Tip: For gap-fill tasks, look at the words which precede and follow the gap for clues about gender and number.

8.20. A

La Festa della Repubblica commemorates the moment in which Italy became a constitutional republic (*la data in cui l'Italia è diventata una repubblica costituzionale*). It is one of the most important national holidays in Italy and takes place on 2nd June (*è una delle feste nazionali più importanti d'Italia e viene festeggiata il 2 giugno*). It involves a military parade (*una parata militare*) followed by a display by the *Frecce Tricolori* (*seguita dall'esibizione delle Frecce Tricolori*). The *Frecce Tricolori* are the Italian equivalent of the 'Red Arrows' in the United Kingdom (UK); *tricolori* (tricoloured) refers to the red, white and green of the Italian flag.

CHAPTER 9

Social Issues

The difficulty rating for each question (Easy [E], Moderate [M] or Hard [H]) can be found in parenthesis next to each question.

9.1. Which of the following is **not** a social issue? (M)

A) l'inserimento sociale
B) il cervello
C) il debito
D) il pregiudizio

Extra Challenge: What, in your opinion, is the most serious social issue in your local area? (Speaking)

9.2. Below are four social issues and four newspaper headlines. Two of the social issues do **not** correspond with the correct headline. Can you identify which **two**? (E)

Il sessismo: Nuova ricerca mostra il danno cerebrale provocato dal consumo delle droghe illegali
La sicurezza stradale: due minori uccisi in un incidente automobilistico a Trieste
Il razzismo: la discriminazione razziale è in aumento nel calcio
La tossicodipendenza: la parità fra i sessi nel luogo di lavoro peggiora

A) il sessismo & il razzismo
B) il razzismo & la sicurezza stradale
C) il sessismo & la tossicodipendenza
D) la tossicodipendenza & la sicurezza stradale

Extra Challenge: Write possible headlines for the following social issues: unemployment (*disoccupazione*) and debt (*debito*). (Writing)

9.3. Ottavio is talking about a forthcoming volunteering opportunity. (H)

Un gruppo di giovani della mia scuola offre volontariamente il proprio tempo per aiutare in una casa di riposo nella nostra città e ho intenzione di unirmi a loro. Infatti giovedì prossimo andrò con loro e avremo l'occasione di cantare nel coro. Dalla morte di mio nonno, ho voglia di passare più tempo con gli anziani e fare la differenza.

Below are some questions and answers about Ottavio's volunteering. Which answer is **correct**?

A) With whom will Ottavio volunteer? A group from church.
B) When will he start volunteering? Every Thursday starting in two months.
C) What will they do? They will play board games with the elderly residents.
D) What sparked this interest in volunteering? The death of Ottavio's grandad.

Extra Challenge: Describe your own volunteering experiences (or the experiences of someone you know). (Speaking)

9.4. Read the short text below where Gino talks about volunteering. (H)

Tre volte alla settimana faccio volontariato in una mensa dei poveri a Napoli. Prepariamo da mangiare e .... i piatti, ma la mia parte preferita è quando parliamo .... insieme. Mi ha fatto .... quanto io sia fortunato ad avere un posto per vivere e del cibo nel frigorifero.

Fill in the gaps with the most appropriate words from the lists below.

A) laviamo, tutti, capire
B) lavare, tutto, saputo
C) lavate, tutte, sapere
D) lavando, tutta, capito

Extra Challenge: Translate the text above into English. (Translation)

9.5. Which of the following is **not** an illness? (E)

A) il tatuaggio
B) la malattia cardiovascolare
C) il cancro
D) l'anoressia

Extra Challenge: Translate the terms above into English. (Translation)

9.6. Read the text below in which Alfonso describes challenges faced by his friend. (H)

Quattro mesi fa il mio amico è dovuto andare in un centro anti-droga per disintossicarsi perché era diventato dipendente dalla cocaina. La riabilitazione è stata molto ardua, particolarmente perché ha avuto una crisi d'astinenza. Per fortuna, l'ho visto per la prima volta la settimana scorsa e mi sembra stia molto meglio.

According to Alfonso's text, which of the following statements is **false**?

A) His friend went to a rehab centre four months ago.
B) He had become addicted to cocaine.
C) He went cold turkey.
D) Alfonso has not yet seen his friend.

Extra Challenge: Translate the text above into English. (Translation)

9.7. Read the text below about the different perspectives on drugs among Beatrice and her friends. (H)

Mi chiamo Beatrice e ho sedici anni. Non c'è dubbio che le droghe siano pericolose ma i miei amici dicono che la droga migliori l'umore e aiuti contro lo stress. Secondo loro, ci si sente più rilassati. Io però non sono d'accordo. A mio avviso, le droghe possono causare la depressione e dipendenza. Non mi interessano per niente!

Which of the opinions below is **not** expressed by Beatrice's friends?

A) Drugs improve your mood.
B) Drugs can be good for stress.
C) Drugs make you feel more relaxed.
D) Drugs can become addictive.

Extra Challenge: Translate the above text into English. (Translation)

9.8. Which of the following is **not** a disadvantage of smoking? (M)

A) Il fumo può portare alla dipendenza.
B) Le sigarette causano problemi respiratori.
C) Ti fa sentire più tranquillo.
D) L'odore e il sapore sono pungenti.

Extra Challenge: Give a brief summary of the advantages and disadvantages of smoking. (Speaking)

9.9. Read the text below about Pasquale's new year's resolution. (H)

Il mio buon proposito per il nuovo anno è di evitare di bere alcolici, almeno per il primo mese dell'anno; il mio cugino inglese lo chiama 'gennaio secco'. Un mese senza bevande alcoliche farà bene al fegato e potrò anche risparmiare un po'!

Which of the following statements is **true**?

A) Pasquale intends to reduce his alcohol intake.
B) His English cousin calls it 'dry February'.
C) A month without alcohol will do his liver good.
D) He will not go out as much.

Extra Challenge: What will your new year's resolution be next year? (Writing)

9.10. What is the major health issue for Roberto in the sentence below? (M)

Ho sempre l'aria stanca. Vado a letto troppo tardi e mi alzo molto presto a causa dell'allenamento di rugby.

A) too much sport
B) body odour
C) breathing bad air
D) lack of sleep

Extra Challenge: Write a list of other potential health issues for young people in Italian. (Writing)

9.11. The four subheadings below about healthy lifestyles are matched with four examples of what one should do to keep healthy. (E)

Which subheading does **not** match its example?

A) La vita sociale – si dovrebbero frequentare gli amici
B) L'alimentazione – ci si dovrebbe rilassare
C) Il riposo – si dovrebbe dormire almeno sette ore a notte
D) Il movimento – si dovrebbe fare dell'esercizio fisico

Extra Challenge: Give an example for the subheadings: *lo stress* and *il fumo*. (Speaking)

9.12. The table below contains examples of healthy living and examples of unhealthy living. (M)

La vita sana	La vita malsana
seguire una dieta equilibrata dormire poco passeggiare spesso respirare aria pulita	vivere una vita sedentaria mangiare spesso i dolci andare in palestra fumare

Can you identify the two examples in the **incorrect** columns?

A) seguire una dieta equilibrata & fumare
B) respirare aria pulita & vivere una vita sedentaria
C) dormire poco & andare in palestra
D) passeggiare spesso & mangiare spesso i dolci

Extra Challenge: Use three of the examples above to talk about healthy living. (Speaking)

9.13. The table below contains items that you would eat (*da mangiare*) and items that you would drink (*da bere*). How many items are in the **incorrect** column? (E)

Da mangiare	Da bere
carne	caffè
torta	birra
gelato	tè
pizza	vino
pasta	pesce
pane	acqua
uova	limonata
burro	latte
aglio	tisana

    A)   Zero
    B)   One
    C)   Two
    D)   Three

Extra Challenge: Translate the vocabulary in the table above into English. (Translation)

9.14. Which of the following lists **only** contains vegetables (rather than a combination of fruit and vegetables)? (H)

    A)   mela, uva, cetriolo, lampone
    B)   ciliegia, pera, anguria, lattuga
    C)   cavolo, piselli, zucchina, cipolla
    D)   melanzana, patata, arancia, pomodoro

Extra Challenge: Make a table of vegetables and fruit in Italian. (Writing)

9.15. Which of the following sentences is the **only** logical one in the list? (M)

    A)   Felipe è vegetariano quindi mangia sempre carne.
    B)   Antonio ha fame, quindi mangerà un succo d'arancia.
    C)   Maria non può mangiare latticini: mangia formaggio e beve spesso latte.
    D)   Luciano ama i dolci, in particolare il gelato.

Extra Challenge: Change the illogical sentences above so that they make sense. (Speaking)

9.16. Read Lina's account below of a recent shopping trip. (H)

Sono andata dal fruttivendolo e ho comprato un chilo di mele, mezzo chilo di ciliegie, sette arance, cento grammi di lamponi ed una scatola di fragole.

Which list contains Lina's food order?

A) 1kg of melons, 200g of raspberries, 3 oranges, 100g of pears, and a box of grapes
B) 1kg of apples, 500g of cherries, 7 oranges, 100g of raspberries, and a box of strawberries
C) 1kg of apples, 250g of blueberries, 6 peaches, 100g of cherries, and a box of blackberries
D) 2kg of apples, 2kg of apricots, 17 bananas, 100g of grapes, and a box of tomatoes

Extra Challenge: Translate the incorrect answers into Italian. (Translation)

9.17. The following phrases include a container and a food/drink item, e.g. *un sacchetto di patatine* (a packet of crisps). Two of the food/drink items need to be switched – can you identify which **two**? (M)

Una bottiglia d'acqua
Un vasetto di torta
Una fetta di yogurt
Un pacchetto di biscotti

A) acqua & biscotti
B) torta & biscotti
C) acqua & yogurt
D) torta & yogurt

Extra Challenge: Make a list of other food and drink items that may be stored in the containers above. (Writing)

9.18.   The following text describes a healthy diet. (H)

Cerco di fare una buona ……….. ogni mattina perché mi sembra molto importante. Oltretutto mangio parecchia frutta e verdura e ……. zucchero. Non bevo ….. bibite gassate.

Fill in the gaps with the most appropriate words from the lists below.

- A)   pranzo, povera, niente
- B)   cena, ricca, nessuno
- C)   dolce, ricco, né
- D)   colazione, poco, molte

Extra Challenge: Write a short paragraph about your eating habits. (Writing)

9.19.   Which of the following body parts is **not** on the top half of the body? (E)

- A)   faccia
- B)   naso
- C)   braccio
- D)   piede

Extra Challenge: Make a list of other body parts on the top half of the body. (Writing)

9.20.   Which of the following body parts is **not** on the bottom half of the body? (E)

- A)   mano
- B)   gamba
- C)   ginocchio
- D)   dito del piede

Extra Challenge: Name as many internal organs in Italian as you can think of, e.g. the heart, lungs and kidneys etc. (Speaking)

CHAPTER 9

Social Issues

Answers and
Detailed Solutions

9.1. B

The only term listed that is not classed as a 'social issue' would be *il cervello*, which means 'the brain'. The other terms are likely to fall into the category of a 'social issue': *l'inserimento sociale* means 'integration', *il debito* means 'debt', and *il pregiudizio* means 'prejudice'.

9.2. C

The two social issues that do not match their headlines are *il sessismo* (sexism) and *la tossicodipendenza* (drug addiction). The headline that matches sexism is *la parità fra i sessi nel luogo di lavoro peggiora* (gender equality in the work place is getting worse), while for drug addiction it is *nuova ricerca mostra il danno cerebrale provocato dal consumo delle droghe illegali* (new research shows brain damage caused by the consumption of illegal drugs). The other two headlines correspond with their description: *la sicurezza stradale* (road safety) goes with *due minori uccisi in un incidente automobilistico a Trieste* (two minors killed in a car accident in Trieste) and *il razzismo* (racism) goes with *la discriminazione razziale è in aumento nel calcio* (racial discrimination is on the rise in football).

9.3. D

Ottavio has been interested in volunteering and spending more time with old people since the death of his grandad (*dalla morte di mio nonno*). He will volunteer with a group from school (*scuola*), not church (*chiesa*). He will start volunteering next Thursday (*giovedì prossimo*) in an old people's home (*una casa di riposo*). Along with his school group, he will have the opportunity to sing in the choir (*avremo l'occasione di cantare nel coro*) rather than play board games (*giocare con giochi da tavolo*).

9.4. A

The first gap is likely to be first-person plural (we/*noi*) in keeping with the first verb in the sentence. As such, *laviamo* (we wash) is the most suitable answer, especially given that the infinitive (*lavare*), the gerund (*lavando*), and the second-person plural (*lavate*) would not make sense. Gino says that his favourite part of volunteering is talking all together; as there is more than one person speaking the plural is needed, e.g. *tutti*. Finally, the volunteering experience has made Gino understand how lucky he is; *mi ha fatto* means 'has made me' and is followed by the infinitive *capire* (to understand), which makes more sense than *sapere* (to know). He finishes the sentence by saying how lucky he is to have a place to live and food in the fridge (*quanto io sia fortunato ad avere un posto per vivere e del cibo nel frigorifero*).

9.5. A

The words *la malattia cardiovascolare* (heart disease), *il cancro* (cancer), and *l'anoressia* (anorexia) are all illnesses, whereas *il tatuaggio* means 'tattoo'.

9.6. D

Three of the statements about Alfonso and his friend are true. Firstly, his friend had to go to a rehab centre four months ago (*quattro mesi fa il mio amico è dovuto andare in un centro anti-droga*). The reason he went to the rehab centre was that he had become addicted to cocaine (*era diventato dipendente dalla cocaine*). Notice the use of the past perfect tense (*trapassato prossimo*) in which the imperfect tense is used with the perfect tense to describe past events which happened before another past event e.g. he **had** become addicted. For more practice with the past perfect refer to question 13.28. in chapter 13. Alfonso describes his friend's rehabilitation as very difficult (*molto ardua*) because he went cold turkey (*ha avuto una crisi d'astinenza*). This means that the false statement is D, Alfonso has not yet seen his friend. This is false because he says *l'ho visto per la prima volta la settimana scorsa* (I saw him for the first time last week). For more practice with the differences between the perfect and imperfect tenses, refer to question 13.19. in chapter 13.

9.7. D

Beatrice says that drugs are dangerous (*le droghe siano pericolose*) and believes that they can cause depression and addiction (*le droghe possono causare la depressione e dipendenza*). Her friends, however, have very different ideas. They believe that drugs improve your mood (*migliori l'umore*), are good for stress (*aiuti contro lo stress*), and help you to feel more relaxed (*ci si sente più rilassati*). Notice how Beatrice disagrees (*non sono d'accordo*) and says that drugs do not interest her at all (*non mi interessano per niente*).

9.8. C

Three of the phrases in question 9.8. outline the disadvantages of smoking. They include the fact that smoking can lead to addiction (*può portare alla dipendenza*), cigarettes cause respiratory problems (*le sigarette causano problemi respiratori*), and the smell and taste are pungent (*l'odore e il sapore sono pungenti*). The only phrase that outlines a potential advantage of smoking, according to some people, is *ti fa sentire più tranquillo* (it makes you feel calmer).

9.9. C

Pasquale's new year's resolution (*il buon proposito per il nuovo anno*) is not only to cut down his alcohol intake but to avoid alcohol altogether; the key word here is *evitare* (to avoid). He is hoping to do what his English cousin calls 'dry January' (*il mio cugino inglese lo chiama 'gennaio secco'*) and not drink for at least the first month of the year (*almeno per il primo mese dell'anno*). He does not mention going out less, but does say that he will be able to save some money (*potrò anche risparmiare un po'*). As a result, the only true statement is C: a month without alcohol will do Pasquale's liver good (*un mese senza bevande alcoliche farà bene al fegato*).

9.10. D

Roberto is not getting enough sleep. The clues are that he always seems tired (*ho sempre l'aria stanca*), he goes to bed late (*vado a letto troppo tardi*), and he gets up very early for rugby training (*mi alzo molto presto a causa dell'allenamento di rugby*).

Exam Tip: Try to pick out key words related to the theme of the text in order to decipher its meaning.

9.11. B

The subheading that does not match its example is *alimentazione* (diet) because the example says, 'one should relax' (*ci si dovrebbe rilassare*). Instead, we would expect to see something like *si dovrebbe mangiare bene* or *seguire una dieta sana* (one should eat well/follow a healthy diet). All the other examples match their subheadings: *la vita sociale* (social life) ⇒ *si dovrebbero frequentare gli amici* (one should hang out with friends), *riposo* (rest) ⇒ *si dovrebbe dormire almeno sette ore a notte* (one should sleep for at least 7 hours per night), and *movimento* (movement) ⇒ *si dovrebbe fare dell'esercizio fisico* (one should do physical exercise).

9.12. C

Dormire poco (to not sleep much) should be in the *vita malsana* column, whereas *andare in palestra* (to go to the gym) should be in the *vita sana* column. The other examples are in the correct columns. In the healthy lifestyle category, there is: *seguire una dieta equilibrata* (to follow a balanced diet), *passeggiare spesso* (to walk often), and *respirare aria pulita* (to breathe clean air). In the unhealthy lifestyle category, there is: *vivere una vita sedentaria* (to live a sedentary life), *mangiare spesso i dolci* (to eat sweet things often), and *fumare* (to smoke).

9.13. B

There is only one mistake in the table: *pesce* means 'fish' and should therefore be in the *da mangiare* category. This is not to be confused with *pesca* (peach). The other items are all in the correct columns and have been translated below.

Da mangiare	Da bere
carne (meat)	caffè (coffee)
torta (cake)	birra (butter)
gelato (ice cream)	tè (tea)
pizza	vino (wine)
pasta	acqua (water)
pane (bread)	limonata (lemonade)
uova (egg)	latte (milk)
burro (butter)	tisana (herbal/fruit tea)
aglio (garlic)	
pesce (fish)	

9.14. C

List C only contains vegetables: *cavolo* (cabbage), *piselli* (peas), *zucchina* (courgette), and *cipolla* (onion). Other vegetables in the lists include: *lettuga* (lettuce), *patata* (potato), *cetriolo* (cucumber) as well as cognates that were not included, such as: *carota, broccoli, spinaci, asparago,* and *avocado.* The fruit in the lists include: *mela* (apple), *uva* (grapes), *lampone* (raspberry), *ciliegia* (cherry), *pera* (pear), *anguria* (watermelon), *arancia* (orange), and *melanzana* (aubergine). There are also many fruits which are cognates, or near-cognates. These include: *banana, melone* and *limone.*

Exam Tip: When revising long lists of vocabulary, such as fruit and vegetables, try to break the list down into smaller chunks, grouped by theme.

9.15. D

The only sentence that makes sense is *Luciano ama i dolci, in particolare il gelato* (Luciano loves desserts, particularly ice cream). The first sentence is illogical because if Felipe was a vegetarian (*Felipe è vegetariano*) he would not eat meat, yet we are told that he always eats meat (*mangia sempre carne*). Secondly, Antonio is hungry (*ha fame*) and it makes little sense for him to eat an orange juice (*mangerà un succo d'arancia*). Finally, if Maria cannot eat dairy products (*non può mangiare latticini*) she would not be able to eat cheese and drink milk (*mangia formaggio e beve spesso latte*).

9.16. B

Option B is correct because *un chilo di mele* is '1kg of apples', *mezzo chilo di ciliegie* is 'half a kilo of cherries', *sette arance* means '7 oranges', *cento grammi di lamponi* means '100g of raspberries', and *una scatola di fragole* is a box of strawberries.

Exam Tip: Remember to agree the noun with the number when talking about quantity, e.g. **un** chil**o**, **due** chil**i**.

9.17. D

Una bottiglia d'acqua (a bottle of water) and *un pacchetto* di biscotti (a packet of biscuits) are both correct. By contrast, *un vasetto* means 'a pot' (or 'a jar') and should therefore be followed by *yogurt*, while *una fetta* is 'a slice' and should be followed by *torta* (cake).

9.18. D

The first gap must be filled with *colazione* (breakfast) because we know it is feminine from *una buona…*, and because *ogni mattina* (each morning) is referred to. The speaker then says, 'I eat lots of fruit and vegetables' (*mangio parecchia frutta e verdure*), and the second gap needs a masculine singular adjective as it is describing *zucchero* (sugar) therefore the only option is *poco*, which in this context means 'little'. Finally, the only word that makes sense in the context is *molte* (many), e.g. *Non bevo molte bibite gassate* (I do not drink many fizzy drinks).

9.19. D

The only body part that is not located on the top half of the body from the list is *piede* (foot). All of the other words refer to body parts on the top half of the body: *faccia* (face), *naso* (nose), and *braccio* (arm). In your own list, you may have included: *testa* (head), *bocca* (mouth), *occhi* (eyes), *orecchi* (ears), *lingua* (tongue), *collo* (neck), *spalla* (shoulder), and *schiena* (back).

9.20. A

The only body part in the list that is not found on the bottom half of the body is *mano* (hand). *Dito* by itself means 'finger' while *dito del piede* means 'toe' (or 'finger of the foot'!). *Ginocchio* is 'knee' while *gamba* is 'leg'. Other important vocabulary related to the body include: *sangue* (blood), *cuore* (heart), *polmoni* (lungs), *pelle* (skin), and *pancia/stomaco* (stomach).

CHAPTER 10

Global Issues

The difficulty rating for each question (Easy [E], Moderate [M] or Hard [H]) can be found in parenthesis next to each question.

10.1. Which of the following phrases could **not** be used to refer to a 'global issue /concern'? (E)

A) un problema globale
B) una questione mondiale
C) un grave incendio
D) una preoccupazione universale

Extra Challenge: Write a short paragraph in Italian about what, in your opinion, are the three biggest issues facing the world today. (Writing)

10.2. Which of the following word pairs are **not** opposites? (E)

A) proteggere - difendere
B) buttare via - riciclare
C) pulire - sporcare
D) sprecare - risparmiare

Extra Challenge: Use each of the verbs above in a sentence. (Speaking)

10.3. Read the text below about Teresa's city. (H)

Sfortunatamente ci sono tanti problemi nella mia città. Innanzitutto, non c'è abbastanza lavoro e abbiamo un problema con la disoccupazione. Per questo tanti giovani non riescono a pagare l'affitto e diventano senzatetto. Inoltre è molto difficile riciclare.

Which of the following is **not** a major issue in Teresa's city?

A) recycling
B) unemployment
C) homelessness
D) pollution

Extra Challenge: What are the five key challenges, in your opinion, that your local area faces? (Speaking)

10.4.   Domenico is talking about poverty in the text below. (H)

Dicono che la povertà sia un circolo vizioso e sono d'accordo. I governi hanno la responsabilità di migliorare la mobilità sociale e fornire un'educazione gratuita a tutti. Per questo due settimane fa ho deciso di partecipare ad una manifestazione contro i tagli al sostegno finanziario per gli alunni più poveri nella nostra società.

Which of the following is **not** mentioned in the text?

A)   Domenico thinks poverty is a vicious circle.
B)   He thinks the government should provide a free education for all.
C)   He went on a demonstration against cuts to students' financial support.
D)   He says that poverty is the biggest problem in society.

Extra Challenge: Translate the text above into English. (Translation)

10.5.   Read the following text in which Serena talks about her city. (H)

Nella mia città si vedono sempre più senzatetto sia alle entrate dei negozi sia alla stazione. Se ci fossero più piani locali e nazionali per aiutare i senzatetto a trovare lavoro o un posto per vivere, non sarebbero più costretti a chiedere soldi ai passanti.

What does Serena believe would be the best strategy for reducing homelessness in her city?

A)   allow the homeless to stay in shops or at the station
B)   more programmes that help homeless people gain stability
C)   give homeless people money
D)   give homeless people food

Extra Challenge: Using the text above as a template, translate into Italian: 'if there were more jobs, there would be fewer homeless people'. (Translation)

10.6. Read the text below about a recent fundraising effort. (M)

Sabato scorso cinque chiese cattoliche nella città di Bologna si sono unite per raccogliere fondi per le famiglie colpite dal recente terremoto. Hanno raccolto seimila euro al fine di poter fornire vestiti e cibo alle vittime del sisma.

Which of the following statements is **false?**

A)   Five Catholic churches came together to raise money.
B)   They were fundraising for families affected by a recent hurricane.
C)   They raised 600 euros.
D)   They aimed to provide clothes and food to the victims.

Extra Challenge: Describe a recent fundraising effort in your local area. (Writing)

10.7. Fill in the gaps in the following text about the environment using the most appropriate three words from the options below. (E)

L'industria chimica e l'uso di carbone e petrolio .... l'aria e causano l'effetto serra. Bisogna considerare energie più .... Inoltre ci sono troppe .... dappertutto e il governo non fa nulla per migliorare il trasporto pubblico.

A)   inquina, durevole, gente
B)   imparano, pulito, treni
C)   inquinano, pulite, macchine
D)   indicano, sporco, persone

Extra Challenge: Translate the text above into English. (Translation)

10.8. Barbara is talking about the environment. (H)

I nostri problemi ambientali peggioreranno a meno che gli esseri umani non cambino il loro comportamento. Secondo me, se avessimo più informazioni a proposito del futuro del nostro pianeta, sarebbe più facile istigare un cambiamento. Per quanto mi riguarda, il problema ambientale più minaccioso è l'inquinamento perché causa malattie respiratorie ed allo stesso tempo danneggia anche la natura. Infatti, ora gli esperti hanno paura che gli effetti dei gas serra siano peggiori di quanto avessimo inizialmente pensato.

Which of the following statements does **not** align with Barbara's views?

A) Changes to human behaviour are essential.
B) More information is needed to bring about change.
C) One of the biggest threats to the planet are our current methods of waste disposal.
D) The experts fear that greenhouse gases will be even more dangerous than first thought.

Extra Challenge: What, in your opinion, is the biggest threat to the environment? (Writing)

10.9. Which of the following should **not** be done by someone who wants to protect the environment? (M)

A) Si dovrebbe ridurre l'inquinamento atmosferico.
B) Si dovrebbe usare solamente la macchina.
C) Si dovrebbero utilizzare i mezzi di trasporto pubblico.
D) Si dovrebbero guidare macchine ecologiche.

Extra Challenge: Say three things you should not do if you want to help the environment, e.g. *non si dovrebbe…* (Speaking)

10.10. Romeo is talking about making his city more environmentally friendly. (E)

La mia città ha bisogno di più zone pedonali, piste ciclabili, e spazi verdi per essere più ecologica.

Romeo mentions three things which the city needs more of. Which of the following does he **not** mention?

A) more green spaces
B) more parking
C) more cycle paths
D) more pedestrian zones

Extra Challenge: Translate into Italian: 'the city needs more public transport and fewer cars'. (Translation)

10.11. Read the sentence below about recycling. (M)

A mio avviso non dobbiamo buttare le cose: in particolare, è meglio riciclare i vestiti, la carta, ed il vetro.

Which of the following is **not** mentioned as something that should be recycled?

A) cans
B) card
C) glass
D) clothes

Extra Challenge: Describe what and how often you recycle. (Writing)

10.12. Which of the following is the most appropriate translation of the sentence below? (H)

During the recycling process, we separate the rubbish into different coloured containers.

A) Durante il processo di riciclare, i bidoni si svuotano in contenitori di colori diversi.
B) Nel processo di riciclaggio, separiate il vetro in contenitori di diversi colori.
C) Durante il processo di riciclaggio, separiamo i rifiuti in contenitori di colori diversi.
D) Nel processo di riciclare, separa le lattine in contenitore di diversi colori.

Extra Challenge: Do you think recycling is important and, if so, why? (Speaking)

10.13. Look at the table below of birds (*uccelli*), insects (*insetti*), and mammals (*mammiferi*). (M)

Uccelli	Insetti	Mammiferi
il pappagallo	la farfalla	il gatto
la colomba	il ragno	il coniglio
la mucca	la formica	il cavallo

One of the animals has been placed in the wrong category. Can you identify which **one**?

- A) la mucca
- B) la farfalla
- C) il ragno
- D) il cavallo

Extra Challenge: List ten other animals in Italian. (Speaking)

10.14. Read Enrico's opinions about deforestation. (H)

Noi giovani abbiamo il compito di piantare più alberi visto che il disboscamento sta rovinando il paesaggio, oltre ad inquinare l'aria fresca e provocare l'estinzione di molte specie animali.

Which of the following statements does Enrico **not** say?

- A) It is the responsibility of young people to plant more trees.
- B) Deforestation ruins the landscape.
- C) Deforestation provides more land for housing.
- D) Deforestation causes the extinction of several species.

Extra Challenge: Translate the text above into English. (Translation)

10.15. Which of the following is the most accurate translation of the sentence below? (M)

I gas serra distruggono il pianeta e contribuiscono all'allargamento del buco dell'ozono.

A)   Greenhouse gases are destroying the planet and contributing to the widening hole in the ozone layer.
B)   Dangerous gases are destroying the planet and contributing to the hole in the ozone layer.
C)   Exhaust fumes are destroying the planet and contributing to the widening hole in the ozone layer.
D)   Biodegradable gases are destroying the planet and contributing to the hole in the ozone layer.

Extra Challenge: Give three examples of causes of greenhouse gases in Italian. (Speaking)

10.16. Which natural disaster is increasingly common according to the sentence below? (E)

L'aumento delle inondazioni in tutto il mondo mi preoccupa.

A)   hurricanes
B)   flooding
C)   earthquakes
D)   droughts

Extra Challenge: Using the sentence above as a template, translate into Italian: 'the increase in temperatures across Europe worries me'. (Translation)

10.17. Which of the following questions could **not** be used to ask about the weather? (M)

A)   Che tempo fa?
B)   Com'è il tempo?
C)   Com'è il tuo tempo libero?
D)   Quali sono le previsioni del tempo per oggi?

Extra Challenge: What is the weather like today? Describe it in Italian. (Speaking)

10.18. In the list below, which of the following is **not** a type of weather in Italian? (E)

A)   Fa caldo.
B)   Bisogna.
C)   È nuvoloso.
D)   Nevica.

Extra Challenge: List five types of weather in the present, past, and future tenses. (Writing)

10.19. Which of the following pairs of phrases do **not** correspond with one another? (H)

A)   Cade la neve ⇒ nevica
B)   È soleggiato ⇒ il sole spende
C)   Ci sarà un temporale ⇒ tuona
D)   Fa freddo ⇒ ci sono 30 gradi

Extra Challenge: Give a weather forecast for tomorrow using the future tense. (Speaking)

10.20. The table below contains phrases that describe the weather yesterday (*ieri*), today (*oggi*), and tomorrow (*domani*). Three phrases have been put into the wrong category as they are in the wrong tense. Can you identify these **three**? (H)

Ieri	Oggi	Domani
faceva cattivo tempo	c'è bel tempo	c'erano circa 20 gradi
le temperature si alzano	sta piovendo	tirerà vento
ha piovuto	farà caldo	nevicherà
c'era il sole	è nuvoloso	farà fresco

A)   Le temperature si alzano, farà caldo, c'erano circa 20 gradi.
B)   Faceva cattivo tempo, è nuvoloso, nevicherà.
C)   Ha piovuto, sta piovendo, tirerà vento.
D)   C'era il sole, c'è bel tempo, farà fresco.

Extra Challenge: Describe yesterday's weather. Ensure that you add appropriate time phrases. (Speaking)

CHAPTER 10

Global Issues

Answers and Detailed Solutions

10.1. C

The following three phrases could be translated to mean 'global issue/concern': *un problema globale, una questione mondiale*, and *una preoccupazione universale*. By contrast, *un grave incendio* means 'a serious fire'.

10.2. A

Proteggere means 'to protect' and its opposite should therefore be something like 'to ruin' (*rovinare*), 'to damage' (*danneggiare*), or 'to destroy' (*distruggere*), rather than 'to defend' (*difendere*). The other answers are opposite pairings: *buttare via* (to throw away) – *riciclare* (to recycle), *pulire* (to clean) – *sporcare* (to make dirty), and *sprecare* (to waste) – *risparmiare* (to save). Another verb for 'to save' when referring to energy is *conservare*.

10.3. D

Pollution is mentioned as being 'not bad' (*non sia male*), which means it is the only one that is not a major issue in Teresa's city. The other issues are mentioned in a negative light. Firstly, there are not many jobs (*non c'è abbastanza lavoro*), which leads to unemployment (*la disoccupazione*). Secondly, young people cannot afford the rent and so become homeless (*non riescono a pagare l'affitto e diventano senzatetto*). Thirdly, it is very difficult to recycle (*è molto difficile riciclare*).

Exam Tip: Often in the reading and listening examinations all the possible answers are mentioned so it is important to think carefully about which apply to the question.

10.4. D

Dominico agrees with the saying that poverty is a cycle (*la povertà sia un circolo vizioso*) and says that governments have a responsibility to improve social mobility and provide a free education for all (*i governi hanno la responsabilità di migliorare la mobilità sociale e fornire un'educazione gratuita a tutti*). He then says that two weeks ago he went on a demonstration against cuts to the financial support offered to the poorest pupils in society (*due settimane fa ho deciso di partecipare ad una manifestazione contro i tagli al sostegno finanziario per gli alunni più poveri nella nostra società*). Although he is clearly passionate about reducing poverty, he does not explicitly mention that he believes it to be the biggest problem in society.

Exam Tip: With longer texts, it may be worthwhile reading through the text twice (or more!) in order to better understand its meaning.

10.5. B

Serena calls for more local and national schemes to help the homeless find a job and a place to live (*più scheme locali e nazionali per aiutare i senzatetto a trovare lavoro o un posto per vivere*) therefore the correct answer is B. She starts the extract by saying that there are more and more homeless people in her city, either at shop entrances or at the station (*si vedono sempre più senzatetto sia alle entrate dei negozi sia alla stazione*). She then argues that if there were more programmes in place (*Se ci fossero più piani locali*), homeless people would not have to ask passers-by for money (*non sarebbero costretti a chiedere soldi ai passanti*).

10.6. B

The true statements are A, C, and D. Five Catholic churches in Bologna came together to raise money last Saturday (*sabato scorso cinque chiese cattoliche nella città di Bologna si sono unite per raccogliere fondi*). The churches raised 600 euros (*hanno raccolto seimila euro*) in order to provide clothes and food to the victims (*fornire vestiti e cibo alle vittime*). The false statement from the list is therefore B, they were fundraising for families affected by a recent hurricane. Instead, the churches were raising money for families affected by a recent earthquake (*raccogliere soldi per le famiglie colpite dal recente terremoto*).

10.7. C

The first blank needs to be filled by a verb in the third-person plural as both chemical industry and the use of coal and petrol (*l'industria chimica e l'uso di carbone e petrolio*) are the subjects of the verb, which rules out answer A. Given the context, only the word *inquinano* (they pollute) would be suitable, as opposed to *imparano* (they learn) or *indicano* (they indicate). Secondly, a feminine plural adjective is needed to describe the feminine plural noun *energie*. *Sporco* (dirty) is masculine, *pulito* (clean) and *durevole* (durable) are both singular, which leaves *pulite* (clean) as the only option. Finally, the last noun must be feminine plural as it is preceded by *troppe* (too many). It could therefore be *macchine* (cars) or *persone* (people), but in this case, it must be *macchine* given the previous answers. The speaker also says that the government are not doing anything to improve public transport (*il governo non fa nulla per migliorare il trasporto pubblico*).

10.8. C

The statement which does not align with Barbara's views is C: one of the biggest threats to the planet are our current methods of waste disposal. Barbara does not mention waste disposal (*il smaltimento rifiuti*) but instead says that the biggest threat to the environment is pollution (*il problema ambientale più minaccioso é l'inquinamento*) because it causes lung problems (*causa malattie respiratorie*) and damages nature (*danneggia anche la natura*). The other three statements correspond with her views. Firstly, she says that 'unless human beings' behaviour changes, our environmental problems will get worse' (*I nostri problemi ambientali peggioreranno a meno che gli esseri umani cambino il loro comportamento*). Notice the use of the subjunctive after the construction *a meno che* (unless) and the use of *non* before the verb. For further practice using the subjunctive refer to question 13.29. in chapter 13. Secondly, she states that 'if we had more information about the future of our planet it would be easier to instigate change' (*se avessimo più informazioni a proposito del futuro del nostro pianeta, sarebbe più facile istigare un cambiamento*). Finally, she says that 'the experts fear that the effects of greenhouse gases will be even worse than they first thought' (*gli esperti hanno paura che gli effetti dei gas serra siano peggiori di quanto avessimo inizialmente pensato*).

10.9. B

The only phrase that would be unhelpful to the environment is *si dovrebbe usare solamente la macchina* (one should only use the car). The other phrases are all positive actions that could benefit the environment: *si dovrebbe ridurre l'inquinamento atmosferico* (one should reduce air pollution), *si dovrebbero utilizzare i mezzi di trasporto pubblico* (one should use public transport), and *si dovrebbero guidare macchine ecologiche* (one should drive eco-friendly cars).

Exam Tip: Making a mindmap with key vocabulary from different topics and asking a friend to test you can be a useful technique when revising for comprehension tasks.

10.10. B

The city needs more *zone pedonali* (pedestrian zones), *piste ciclabili* (cycle paths), and *spazi verdi* (green space). Therefore, the only option not mentioned is parking (*parcheggio*).

Notice how the adjective *pedonali* goes after the noun, which is the norm in Italian, and the plural of *zona* is *zone*.

10.11. A

Cans (*le lattine*) are not mentioned in the text as a material that should be recycled. The speaker says that we must not throw things away (*non dobbiamo buttare le cose*). Instead, it is better for us to recycle (*è meglio riciclare*), particularly clothes (*i vestiti*), card (*la carta*), and glass (*il vetro*).

10.12. C

The most appropriate translation is C for a number of reasons. Firstly, *durante* is a better translation for 'during' than *nel* (although *nel corso di* could also work). Secondly, to translate 'recycling' it is better to use the noun *reciclaggio* than the infinitive *riciclare*. Thirdly the most appropriate translation of 'we separate' would be *separiamo*, although the impersonal *si separa* could also work. 'Rubbish' in Italian is *i rifiuti*, whereas *i bidoni/i cestini* are 'bins', *il vetro* is 'glass' and *le lattine* are 'cans'. Finally, 'into different coloured containers' is best translated as *in contenitori di colori diversi*, as the adjective generally goes after the noun in Italian.

10.13. A

La mucca is a cow, and therefore should go in the mammal (*mammiferi*) category. See the following table for translations of the other terms.

Uccelli	Insetti	Mammiferi
il pappagallo (parrot)	la farfalla (butterfly)	il gatto (cat)
la colomba (dove)	il ragno (spider)	il coniglio (rabbit)
	la formica (ant)	il cavallo (horse)
		La mucca (cow)

10.14. C

Enrico starts by saying that 'we young people have a responsibility to plant more trees' (*noi giovani abbiamo il compito di piantare più alberi*). His reasoning for this is that deforestation is harmful in three distinct ways: it ruins the landscape (*il disboscamento sta rovinando il paesaggio*), it is polluting fresh air (*inquinare l'aria fresca*), and it is causing the extinction of several species (*provocare l'estinzione di molte specie animali*).

10.15. A

The most appropriate translation is A. *I gas serra* are 'greenhouse gases', whereas 'dangerous gases' would be *i gas pericolosi*, 'exhaust fumes' would be *fumi di scarico*, and biodegradable is a near-cognate – *biodegradabile*. Notice how both verbs are conjugated in the third-person plural (e.g. *distruggono, contribuiscono*) as the subject is plural (greenhouse ga**ses**).

10.16. B

The speaker is worried (*mi preoccupa*) about the increase in **floods** across the world (*l'aumento delle inondazioni in tutto il mondo*). The following natural disasters were not mentioned: hurricanes (*gli uragani*), earthquakes (*i terremoti*), and droughts (*le siccità*).

10.17. C

The first two questions are very similar: *che tempo fa?* (what is the weather like?) and *com'è il tempo?* (how is the weather?). The final question *quali sono le previsioni del tempo per oggi?* refers to the weather forecast (*previsioni*). Question C is unrelated to weather as *tempo libero* means 'free time'. *Tempo* is a homonym because it means both 'time' and 'weather'; make sure you check the context to decipher which meaning is being referred to when this term is used. Other homonyms in Italian include: *fine*, which means 'goal/aim' in the masculine (*il fine*) and 'end' in the feminine (*la fine*); *metro* which means 'metre' in the masculine (*il metro*) and 'underground' in the feminine (*la metro*).

10.18. B

The only word which is not a weather type is *bisogna*, which means 'he/she/it needs'. All the other words/phrases in the list are weather types: *fa caldo* (it is hot), *è nuvoloso* (it is cloudy), and *nevica* (it is snowing).

10.19. D

The phrases that do not correspond are *fa freddo* (it is cold) and *ci sono 30 gradi* (it is 30 degrees). The other weather phrases correspond to their respective pair: *cade la neve* (snow is falling), and *nevica* (it snows), *è soleggiato* (it is sunny), and *il sole spende* (the sun is shining), and more tenuously, *ci sarà un temporale* (there will be a storm) and *tuona* (there is thunder). Remember that in Italian, just like in English, there are often many ways of saying the same or a similar thing.

10.20. A

The phrases in list A are not in the correct columns because they are not in the right tense. Firstly, *le temperature si alzano* means 'temperatures are rising', which is in the present rather than the past tense. Secondly, *farà caldo* means 'it will be hot', and so should be in the *domani* category. Thirdly, *c'erano circa 20 gradi* translates as 'it was about 20 degrees', and so should go in the *ieri* column. See the following table for translations of all the weather phrases.

Ieri	Oggi	Domani
faceva cattivo tempo (it was horrible weather) ha piovuto (it rained) c'era il sole (it was sunny) **c'erano circa 20 gradi (it was about 20 degrees)**	c'è bel tempo (it is nice weather) sta piovendo (it is raining) è nuvoloso (it is cloudy) **le temperature si alzano (temperatures are rising)**	ci sarà vento (it will be windy) nevicherà (it will snow) farà fresco (it will be cool) **farà caldo (it will be hot)**

For further practice recognising different tenses, see question 13.30. in chapter 13.

CHAPTER 11

Miscellaneous Vocabulary

The difficulty rating for each question (Easy [E], Moderate [M] or Hard [H]) can be found in parenthesis next to each question.

11.1. Which of the following is **not** a question word in Italian? (E)

A) quando
B) qual
C) che
D) quindi

Extra Challenge: Ask three questions in Italian using the three question words above. (Speaking)

11.2. Which of the following question words changes its form according to the noun in the question? (E)

A) dove
B) chi
C) quanto
D) che

Extra Challenge: Ask a question in Italian starting with each of the question words above. (Speaking)

11.3. Read the following four pairs of questions and answers. In which pair does the answer **not** match with the question? (M)

A) Che ore sono? Le tre meno un quarto.
B) Quando è il concerto? Dieci canzoni.
C) Con chi vai al supermercato? Due amici.
D) Dove abitano i vostri nonni? In campagna, vicino a Torino.

Extra Challenge: Give alternative answers to the four questions posed above. (Speaking)

11.4. Which of the following terms would **not** be used to describe the dimensions of an object? (E)

A) altezza
B) bellezza
C) lunghezza
D) larghezza

Extra Challenge: Translate into Italian: 'the length of the box is 1 metre. Its height is 20cm and its width is 30cm'. (Translation)

11.5. Which of the following terms does **not** relate to size? (M)

A) la dimensione
B) la taglia
C) la misura
D) la pelle

Extra Challenge: Make a list of adjectives in Italian that relate to size, such as long, wide, tall etc. (Writing)

11.6. Out of the four sentences below, three contain a shape. Which sentence does **not** contain a shape? (H)

A) Roberta ha disegnato un triangolo nel quaderno.
B) Il cerchio sul soffitto è bianco.
C) Il biglietto d'auguri ha la forma di un quadrato.
D) Michele vuole un buono sconto sulla scrivania.

Extra Challenge: Translate the sentences above into English. (Translation)

11.7. Fabiano is saying goodbye to his neighbour. Which of the following would **not** be a suitable phrase to use? (E)

A) arrivederci
B) ci vediamo presto
C) benvenuto
D) a domani

Extra Challenge: Give five examples of how Fabiano might greet his neighbour in Italian, e.g. good afternoon. (Speaking)

11.8. Olimpia just bumped into someone in the corridor. Which of the following phrases should she **not** use in this situation? (M)

A) in bocca al lupo
B) scusa
C) è colpa mia
D) mi dispiace

Extra Challenge: Write a role play dialogue involving someone bumping into another person in Italian. (Writing)

11.9. The following words are colours in Italian. How many are spelt **incorrectly**? (M)

verde, giallo, blu, roso, rosa, grigio, nerro, bianco, brunno, viola, arancione

A) Two
B) Three
C) Four
D) Five

Extra Challenge: Write five sentences in Italian using five of the colours above. (Writing)

11.10. Out of the four sentences below, three contain a material. Which sentence does **not** contain a material? (H)

A)   Daniele usa del legno per costruire un giocattolo.
B)   Mi va una merenda.
C)   La bottiglia è fatta di vetro.
D)   Mi piace questa gonna di cuoio.

Extra Challenge: Make a list of other materials in Italian. (Writing)

11.11. The following sentences relate to distance and location. They are grouped into pairs with similar meanings. Which pair of sentences do **not** have a similar meaning? (H)

A)   L'ospedale è molto lontano – L'ospedale è a due passi.
B)   Mia nonna abita alla periferia della città – La casa di mia nonna è nei sobborghi.
C)   Ci sono negozi dappertutto – Ci sono negozi in ogni luogo.
D)   Abito in occidente – Abito in un paese occidentale.

Extra Challenge: Translate the sentences above into English. (Translation)

11.12. Which of the following is the most appropriate translation of the sentence below? (H)

You will find the cat outside the house, under the bench in the middle of the garden.

A) Troverai il gatto fuori di casa, sotto la panca in mezzo al giardino.
B) Troverai il gatto in cima alla casa, sopra la panca lontano dal giardino.
C) Troverai il gatto in fondo alla casa, sotto la panca vicino al giardino.
D) Troverai il gatto dentro la casa, sopra la panca intorno al giardino.

Extra Challenge: Translate the following sentence into Italian: 'You will find the dog inside the house, behind the table in the kitchen'. (Translation)

11.13. Which of the following is the most appropriate translation of the sentence below? (H)

The customers were unhappy because the train arrived late.

A) I clienti erano scontenti perché il treno è arrivato in ritardo.
B) Le persone sono state tristi perché il treno è stata in ritardo.
C) La gente erano felici perché il treno è arrivato in orario.
D) La clientela era infelici perché il treno non è arrivati puntualmente.

Extra Challenge: Translate the following sentence into Italian 'the students were happy because the train was on time'. (Translation)

11.14. Which of the following is the **only** negative opinion? (E)

A) La politica mi interessa tanto; oggigiorno è più importante che mai!
B) Mi piace la storia dell'arte perché è molto interessante.
C) I colori mi sembrano brutti.
D) La vista dal balcone era spettacolare.

Extra Challenge: Write four positive and four negative opinions using a variety of sentence structures. (Writing)

11.15. Which of the following sentences does **not** contain a comparison? (H)

A)　La torta è più buona della pasta.
B)　Penso che i biglietti siano gratis.
C)　Le biblioteche sono meno rumorose dei ristoranti.
D)　Paolo è arrogante tanto quanto Pietro.

Extra Challenge: Compare the personalities of two of your friends (or family members), using at least four comparisons. (Speaking)

11.16. The following table contains a list of opposite comparatives and superlatives. Can you identify which **two** words should be swapped? (H)

ottimo	pessimo
meglio	minimo
migliore	peggiore
maggiore	minore
massimo	peggio

A)　minimo / peggio
B)　massimo / pessimo
C)　peggiore / minore
D)　maggiore / meglio

Extra Challenge: Write three sentences in Italian using the pairs of opposites listed above. (Writing)

11.17. Which of the following is **not** a time phrase related to the past? (E)

A)　ieri
B)　la settimana scorsa
C)　domani
D)　il mese scorso

Extra Challenge: Use each of the time phrases above in a sentence, ensuring that you select the correct tense. (Speaking)

11.18. Which of the following terms does **not** relate to a time of the day? (M)

A) mezzanotte
B) primavera
C) la sera
D) la mattina

Extra Challenge: Give three examples of things you do at different times of day. (Writing)

11.19. Read the text below in which Angelo talks about healthy eating. (H)

Provo sempre a mangiare in ………….. sana. Amo la frutta ……… le pere e le albicocche secche …….. non mi piacciono le verdure, ………….. i broccoli ed il cavolfiore.

Which of the following words would be most appropriate to fill in the gaps?

A) modo, forse, ma, se
B) maniera, come, però, specialmente
C) luogo, altrimenti, comunque, soprattutto
D) vita, per esempio, insomma, cioè

Extra Challenge: Write a short paragraph on a topic of your choosing, using at least five conjunctions. (Writing)

11.20. Look at the lists of words below. Which of the following is the **only** list that does not contain words with similar meanings? (M)

A) quindi, dunque, perciò
B) nonostante, comunque, tuttavia
C) per fortuna, purtroppo, soprattutto
D) inoltre, anche, per di più

Extra Challenge: Use at least three of the conjunctions above in three separate sentences. (Speaking)

CHAPTER 11

Miscellaneous Vocabulary

Answers and Detailed Solutions

11.1. D

Quindi is not a question word, as it means 'therefore' whereas the other items are all question words: *quando* (when), *qual* (which), and *che* (what).

11.2. C

Quanto is the only question word mentioned that changes its form according to the noun in the question. For example, asking 'how old are you?' in Italian is literally translated as 'how many years do you have?', *quanti anni hai?* Notice that the 'how much' is changed to its masculine plural form because the noun *anni* (years) is masculine plural. If we were asking how many houses there are we would need to change *quanto* to its feminine plural form, *quante*, e.g. *quante case ci sono?* (how many houses are there?). Question words such as *dove, chi*, and *che* are static and do not change according to the nouns in the question.

11.3. B

The pair in which the question does not match with the answer is B. The question is *quando è il concerto?* (when is the concert?), whereas the answer is *dieci canzoni* (ten songs). Instead the answer would need to change to something like *alle dieci* (at 10 o'clock), or the question could change to *quante canzoni?* (how many songs?). The other question and answer pairings correspond with one another: *che ore sono?* (what time is it?) *le tre meno un quarto* (quarter to three), *con chi vai al supermercato?* (with whom do you go to the supermarket?) *due amici* (two friends), and *dove abitano i vostri nonni?* (where do your grandparents live?) *in campagna, vicino a Torino* (in the countryside near Turin).

11.4. B

Height in Italian is *altezza*, length is *lunghezza*, and width is *larghezza*. These nouns are similar to the adjectives *alto* (high), *lungo* (long), and *largo* (wide). *Bellezza* means 'beauty' and is therefore the only word that does not refer to dimensions.

Exam Tip: Look for patterns in words in order to help you deduce meanings. This is particularly true for prefixes and suffixes.

11.5. D

La pelle means 'skin' and therefore is not related to size, unlike the following words: *la dimensione, la taglia* (size), and *la misura* (size/measurement). Adjectives relating to size include: *alto* (tall/high), *basso* (short/low), *largo* (wide), *stretto* (narrow), *lungo* (long), *profondo* (deep), *minuscolo* (tiny), and *enorme* (huge).

11.6. D

The three shapes mentioned in the sentences include *un triangolo* (a triangle), *il cerchio* (the circle), and *un quadrato* (a square). The sentences translate as: *Roberta ha disegnato un triangolo nel quaderno* (Roberta drew a triangle in the notebook), *il cerchio sul soffitto è bianco* (the circle on the ceiling is white), and *il biglietto d'auguri ha il formo di un quadrato* (the birthday card is a square). Therefore, the sentence without a shape is *Michele vuole un buono sconto sulla scrivania* (Michele wants a discount on the desk).

11.7. C

If Fabiano was saying goodbye to his neighbour he would be unlikely to say *benvenuto* (welcome). He is much more likely to use one of the following phrases: *arrivederci* (goodbye), *ci vediamo presto* (see you soon), or *a domani* (see you tomorrow). When greeting his neighbour he might say *buon giorno* (good day), *ciao* (hi), or *buona sera* (good evening).

11.8. A

In bocca al lupo means 'good luck' (although it literally translates as 'into the mouth of the wolf') and would therefore not be an appropriate phrase to use if you had bumped into someone. Instead, *scusa* (excuse me), *è colpa mia* (it is my fault), or *mi dispiace* (sorry) would be more appropriate responses.

11.9. B

Three of the colours in the list are misspelt: *nero* (black) has one *r*, *rosso* (red) needs two *s*'s, and *bruno* (brown) should only have one *n*. The other colours translate as follows: *verde* (green), *giallo* (yellow), *rosa* (pink), *grigio* (grey), *blu* (blue), *bianco* (white), *viola* (purple), and *arancione* (orange).

Exam Tip: Check your spelling carefully when writing in Italian.

11.10. B

The only sentence that does not include a material is B: *mi va una merenda* (I would like a snack). The three materials mentioned are *legno* (wood), *vetro* (glass), and *cuoio* (leather). The sentences therefore translate as follows: *Daniele usa del legno per costruire un giocattolo* (Daniele uses the wood to make the toy), *la bottiglia è fatta di vetro* (the bottle is made of glass), and *mi piace questa gonna di cuoio* (I like this leather skirt). Other materials in Italian include: *la carta* (paper), *il cotone* (cotton), *il ferro* (iron), *l'oro* (gold), and *la seta* (silk).

11.11. A

L'ospedale è molto lontano (the hospital is very far) does not correspond with *l'ospedale è a due passi* (the hospital is very nearby). The other three pairs of sentences do have similar meanings: *Mia nonna abita alla periferia della città* (my grandmother lives on the outskirts of town) – *La casa di mia nonna è nei sobborghi* (my grandmother's house is in the suburbs), *ci sono negozi dappertutto* (there are shops everywhere) – *ci sono negozi in ogni luogo* (there are shops everywhere), and *abito in occidente* (I live in the West) – *abito in un paese occidentale* (I live in a western country).

11.12. A

The most appropriate translation is A: *Troverai il gatto fuori di casa, sotto la panca in mezzo al giardino*. The key words needed here are 'outside' (*fuori*), 'under' (*sotto*), and 'in the middle of' (*in mezzo a*). The incorrect words and phrases included: 'at the top of' (*in cima a*), 'at the bottom of' (*in fondo a*), 'inside' (*dentro*), 'above' (*sopra*), 'far' (*lontano da*), 'near' (*vicino a*), and 'around' (*intorno a*).

11.13. A

The most appropriate translation is A: *i clienti erano scontenti perché il treno è arrivato in ritardo*. Firstly, *i clienti* are 'clients' or 'customers', whereas *le persone* and *la gente* refer to 'people' and *la clientela* is 'the clientele'. Secondly, 'unhappy' could be translated as *infelici* or *scontenti*, whilst *tristi* is 'sad'. Thirdly, 'late' can be translated *in ritardo*, not *puntualmente* (punctually) or *in orario* (on time).

11.14. C

I colori mi sembrano brutti translates to 'the colours seem ugly to me' and is therefore the only negative opinion. The positive opinions given are as follows: *la politica mi interessa tanto; oggigiorno è più importante che mai* (politics interests me so much: nowadays it is more important than ever), *mi piace la storia dell'arte perché è molto interessante* (I like the history of art because it is very interesting), and *la vista dal balcone era spettacolare* (the view from the balcony was amazing).

Exam Tip: When giving opinions in Italian, try to use a variety of structures and always justify and develop your opinions.

11.15. B

The only sentence not to contain a comparative element is B: *penso che i biglietti siano gratuiti* (I think the tickets are free). Notice the use of the subjunctive in this sentence (*siano*) as *penso che* (I think that) contains an element of doubt. For more information about the subjunctive, refer to question 13.29. in chapter 13. The other three sentences feature a comparison of some sort: *La torta è più buona della pasta* (the cake is nicer than the pasta), *le biblioteche sono meno rumorose dei ristoranti* (libraries are less noisy than restaurants), and *Paolo è arrogante tanto quanto Pietro* (Paul is as arrogant as Peter). When making comparisons, use *più/meno… di* when comparing two different nouns (e.g. *il cinema è più divertente del teatro*). By contrast, use *più/meno…che* when comparing two qualities of the same noun (e.g. *Marco è **più** amichevole **che** scortese* [Marco is more friendly than rude]), or in front of an infinitive (e.g. *è **meno** facile cantare **che** ballare* [it is less easy to sing than to dance]).

11.16. A

The words that should be swapped over are *minimo* (minimum), which is the opposite of *massimo* (maximum), and *peggio* (worse), which should go next to *meglio* (better). The list of comparatives and superlatives are translated into English in the following table.

ottimo (best, excellent)	pessimo (worst, awful)
meglio (better)	peggio (worse)
migliore (the best)	peggiore (the worst)
maggiore (greater, bigger)	minore (smaller, minor)
massimo (maximum)	minimo (minimum)

11.17. C

Domani means 'tomorrow' and is therefore the only time phrase not related to the past. The other phrases can be used to describe events that have happened in the past: *ieri* (yesterday), *la settimana scorsa* (last week), and *il mese scorso* (last month). Time phrases in reading comprehension tasks can provide a useful signpost as to when the events are taking place.

Exam Tip: Using a variety of time phrases in your writing and speaking is very important as it indicates to the listener or reader when and how often an event takes place.

11.18. B

Primavera means spring and is therefore the only word not related to a time of day. The other words are related to a time of day and include: *mezzanotte* (midnight), *la sera* (evening), and *la mattina* (morning). Other times of day include: *mezzogiorno* (midday), *pomeriggio* (afternoon), *alba* (dawn), and *tramonto* (dusk/sunset).

11.19. B

Angelo begins by saying 'I try to eat healthily' (*provo sempre a mangiare in maniera sana*). Although *in modo sano* also means 'healthily', in this instance *modo* would not fit because the adjective was feminine (*sana*) rather than masculine (*sano*). The words *luogo* (place) and *vita* (life) do not work in the context. Angelo then says, 'I love fruit' (*amo la frutta*) and gives the examples of pears and dried apricots (*le pere e le albicocche secche*). The two phrases that would be suitable are *per esempio* (for example) and *come* (like/such as). *Forse* (maybe) and *altrimenti* (otherwise) do not fit with the sentence. Thirdly, Angelo gives a contrasting opinion saying that he does not like vegetables (*non mi piacciono le verdure*), therefore *ma* (but), *però* (but), and *comunque* (however) are all appropriate. *Insomma* means 'in conclusion' or 'so' and does not work in the context of the sentence. Finally, Angelo gives examples of particular vegetables he dislikes, so the two appropriate choices would be *specialmente* (especially) or *soprattutto* (above all), whereas *se* (if) and *cioè* (that is to say) do not work. The answer is therefore B as it contains only words suitable for the given text.

11.20. C

The list of words that do not have similar meanings are in option C: *per fortuna* (fortunately), *purtroppo* (unfortunately), *soprattutto* (above all). The other lists contain words with similar meanings. In list A, *quindi, dunque*, and *perciò* all mean 'therefore'. In list B, *nonostante, comunque*, and *tuttavia* mean 'however' or 'nevertheless'. Finally, list C contains *inoltre* (furthermore), *anche* (also), and *per di più* (moreover), all of which have a similar meaning.

Exam Tip: It is important to use a range of connectives in your writing, in order to link clauses and ideas together. Try to avoid repetition!

CHAPTER 12

Articles, Nouns and Pronouns

The difficulty rating for each question (Easy [E], Moderate [M] or Hard [H]) can be found in parenthesis next to each question.

12.1. 'The' is a definite article and can be said in multiple ways in Italian, depending on the gender and number of the noun. (E)

Which of the following lists contains **all** the definite articles in Italian?

A) il, la, dei, lo, degli, le
B) il, lo, l', la, i, gli, le
C) il, la, gli, le
D) il, lo, la, i, gli

Extra Challenge: Give an example of a noun in Italian with each of the definite articles above.

12.2. Which definite article would you need before all of the following nouns: (E)

poeta, tempo, sole, cotone, cappuccino, dolore

A) il
B) gli
C) la
D) le

Extra Challenge: Translate the list of nouns above.

12.3. Which definite article would you need before the following nouns? (E)

nebbia, pagina, mela, fine, ditta, Chiesa, decisione, qualità, lavatrice, mano

A) gli
B) i
C) le
D) la

Extra Challenge: Translate the list of nouns above.

12.4. Which of the following nouns is **not** masculine in Italian? (E)

A) porta
B) opuscolo
C) film
D) clima

Extra Challenge: Which other word in the list would you expect to be feminine and why?

12.5. How do Italian nouns ending in –o and –a respectively in the singular end in the plural? (E)

A) both i
B) both e
C) i & a
D) i & e

Extra Challenge: Give five examples of nouns in their plural form in Italian.

12.6. Which of the following lists feature **only** plural nouns? (M)

A) forbici, laghi, cipolle, elicotteri
B) regalo, musica, verità, violini
C) squadre, spazzolino da denti, casco, fiori
D) informazione, rumore, zona, pedone

Extra Challenge: Change all the singular nouns above into their plural forms.

12.7. Which of the following complications regarding plural nouns in Italian is **false**? (M)

A) Nouns ending in -co, -ca, -go or -ga often require a 'h' in the plural to preserve the sound.
B) Shortened and borrowed words often stay the same in the plural.
C) Words ending –gio or –cio keep their 'o' in the plural.
D) Some nouns stay the same in the plural as they are in the singular.

Extra Challenge: Give three examples of nouns that do **not** change in the plural in Italian.

12.8. Which of the following sentences **correctly** transforms the nouns in the text below from singular to plural? (M)

Abito in una casa con un giardino, una piscina, un salotto, un televisore ed una torre.

A) Abito in due case con tre giardine, quattro piscina, cinque salotta, sette televisori e due torre.
B) Abito in due case con tre giardine, quattro piscina, cinque salotti, sette televisori e due torre.
C) Abito in due case con tre giardini, quattro piscine, cinque salotti, sette televisori e due torri.
D) Abito in due case con tre giardini, quattro piscine, cinque salotte, sette televisore e due torri.

Extra Challenge: Say a sentence in Italian using at least 5 nouns in their plural forms.

12.9. Indefinite articles, translating to 'a' or 'an' in English, also vary according to the gender and number of the noun. (M)

How many indefinite articles are there in Italian?

A) Two
B) Three
C) Four
D) Five

Extra Challenge: Give an example of each indefinite article with a noun.

12.10. Which indefinite article is needed before the following nouns? (E)

ora, entrata, opera, autostrada, istruzione

A) un
B) uno
C) una
D) un'

Extra Challenge: Translate the nouns in the list above into English.

12.11. Partitive articles consist of: (M)

A) the preposition *di* + the definite article
B) the preposition *a* + the definite article
C) the preposition *di* + the indefinite article
D) the preposition *a* + the indefinite article

Extra Challenge: Give three ways of saying 'some' in Italian.

12.12. Which list displays the partitive articles needed to fill in the gaps in the phrases below? (M)

1) Mangia ...... cioccolata, 2) Litighiamo a causa ...... vestiti, 3) Parlo con ...... studenti, 4) Bevo ..... limonata.

A) 1. della 2. della 3. degli 4. dell'
B) 1. del 2. delle 3. del 4. dello
C) 1. della 2. dei 3. degli 4. della
D) 1. dello 2. degli 3. dei 4. della

Extra Challenge: Translate the four phrases above into English.

12.13. Often the partitive article in the singular (*del, della* etc.) and in the plural (*dei, delle* etc.) can be replaced respectively by which words/phrases? (M)

A) singular: **qualche**, plural: **un po' di**
B) singular: **un po' di**, plural: **alcuni/e**
C) singular: **qualche**, plural: **qualchi**
D) singular: **alcuni/e**, plural: **qualche**

Extra Challenge: Give three examples of saying 'some' without using the partitive article.

12.14. When conjugating verbs in Italian, in what order do personal subject pronouns go? (E)

A) tu, voi, noi, io, loro, lui/lei
B) lui/lei, loro, io, noi,
C) io, tu, lui/lei, noi, voi, loro
D) io, noi, tu, voi, lui/lei, loro

Extra Challenge: Use each of the personal subject pronouns above in a sentence.

12.15. Which personal subject pronoun is used to say 'they', when referring to a group of girls? (E)

A) lora
B) loro
C) lori
D) lore

Extra Challenge: Translate the following sentence into Italian: 'they go to the shops'.

12.16. Which of the following does **not** use the correct direct object pronoun in the answer to the question? (H)

A) Mi ascolti? Si, te ascolto.
B) Bevi il tè? Si, lo bevo.
C) Vedi i ragazzi? No, non li vedo.
D) Compri la pasta? Si, la compro.

Extra Challenge: Give three of your own examples of the direct object pronoun.

12.17. Which would be the most appropriate translation for the following sentence? (H)

Have you seen the film? I am going to see it tonight.

A) Hai visto il film? Vado a vederla stasera.
B) Hai visto il film? Vado a guardarla stasera.
C) Hai visto il film? Vado a vederlo stasera.
D) Hai visto il film? Vado a guadagnarlo stasera.

Extra Challenge: Translate the following sentences into Italian: 'Have you eaten the main course? I am going to eat it now'.

12.18. Which of the following sentences does **not** contain an indirect object pronoun? (H)

A)   Mia mamma mi manda un messaggio.
B)   Ci dicono l'obiettivo.
C)   Devo telefonarle stasera.
D)   Vediamo la partita insieme.

Extra Challenge: Translate the sentences above into English.

12.19. Which of the following possessive pronouns would **not** be used for 'yours'? (H)

A)   il tuo
B)   i vostri
C)   la nostra
D)   le Sue

Extra Challenge: Translate the following words into Italian: 'mine', 'his' and 'theirs'.

12.20. Which is the relative pronoun in the following sentence? (H)

La donna che ho incontrato ama il libro che hai scritto.

A)   che
B)   il
C)   incontrato
D)   libro

Extra Challenge: Write three sentences using relative pronouns.

12.21. The relative pronoun *cui* is used after prepositions in Italian. Which of the following translations is **incorrect**? (H)

A)   la città in cui abito = the city in which I live
B)   la regione su cui viene = the region from which he comes
C)   l'uomo a cui telefonano = the man whom they phone
D)   la ragazza con cui gioco a tennis = the girl with whom I play tennis

Extra Challenge: Give three more examples of sentences using *cui*.

12.22. Demonstrative pronouns are used to indicate which object is being referred to. In the following sentence, which demonstrative pronoun is **incorrect**? (M)

Quelle torte sono più gustose di queste.
Quello caramella è meno sano di questa.

A) quelle
B) queste
C) quello
D) questa

Extra Challenge: Translate the following sentence into Italian: 'those students are more polite than these'.

12.23. Which of the following sentences is grammatically incorrect? (H)

A) Alcuno ama bere.
B) Qualcuno deve pulire la casa regolarmente.
C) Qualcosa cambierà.
D) Nessuno vuole parlare con me.

Extra Challenge: Translate the following into Italian: 'some people do not agree', 'someone waits patiently', 'something must change', and 'no-one told me'.

12.24. Which of the following translation pairings of indefinite pronouns is **incorrect**? (E)

A) Troppo – too much
B) Niente – no-one
C) Ciascuno - each
D) Certo - some

Extra Challenge: Use each of the indefinite pronouns above in a sentence.

12.25. Which of the following provides the **correct** list of reflexive pronouns in Italian? (M)

A) mi, ti, gli, le, ci, vi and gli
B) mi, ti, lo, la, ci, vi, li and le
C) io, tu, lui, lei, noi, voi and loro
D) mi, ti, si, ci, vi and si

Extra Challenge: What type of pronouns are the other three lists?

12.26. Which of the following means 'here it is'? (E)

A) dietro
B) eccolo
C) stesso
D) dubbio

Extra Challenge: Use each of the words above in a sentence.

12.27. Which translation would be most appropriate for the following sentence? (H)

I like to go there every day.

A) Mi piace andarci ogni giorno.
B) Mi piace ci andare ogni giorno.
C) Tutto giorno mi piacciono andare.
D) Mi piace andare lì tutti giorni.

Extra Challenge: Translate the following sentence into Italian: 'we go there every year'.

12.28. Which of the following translation pairings is **incorrect**? (H)

A) Quanti ne hai? – How many of them do you have?
B) I miei genitori ne parlano – My parents are talking about it.
C) Ne voglio di più – I want all of it.
D) Ne abbiamo paura – We are scared of it.

Extra Challenge: In which situations should one use *ne*?

12.29. Double pronouns generally involve an indirect object pronoun followed by a direct object pronoun, e.g. *ce lo danno* (they give it to us). Which of the following means 'I bring it to him'? (H)

A) glielo porto
B) glilo porto
C) lo gli porto
D) logli porto

Extra Challenge: Translate the following sentence into Italian: 'she sends it to him'.

12.30. Expressions using *avere* + noun are very common in Italian. The following table gives several examples of these expressions, but **two** of the translations are in the wrong place. Can you identify the **two** English translations that should be swapped? (M)

Italiano	English
avere sonno	to be sleepy
avere fame	to be thirsty
avere bisogno di	to need
avere sete	to be hungry
avere freddo	to be cold
avere caldo	to be hot
avere voglia di	to want
avere paura di	to be scared of
avere ragione	to be right
avere torto	to be wrong

A) 'to be hot' and 'to be cold'
B) 'to want' and 'to need'
C) 'to be sleepy' and 'to be scared of'
D) 'to be hungry' and 'to be thirsty'

Extra Challenge: Conjugate the verb *avere* in the present tense and create a sentence with each of the expressions above. E.g. *Mio fratello ha sonno perché ha giocato a calcio.*

CHAPTER 12

Articles, Nouns and Pronouns

Answers and
Detailed Solutions

12.1. B

The definite articles in Italian are: *il* (masculine singular starting with consonant), *lo* (masculine singular starting with z, ps, gn or s + consonant), *l'* (masculine and feminine singular beginning with vowel), *la* (feminine singular starting with consonant), *i* (masculine plural starting with consonant), *gli* (masculine plural starting with z, ps, gn or s + consonant), and *le* (feminine plural).

Examples of definite articles:

Definite article	Example
il	il palcoscenico (stage)
lo	lo scambio (exchange)
la	la scherma (fencing)
l'	l'anello (ring)
i	i sottotitoli (subtitles)
gli	gli occhiali (glasses)
le	le ferie (holidays)

12.2. A

Singular masculine nouns starting with a consonant (except nouns starting with z, ps, gn or s + consonant) use *il* as their definite article. Most nouns ending in –o are masculine, e.g. *il tempo* (time/weather), *il cappuccino*. The most common exceptions to this rule include: *mano* (hand), *moto* (motorbike), *radio*, *auto* (car), *pallavolo* (volleyball), and *metro* (underground), which are all feminine and therefore use *la/l'*. Many nouns ending in –e are also masculine, e.g. *il sole* (sun), *il cotone* (cotton), as are nouns ending in –ore, e.g. *il dolore* (pain). There are also exceptionally a few masculine nouns ending in –a, e.g. *il poeta*, *il problema*.

12.3. D

All the words in the list would need the definite article *la*, because they are all feminine. Notice that nouns ending in *-a* are generally feminine. Exceptions to this rule include nouns ending in *-ma* (e.g. *il problema, il cinema*), which end in *-i* in the plural, e.g. *i problemi*. Nouns which end in *-tà, -trice,* and *-zione* are feminine, e.g. *città/direttrice/azione*. Singular nouns ending in *-e* can be masculine, e.g. *il fiume* (the river)/*lo studente*, or feminine, e.g. *la luce* (the light)/*la decisione*.

12.4. A

The only option that is not masculine is A, *porta* (door), which is feminine. Borrowed words such as *film* are often masculine and *opuscolo* (brochure) is masculine, as it ends in *-o*. *Clima* (climate) is also masculine, and is an exception to the rule given that it ends in *-a*.

12.5. D

Singular masculine nouns ending in *-o* end in *-i* in the plural (e.g. *un libro* ⇒ *due libri*). Singular feminine nouns ending in *-a* end in *-e* in the plural (e.g. *una ragazza* ⇒ *tre ragazze*). As we will explore in the next question and solution, there are some exceptions to these rules and certain complications with plural nouns.

12.6. A

Only the list including *forbici* (scissors [f]), *laghi* (lakes), *cipolle* (onions), and *elicotteri* (helicopters) contains all plurals. *Verità* (truth[s]) is the only noun that could be singular or plural depending on the context and the preceding article. Other words such as *spazzolino da denti* (toothbrush), *casco* (helmet), *rumore* (noise), and *pedone* (pedestrian) are all singular.

12.7. C

Nouns ending in *-gio* and *-cio* lose their 'o' in the plural: *un viaggio* (a journey) ⇒ *quattro viaggi, un edificio* (a building) ⇒ *cinque edifici*). A notable exception is *il braccio* (arm), which becomes feminine in the plural, *le braccia*. Shortened words (*foto, moto*), monosyllabic words (*re* [king], *gru* [crane]), nouns borrowed from other languages (*film, gol*), and nouns ending with a vowel with an accent (*identità, caffè*) stay the same in the plural as they are in the singular. Nouns ending in -co, -ca, -go or -ga preserve their sound by adding an 'h' to the plural e.g. *tedesco* (German) ⇒ *tedeschi, domenica* (Sunday) ⇒ *domeniche, chirurgo* (surgeon) ⇒ *chirurghi, strega* (witch) ⇒ *streghe*. Although there are several exceptions to this rule, the most common is that *amico* (friend) becomes *amici* in the plural.

12.8. C

The first noun to transform into the plural is *casa* (house), which becomes *case* (houses). The second noun is *giardino* (garden), which becomes *giardini* (gardens), as it is masculine. Thirdly, *piscina* (swimming pool) becomes *piscine* (swimming pools) and fourthly, *salotto* (living room) becomes *salotti* (living rooms). The fifth noun, *televisore*, which ends in an –e in the singular, becomes *televisori*, ending in an –i in the plural. The same applies to the final noun, *torre*, which becomes *torri* in the plural.

12.9. C

There are four indefinite articles in Italian. They are: *un* (masculine singular), *uno* (masculine singular starting with z, ps, gn or s + consonant), *una* (feminine singular), and *un'* (feminine singular starting with a vowel).

Examples of indefinite articles in Italian:

un	un ragazzo (a boy)
uno	uno schermo (a screen)
una	una rivista (a magazine)
un'	un'onda (a wave)

12.10. D

The indefinite article *un'* is needed for the words in the list because they are all feminine and start with a vowel. Remember that nouns ending in –ione (*creazione, ragione*) are feminine.

12.11. A

Partitive articles are used to introduce part of a whole. In English, we would often translate this as 'some'. Partitive articles consist of *di* + the definite article. However, it is important to note that *di* changes according to the article. See the table below for how *di* changes.

Definite article	Di + definite article	Example
il	del	il pane (bread) ⇒ del pane (some bread)
lo	dello	lo zucchero (sugar) ⇒ dello zucchero (some sugar)
la	della	la pizza ⇒ della pizza
l'	dell'	l'ospedale ⇒ dell'ospedale
i	dei	i documento ⇒ dei documenti
gli	degli	gli alcolici ⇒ degli alcolici
le	delle	le persone ⇒ delle persone

12.12. C

The first gap needs *della*, as *cioccolata* is a feminine singular noun. Secondly, *dei* is required as *vestiti* (clothes) is masculine plural. Thirdly, we need *degli* as *studenti* is masculine plural starting with s + consonant. Finally, *della* is needed as *limonata* (lemonade) is also feminine singular.

12.13. B

Un po' di means 'a little of' and, in most cases, can directly replace the partitive article (e.g. *del caffè* ⇒ *un po' di caffè*). *Alcuni* (masculine) and *alcune* (feminine) mean 'some' and can often be used to replace plural partitive articles (e.g. *alcuni libri/alcune persone*). On the other hand, *qualche*, which also means 'some' can only be used with singular nouns (e.g. *ho qualche messaggio* - I have some messages).

12.14. C

Personal subject pronouns replace the subject to which the verb is referring. In English, the personal subject pronoun in the sentence 'she runs quickly' is 'she'. However, in Italian often the personal subject pronoun is not needed, as the subject of the verb is obvious from the form of the verb, e.g. *io vado* ⇒ *vado* (I go). It is often in ambiguous cases (e.g. *lui/lei*) when personal subject pronouns are used, or to add emphasis. To make Italian verb conjugation (slightly!) easier the personal pronouns always follow in the same order:

Personal Pronoun	English
io	I
tu	You (singular)
lui/lei	He/she
noi	We
voi	You (plural)
loro	They

Exam Tip: It is important to note that *Lei*, when capitalised, means 'you' (in a formal sense).

12.15. B

Unlike many adjectives and nouns, personal subject pronouns do not end in -e in the feminine plural but instead *loro* refers to 'they' regardless of gender.

12.16. A

The incorrect direct object pronoun is *te* in *si, te ascolto*. Instead, the answer should be *si, **ti** ascolto* (yes, I am listening **to you**). Direct object pronouns are as follows in Italian: *mi, ti, lo/la/l', ci, vi* and *li/le*. Direct object pronouns can be used to replace the name of a person or object and go **before** the verb. The other question-answer pairings translate as follows: *bevi il tè? Si, **lo** bevo* (do you drink tea? Yes, I drink **it**), *vedi i ragazzi? No, non **li** vedo* (do you see the guys? No I do not see **them**), and *compri la pasta? Si, **la** compro* (do you buy pasta? Yes, I buy **it**).

12.17. C

The direct object pronoun goes after the infinitive in this translation (just as it does in English). The reason for this is that the direct object refers to the second verb rather than the first (conjugated) verb. As such, 'I am going to see it' should be *vado a vederlo* as the direct object is describing the film (*il film*) which is masculine. As such, *vederla* would not be appropriate. The verb *vedere* translates as 'to see', while *guardare* means 'to watch' and *guadagnare* means 'to earn'.

Exam Tip: When reading in Italian, look out for direct object pronouns and try to identify which nouns they replace in order to understand the meaning of the sentence.

12.18. D

Indirect object pronouns precede a conjugated verb and are as follows in Italian: *mi, ti, Le* (you [formal]), *gli* (to/for him), *le* (to/for her), *ci, vi, Loro* (you [formal]), and *loro* (to/for them). They are used to replace the indirect object and answer questions like 'to whom?' or 'for whom?'. The following sentences contain an indirect object pronoun (which is highlighted in **bold**): *Mia mamma **mi** manda un messaggio* (my mum sends **me** a message), ***ci** dicono l'obiettivo* (they tell **us** the objective), *devo telefonar**le** stasera* (I have to phone **her** this evening). The one sentence that does not contain an indirect object pronoun is therefore D: *vediamo la partita insieme* (we are watching the match together).

12.19. C

Possessive pronouns are used to describe to whom something belongs and must agree in number and gender with the noun they replace. Examples of possessive pronouns in English are 'mine', 'yours', 'his', etc. In Italian, the definite article is generally used before the possessive pronoun, e.g. *è **la** tua* (it is yours). The following table provides a list of the different possessive pronouns to be used with masculine, feminine, and plural nouns. As you can see from the table, *il tuo, i vostri*, and *le Sue* can all be used to mean 'yours', whereas *la nostra* means 'ours'.

	Masculine Singular	Feminine Singular	Masculine Plural	Feminine Plural
Mine	il mio	la mia	i miei	le mie
Yours (singular)	il tuo	la tua	i tuoi	le tue
His/hers	il suo	la sua	i suoi	le sue
Yours (formal)	il suo	la sua	i suoi	le sue
Ours	il nostro	la nostra	i nostri	le nostre
Yours (plural)	il vostro	la vostra	i vostri	le vostre
Theirs	il loro	la loro	i loro	le loro

12.20. A

Relative pronouns replace a noun and link two clauses together. In English, we would use 'that', 'who', and 'which'. The sentence *la donna che ho incontrato ama il libro che hai scritto* means 'the woman **who** I met loves the book **that** you wrote'. As such, the relative pronoun in the sentence is *che*.

12.21. B

The incorrect use of the relative pronoun is in the sentence *la regione su cui lui viene*. Instead, 'from which' should be translated as *da cui*: *la regione da cui viene* (the region from which he comes). The other translations are correct: *in cui* (in whom/which), *a cui* (to whom/which), and *con cui* (with whom/which).

12.22. C

The incorrect demonstrative pronoun is *quello* (that), which should be *quella* because it is describing a sweet (*caramella*), which is feminine. The sentences translate as follows: *quelle torte sono più gustose di queste* (those cakes are more tasty than these), and *quella caramella è meno sano di questa* (that sweet is less healthy than this one).

12.23. A

Option A is grammatically incorrect, as *alcuno* means 'some' and cannot be used to mean 'someone', which is *qualcuno*. The other options are correct: *qualcuno deve pulire la casa* (someone must clean the house), *qualcosa cambierà* (something will change), and n*essuno vuole parlare con me* (no-one wants to talk to me).

12.24. B

B is the incorrect pairing because 'no-one' in Italian is *nessuno*, while *niente* means 'nothing'. The other indefinite pronouns are translated correctly: *troppo* (too much), *ciascuno* (each), and *certo* (some).

12.25. D

The list of reflexive pronouns is option D: *mi, ti, si, ci, vi* and *si*. Reflexive pronouns are used with reflexive verbs to indicate that the action is happening back onto the subject of the verb. For more information on using reflexive pronouns and verbs see questions 13.6 and 13.7. in chapter 13. Option A lists **indirect object** pronouns (*mi, ti, gli, le, ci, vi* and *gli*), option B contains a list of **direct object** pronouns (*mi, ti, lo, la, ci, vi, li* and *le*), and option C is a list of **personal subject** pronouns (*io, tu, lui, lei, noi, voi* and *loro*).

12.26. B

Ecco means 'here … is' and is often used with direct object pronouns, e.g. *eccolo* (here it is), *eccomi* (here I am), *eccola* (here she is), *eccoli* (here they are). *Dietro* means 'behind', *stesso* means 'same', and *dubbio* means 'doubt'.

12.27. A

The most appropriate translation for the sentence is *mi piace andarci ogni giorno*. The pronoun *ci* is used to mean 'there', and is also used to replace a noun preceded by *a, in, su*, and *con*.

12.28. C

The incorrect translation pairing is *ne voglio di più* – I want all of it: *ne voglio di più* means 'I want some more (of it)', whereas *lo voglio tutto* would be 'I want all of it'. The other translation pairings are correct, and show how *ne* can be used in Italian. It can be used to replace a noun introduced by an expression of quantity, e.g. 'of them' (*quanti ne hai?* – how many of them do you have?). It can also be used to replace a verb/verbal expression + di, e.g. 'about it/of it' (*i miei genitori ne parlano* – My parents are talking about it; *ne abbiamo paura* – We are scared of it).

12.29. A

Gli (to him) and *le* (to her) become *glie* before direct object pronouns, which is why *glielo porto* is 'I bring it to him'. See the table below for double pronoun combinations:

Indirect Object Pronoun	Double Pronoun
mi	me lo, me la, me li, me le, me ne
ti	te lo, te la, te li, te le, te ne
gli/le/le	glielo, gliela, glieli, gliele, gliene
ci	ce lo, ce la, ce li, ce le, ce ne
vi	ve lo, ve la, ve li, ve le, ve ne
si	se lo, se la, se li, se le, se ne

12.30. D

'To be hungry' in Italian is *avere fame* (translated literally 'to have hunger') and 'to be thirsty' is *avere sete* (literally 'to have thirst'). Notice that many of the expressions in the table would be translated 'to be....' in English, but in Italian we use *avere* (to have).

Exam Tip: Using expressions with *avere* + noun in your writing and speaking demonstrates a more natural and native-like competence.

CHAPTER 13

Verbs and Tenses

The difficulty rating for each question (Easy [E], Moderate [M] or Hard [H]) can be found in parenthesis next to each question.

13.1. How do verbs in their infinitive form end in Italian? (E)

A)   -ere & -ire
B)   -are, -ere & -ore
C)   -are, -ere & -ire
D)   -ire & -ore

Extra Challenge: Give two examples of each type of verb.

13.2. How do you conjugate -ARE verbs in the present tense? (E)

A)   Remove the -are and add the following endings: -o, -i, -a, -iamo, -ate, -ano.
B)   Remove the -re and add the following endings: -o, -i, -a, -iamo, -ate, -ano.
C)   Remove the -e and add the following endings: -o, -i, -a, -iamo, -ate, -ano.
D)   Keep the -are and add the following endings: -o, -i, -a, -iamo, -ate, -ano.

Extra Challenge: Conjugate the verbs *comprare* (to buy) and *nuotare* (to swim) in the present tense.

13.3. *Credere* (to believe) is a regular -ERE verb. Which list outlines the correct conjugation of this verb in the present tense? (E)

A)   crede, credisti, crede, crediamo, credete, credeno
B)   credo, credi, creda, crediemo, credeste, credono
C)   crede, credi, credo, crediamo, credete, credino
D)   credo, credi, crede, crediamo, credete, credono

Extra Challenge: Conjugate the verbs *spendere* (to spend) and *perdere* (to lose) in the present tense.

13.4. -IRE verbs are slightly more complicated than -ARE and -ERE verbs as they can be conjugated in the present tense in **two** ways, according to the verb. The subject pronouns *noi* and *voi* stay the same in both types of -IRE conjugation in the present tense, while subject pronouns *io, tu, lui/lei* and *loro* change between type 1 and type 2.

Finire (to finish) is a type 1 -IRE verb and *dormire* (to sleep) is a type 2 -IRE verb. Which is the correct conjugation in the first-person singular (*io*) of these two verbs? (E)

    A)   finisco & dormo
    B)   fino & dormisco
    C)   finisco & dormisco
    D)   fino & dormo

Extra Challenge: Conjugate the verbs *pulire* (to clean – type 1) and *partire* (to leave – type 2) in the present tense.

13.5. Which list **correctly** conjugates the four verbs in the sentences below? (M)

    1)   Io .... sempre in ritardo. (arrivare)
    2)   Lui .... una casa. (costruire)
    3)   Loro .... male. (sentire)
    4)   Noi .... un buon libro. (leggere)

    A)   1. arrivo, 2. costruisce, 3. sentono, 4. leggiamo.
    B)   1. arrivo, 2. costruisci, 3. sentino, 4. leggemo.
    C)   1. arrivi, 2. costrui, 3. sentino, 4. leggiemo.
    D)   1. arriva, 2. costrue, 3. sentono, 4. leggiamo.

Extra Challenge: Translate the sentences above into English.

13.6. When are reflexive verbs used? (M)

    A)   when the subject and object of a verb are different e.g. I watched him
    B)   when the subject and the object of the verb are the same e.g. I enjoyed myself
    C)   after infinitives
    D)   before infinitives

Extra Challenge: Can you think of some examples of reflexive verbs in Italian?

13.7. Which of the following is **not** a reflexive verb in the present tense? (M)

A) io mi alzo
B) tu ti siedi
C) loro si innamorano
D) noi lo guardiamo

Extra Challenge: Conjugate the whole verb in the examples above.

13.8. Which of the following is the most accurate translation of the sentence below? (M)

I like books but I do not like reading.

A) Mi piacciono i libri ma non mi piace leggere.
B) Mi piacciono il libro ma non mi piace leggere.
C) Mi piace i libri ma non mi piace la letteratura.
D) Piacio i libri ma non mi piace leggere.

Extra Challenge: Translate the following sentence into Italian: 'I like films but I do not like watching the television'.

13.9. Which of the following lists have the **correct** conjugation in the first-person singular (*io*) of the verbs *dire* (to say), *fare* (to do), *essere* (to be), and *avere* (to have)? (M)

A) dicho, fao, sono, avo
B) diccio, faccio, esso, ho
C) dico, faccio, sono, ho
D) dicco, facco, sonno, avo

Extra Challenge: Conjugate the same verbs in the third-person singular (*lui/lei*).

13.10. *Andare* (to go) is a key verb in Italian and is often used in the present tense. (E)

How is the verb *andare* conjugated in the present tense?

- A) ando, andai, anda, andiamo, andate, andanno
- B) vado, vas, va, viamo, vate, vanno
- C) vado, vai, va, andiamo, andate, vanno
- D) vado, vai, va, andiamo, andate, andanno

Extra Challenge: Translate the following sentence into Italian: 'We are going to a party'.

13.11. Impersonal verbs take the third-person singular (*lui/lei*) form when conjugated, and are often used in English when the subject is 'there' or 'it'. Weather expressions are examples of impersonal verbs, as you would only tend to use them in the third-person singular, e.g. *piove* (it rains). (H)

Which type of verbs follow the impersonal verbal phrases below?

È necessario (it is necessary)
È essenziale (it is essential)
Bisogna (it is needed)
Occorre (it is needed)

- A) reflexive verbs
- B) infinitives
- C) modal verbs
- D) conjugated verbs

Extra Challenge: Give four examples of sentences using the four sentence starters above.

13.12. It is very common in Italian to use impersonal constructions with *si* when the subject of the verb is not specific. This verb can be conjugated in the third-person singular, e.g. *si deve* (one must), or the third-person plural, e.g. *si mangiano molte caramelle* (lots of sweets are eaten). (H)

Using this construction, how would you translate 'it is not known' into Italian?

A) non so
B) non si sappiamo
C) non sa
D) non si sa

Extra Challenge: Translate the following into Italian: 'one can decide afterwards'.

13.13. The gerund (*il gerundio*) in Italian is the equivalent of –ing in English, e.g. writ**ing**, do**ing**, play**ing**, etc. You often use the gerund after the conjugated version of the verb *stare* (to be). To form the gerund in Italian, you remove the –are, -ere, and –ire from the infinitive and add: (H)

A) –ando and -endo
B) –ando, -endo, and –indo
C) –ato, -eto, and -ito
D) –anto, -ento, and -into

Extra Challenge: Give six examples of gerunds in Italian.

13.14. How do you form the perfect tense (*passato prossimo*) in Italian? (E)

A) with the stem of the verb followed by the appropriate ending
B) with an auxiliary verb (avere or essere) followed by a past participle
C) with a past participle followed by an auxiliary verb (avere or essere)
D) with an infinitive followed by a past participle

Extra Challenge: Give three examples of the perfect tense (*passato prossimo*).

13.15. When turning regular infinitives into past participles, remove the -are and add -ato, remove the -ire and add -ito, and remove the -ere and add: (M)

A)   -ieto
B)   -aeto
C)   -eto
D)   -uto

Extra Challenge: Turn the following infinitives into past participles: *fumare* (to smoke), *costruire* (to build), and *godere* (to enjoy).

13.16. Which of the following verbs does **not** have an irregular past participle? (H)

A)   prendere (to take)
B)   potere (to be able to)
C)   vincere (to win)
D)   succedere (to happen)

Extra Challenge: Use each of the verbs above in a sentence in the perfect tense.

13.17. Which list contains **only** verbs that take *essere* as the auxiliary in the perfect tense? (M)

A)   dare, fare, bere, mangiare, sentire, giocare
B)   nascere, arrivare, partire, uscire, entrare
C)   ritornare, mancare, vincere, stare, piovere
D)   diventare, pensare, cambiare, cenare, salire

Extra Challenge: Which other verbs take *essere* as the auxiliary in the perfect tense?

13.18. What do you need to do when using *essere* as an auxiliary in the perfect tense? (E)

A)   agree the past participle with the object of the verb
B)   add –oto to the past participle
C)   agree the past participle with the subject of the verb
D)   add a direct object pronoun to the verb

Extra Challenge: Give four examples of the perfect tense in Italian, with verbs that take *essere* as their auxiliary.

13.19. In which of the following instances would it **not** be appropriate to use the imperfect tense? (E)

A) When describing the ongoing state of something in the past e.g. the woman **had** red hair, the views **were** spectacular.

B) When describing an ongoing event in the past that coincided or was interrupted by another event e.g. the teacher **was reading**, when the student arrived.

C) When describing an action in the past that used to happen e.g. he **used to** watch the tennis on television.

D) When describing a one-off event in the past e.g. I **ate** spaghetti for lunch.

Extra Challenge: Translate the four examples above into Italian.

13.20. Which of the following **correctly** conjugates the verbs *andare* (to go), *avere* (to have), and *pulire* (to clean) in the imperfect tense? (M)

A) tu andavi, io avevo, noi pulivamo
B) tu andevi, io aveva, noi pulevamo
C) tu andavate, io avevemo, noi pulavamo
D) tu andeva, io avevi, noi pulivate

Extra Challenge: Conjugate the verb *mangiare* (to eat) in the imperfect tense with each subject pronoun.

13.21. There are three main irregular verbs in the imperfect tense. Which ones are they? (H)

A) vedere, volere, avere
B) stare, andare, dovere
C) essere, dire, fare
D) essere, avere, dare

Extra Challenge: How are the three irregular verbs above conjugated in the imperfect tense?

13.22. Look at the verbs below. How many are in the future tense? (E)

scrivi guiderà partiremo crederai ordino ricorderanno
spiegherò viaggiavamo ascoltavo insegnano

- A) three
- B) four
- C) five
- D) six

Extra Challenge: Translate the verbs above into English.

13.23. Which of the following is the **correct** conjugation of the verb *giocare* in the first-person singular (*io*) of the future tense? (M)

- A) gioco
- B) giocherò
- C) giocavo
- D) giocherai

Extra Challenge: Conjugate the whole of the verb *restare* (to stay) in the future tense.

13.24. Many verbs in the future tense have irregular future stems. Which list below features **only** verbs with irregular future stems? (H)

- A) andare, potere, vivere
- B) cantare, dovere, correre
- C) sapere, scoprire, misurare
- D) dormire, essere, sbagliare

Extra Challenge: What are the future stems of the verbs above?

13.25. Which of the following sets of endings are needed to form the conditional tense? (E)

- A) –ai, -asti, -abbe, -ammo, -aste, -abbero
- B) –ò, -ai, -à, -emo, -ete, -anno
- C) –evo, -evi, -eva, -evamo, -evate, -evano
- D) –ei, -esti, -ebbe, -emmo, -este, -ebbero

Extra Challenge: When is the conditional tense used in Italian?

13.26. Verbs in the conditional tense have the same stem as in the future tense. Which of the following sentences contains a conditional verb with an irregular stem? (H)

A) Con più soldi **andrei** negli Stati Uniti.
B) **Dormirei** bene.
C) Mi **piacerebbe** un bambino.
D) I suoi genitori **canterebbero**.

Extra Challenge: Give four more examples of conjugated verbs in the conditional tense with irregular stems.

13.27. The conditional perfect is used to say what would/could/should have happened in the past. How is the conditional perfect formed in Italian? (H)

A) the imperfect of the verb's auxiliary (*avere* or *essere*) + past participle
B) the conditional of the verb's auxiliary (*avere* or *essere*) + past participle
C) the future tense of the verb + past participle
D) the perfect tense of the verb + past participle

Extra Challenge: Give three examples of the conditional perfect.

13.28. The past perfect tense (*trapassato prossimo*) describes an action or event that took place before another action in the past, e.g. I **had seen** the film already when we went to the cinema. In this example, 'had seen' is the past perfect, whereas 'we went' is in the perfect tense (*passato prossimo*). (H)

Which of the following means 'they had found a dog'?

A) Avevano trovato un cane.
B) Avranno trovato un cane.
C) Avrebbero trovato un cane.
D) Hanno trovato un cane.

Extra Challenge: Translate 'they had seen the match' into Italian.

13.29. The subjunctive (*congiuntivo*) is used in Italian in a variety of contexts, including: expressing doubt, uncertainty, desire, opinions, and set expressions. The subject of the verb in the subjunctive is generally different to the subject of the original verb, e.g. **I** think that **you** are kind (the subjunctive would **not** be used for 'I think that I am kind'). (H)

Which of the following sentences should **not** use the subjunctive?

A) Credo che sia un film strano. (I think that it is a strange film)
B) È necessario che tu faccia attenzione. (it is necessary that you take care)
C) Dubito che lui compri i dolci. (I doubt that he buys sweet things)
D) Voglio che io vado al cinema. (I want to go to the cinema)

Extra Challenge: How is the present subjunctive formed in Italian?

13.30. The following table shows conjugated Italian verbs in the past (perfect and imperfect), present and future tenses. (M)

There are three mistakes in the table (one in each column) – can you identify all **three**?

Past (perfect & imperfect)	Present	Future
ho mangiato	ascolto	comprerà
dicevi	iniziano	facevate
siamo andati	berrò	pagheremo
guaderò	risparmiamo	parlerai
andavamo	spende	aprirò

A) dicevi, iniziano, facevate
B) guarderò, berrò, facevate
C) andavamo, berrò, pagheremo
D) siamo andati, risparmiamo, parlerai

Extra Challenge: Translate the verbs above and conjugate them in the other tenses.

CHAPTER 13

Verbs and Tenses

Answers and
Detailed Solutions

13.1. C

There are three types of infinitives in Italian: -ARE, -ERE & -IRE. To conjugate any verb in any tense, it is important to start with the infinitive. -ARE verbs are the most common, e.g. *cantare* (to sing), *comprare* (to buy).

13.2. A

-ARE verbs are the most common out of the three types of Italian infinitives, therefore it is important to be able to conjugate these verbs in the present tense. To do this, you remove the -are and add the following endings: -o, -i, -a, -iamo, -ate and -ano. An example of this is the verb *portare* (to carry/bring/wear), which is conjugated below:

PORTARE
(io) port**o**
(tu) port**i**
(lui/lei) port**a**
(noi) port**iamo**
(voi) port**ate**
(loro) port**ano**

Examples of regular -ARE verbs include: *accettare* (to accept), *cenare* (to have dinner), *costare* (to cost), *dimenticare* (to forget), *durare* (to last), *meritare* (to deserve), *prenotare* (to reserve/book), *ringraziare* (to thank), *rubare* (to steal), *scappare* (to escape), and *sembrare* (to seem).

13.3. D

Regular -ERE verbs are less common than -ARE verbs, and include, among others, *vivere* (to live), *leggere* (to read), *scrivere* (to write), and *rispondere* (to answer). These verbs are conjugated by removing the *-ere* and adding the following endings, according to the personal subject pronoun: -o, -i, -e, -iamo, -ete, and -ono. The verb *credere* (to believe) is therefore conjugated in the present tense as follows:

CREDERE
(io) cred**o**
(tu) cred**i**
(lui/lei) cred**e**
(noi) cred**iamo**
(voi) cred**ete**
(loro) cred**ono**

Further examples of -ERE verbs include: *aggiungere* (to add), *cadere* (to fall), *chiudere* (to close), *descrivere* (to describe), *perdere* (to lose), *piangere* (to cry), *ricevere* (to receive), *ridere* (to laugh), *smettere* (to stop), *sorridere* (to smile), and *spingere* (to push).

13.4. A

As *finire* is a type 1 -IRE verb, it is conjugated by removing the -ire and adding the following endings according to the subject of the verb: -isco, -isci, -isce, -iamo, -ite and -iscono. Therefore, in the first-person singular (*io*) the verb is conjugated *finisco* (I finish). By contrast, *dormire* is a type 2 verb and is conjugated by removing the -ire and adding the following endings: -o, -i, -e, -iamo, -ite, and -ono. Notice that type 2 -IRE verbs follow the same conjugation pattern as -ERE verbs, with the exception of the second-person plural (*voi*), which changes from –ete with -ERE verbs to –ite with -IRE verbs.

Pronoun	-ire (Type I)	-ire (Type II)
io	-**isc**o	-o
tu	-**isc**i	-i
lui/lei	-**isc**e	-e
noi	-iamo	-iamo
voi	-ite	**-ite**
loro	-**isc**ono	-ono

There is no particular rule to distinguish between type 1 and type 2 -IRE verbs and they need to be learnt. Fortunately, however, there are not too many of them. Refer to the table below for some common -IRE verbs.

-ire (Type I)	-ire (Type II)
finire (to finish)	dormire (to sleep)
spedire (to send)	sentire (to feel)
costruire (to build)	vestire (to dress)
capire (to understand)	partire (to leave)
suggerire (to suggest)	coprire (to cover)
preferire (to prefer)	riempire (to fill)

13.5. A

Applying the rules set out in questions 13.2., 13.3., and 13.4., we see that the first-person singular (*io*) of *arrivare* is *arrivo* (I arrive), the third-person singular of *costruire*, a type 1 IRE verb, is *costruisce* (he builds), the third-person plural of *sentire*, a type 2 IRE verb, is *sentono* (they hear), and the first-person plural of *leggere* is *leggiamo* (we read).

Exam Tip: Sustained practice of verb conjugation in the present tense will not only improve your language production (speaking and writing) but also your comprehension (listening and reading) of the Italian language. So keep up the good work!

13.6. B

Reflexive verbs are needed when the subject and object of the verb are the same, and can be recognised by the presence of a reflexive pronoun. Reflexive verbs are far more common in Italian than in English. For instance, in English we would say 'I wash'. The Italian version would be *mi lavo* (I wash myself). In order to form a reflexive verb in its infinitive, remove the -e from the -ARE, -ERE, or -IRE and add the reflexive pronoun *si*, e.g. *chiamare* (to call) ⇒ *chiamarsi* (to call oneself).

Reflexive verbs are conjugated in the same way as regular -ARE, -ERE and -IRE verbs, the only difference is that a reflexive pronoun is needed before the verb, e.g. *mi* chiamo *Erica* (I call myself/I am called Erica). See the table below for which reflexive pronoun to use with which part of the verb.

E.g. *chiamarsi* (to call oneself)

Subject pronoun	Reflexive pronoun	*Chiamarsi*
io	mi	mi chiamo
tu	ti	ti chiami
lui/lei	si	si chiama
noi	ci	ci chiamiamo
voi	vi	vi chiamate
loro	si	si chiamano

Other examples of reflexive verbs include: *addormentarsi* (to fall asleep), *alzarsi* (to get up), *dispiacersi* (to be sorry), *divertirsi* (to enjoy oneself), *interessarsi a* (to be interested in), *lamentarsi* (to complain), *preoccuparsi* (to worry), *sedersi* (to sit down), *trovarsi* (to be located), and *truccarsi* (to put make up on).

13.7. D

Noi lo guardiamo (we watch him/it) is not a reflexive verb as the object of the verb (him/it) is different to its subject (we). It would only be reflexive if it became *noi ci guardiamo* (we watch each other). The other three examples are reflexive verbs: *io mi alzo* (I get up), *tu ti siedi* (you sit down), and *loro si innamorano* (they fall in love).

13.8. A

Piacere means 'to please'. Although in English we would translate *mi piace* as 'I like', the literal translation would be 'it is pleasing to me'. As the subject of the verb is generally 'it' or 'they', the verb needs to be conjugated in the third-person singular or plural respectively, e.g. *mi piace*, *mi piacciono*. Therefore, when a singular noun or an infinitive is used, we use the singular, e.g. *mi piace leggere* (I like to read). When a plural noun is used, we need the plural verb, e.g. *mi piacciono i libri.*

Exam Tip: Take care when saying 'I like' that you have got the correct form: *mi piace* or *mi piacciono.*

13.9. C

The correct conjugations of the verbs *dire, fare, essere,* and *avere* in the first-person singular are: *dico* (I say), *faccio* (I do), *sono* (I am), and *ho* (I have). The full conjugation of the four verbs can be found in the table below.

Subject	*Dire* (to say)	*Fare* (to do)	*Essere* (to be)	*Avere* (to have)
io	dico	faccio	sono	ho
tu	dici	fai	sei	hai
lui/lei	dice	fa	è	ha
noi	diciamo	facciamo	siamo	abbiamo
voi	dite	fate	siete	avete
loro	dicono	fanno	sono	hanno

Exam Tip: It is a good idea to learn the key irregular verbs in the present tense as they recur frequently in reading, writing, speaking, and listening tasks.

13.10. C

Andare is an irregular verb and its conjugation in the present tense is as follows: *vado, vai, va, andiamo, andate, vanno.* Notice how the first-person plural (*noi*) and second-person plural (*voi*) are more similar to the stem of the verb. The translation of 'we are going to a party' is therefore *andiamo ad una festa.*

13.11. B

Impersonal verbs or verbal phrases such as *è necessario* (it is necessary), *è essenziale* (it is essential), *bisogna* (it is needed…), and *occorre* (it is needed…) are followed by infinitives, regardless of the tense. For instance, *è essenziale bere molto* (it is essential to drink lots).

13.12. D

'It is not known' or 'no-one knows' in Italian would be *non si sa*. *Non so*, by contrast, means 'I do not know' and *non sa* means 'he/she does not know'. The translation of 'one can decide afterwards' would be *si può decidere dopo*.

13.13. A

In Italian, the gerund is formed by removing the ending of the infinitive and adding –ando (for –ARE verbs) and -endo (for –ERE and –IRE verbs), e.g. *parlando* (speaking), *vendendo* (selling), and *morendo* (dying). The gerund is often used with the conjugated version of *stare* to form the present continuous, e.g. *stanno mentendo* (they are lying). Note, however, that the simple present tense can be, and often is, used to say –ing as well. For example, *cosa dite?* and *cosa state dicendo?* can both be translated into English as 'what are you saying?'.

13.14. B

The perfect tense (*passato prossimo*) is used to speak of a completed action in the past. To form the perfect tense, you first need the present tense of either *avere* (to have) or *essere* (to be), depending on the verb you are talking about. Most verbs take *avere* as their auxiliary verb, although you will need to learn the verbs that take *essere* (see question 13.17. in chapter 13 for more practice with this). Once you have the correct auxiliary verb conjugated with the correct subject, you add a past participle. Generally, to create the past participle remove the –are, –ere, and -ire, and add –ato, -uto, and -ito respectively. Be aware, however, that many past participles in Italian are irregular (refer to question 13.16. to practise this). See the tables below for a verb that takes *avere* as its auxiliary and a verb that takes *essere* as its auxiliary in the perfect tense.

Verb taking *avere* as auxiliary

Subject pronoun	*dimenticare* (to forget)
io	ho dimenticato
tu	hai dimenticato
lui/lei	ha dimenticato
noi	abbiamo dimenticato
voi	avete dimenticato
loro	hanno dimenticato

Verb taking *essere* as auxiliary

Subject pronoun	Arrivare (to arrive)
io	sono arrivato/a/i/e
tu	sei arrivato/a/i/e
lui/lei	è arrivato/a/i/e
noi	siamo arrivato/a/i/e
voi	siete arrivato/a/i/e
loro	sono arrivato/a/i/e

13.15. D

Past particles from verbs ending in -ERE use –uto, e.g. *cadere* (to fall) ⇒ *ca**duto***. However, many –ERE verbs have irregular past participles, e.g. *chiedere* (to ask) ⇒ *chiesto*, *scrivere* (to write) ⇒ *scritto*, *leggere* (to read) ⇒ *letto*, and *ridere* (to laugh) ⇒ *riso*.

13.16. B

The only verb in the list with a regular past participle in Italian is *potere* (to be able to), as its past participle is *potuto*. See the table below with a list of common irregular past participles.

Infinitive	English	Past participle
aprire	to open	aperto
bere	to drink	bevuto
dire	to say	detto
fare	to do	fatto
perdere	to lose	perso
permettere	to allow	permesso
prendere	to take	preso
rompere	to break	rotto
scegliere	to choose	scelto
succedere	to happen	successo
vedere	to see	visto
vincere	to win	vinto

13.17. B

Only list B exclusively features verbs that take *essere* as their auxiliary. While list C and D contain a mixture of verbs that use both *essere* and *avere*, list A solely features verbs that take *avere* in the perfect tense.

The most common verbs that take *essere* as their auxiliary are:

Italiano	English
andare	to go
arrivare	to arrive
cadere	to fall
diventare	to become
essere	to be
morire	to die
nascere	to be born
partire	to leave
rimanere	to remain
ritornare	to return
riuscire	to succeed
salire	to go up
scendere	to go down
stare	to be
uscire	to go out

13.18. C

When the verb *essere* is used an auxiliary verb in the perfect tense, the past participle must agree with the subject of the verb. For example, when talking about a female or a feminine noun, the past participle must end in –a, e.g. *lei è nata* (she was born). When the subject of the verb is a group of males or a plural masculine noun, the past participle must end in –i, e.g. *gli uomini sono arrivati* (the men arrived). Finally, when the subject of the verb is a group of females or a plural feminine noun, the past participle must end in –e, e.g. *le ragazze sono partite* (the girls left).

13.19. D

The perfect tense (see questions 13.14., 13.15., 13.16., 13.17., and 13.18. in chapter 13) is used when we are talking about one-off events that occurred in the past, e.g. I **ate** pasta for lunch (*ho mangiato la pasta per pranzo*), my brother **saw** a good film (*mio fratello ha visto un buon film*). The imperfect tense, however, is used for describing an ongoing action or state in the past (even if the time period is not specified), and events that were happening when they were interrupted. In example B, the phrase 'the teacher **was reading**' (*il professore leggeva*) would require the imperfect tense in Italian, while the second half of the sentence 'when the student **arrived**' (*quando lo studente è arrivato*) would be in the perfect tense as it describes a one-off, completed action/event. The other examples would also require the imperfect tense: 'the woman **had** red hair' (*la donna aveva i capelli rossi*) and 'he **used to** watch the tennis on television' (*guardava il tennis sulla televisione*).

Exam Tip: When writing or speaking about events in the past, think carefully about whether the imperfect or perfect tense is needed.

13.20. A

To conjugate verbs in the imperfect tense in Italian, you remove the -re from the infinitive and add the following endings, according to the subject pronouns: -vo, -vi, -va, -vamo, -vate, and -vano. There are very few irregulars in the imperfect tense (see question 13.21. for more details). You can refer to the table below for the conjugation of the verbs *andare* (to go), *avere* (to have), and *pulire* (to clean) with each subject pronoun:

	Andare	**Avere**	**Pulire**
Io	andavo	avevo	pulivo
Tu	andavi	avevi	pulivi
Lui/lei	andava	aveva	puliva
Noi	andavamo	avevamo	pulivamo
Voi	andavate	avevate	pulivate
Loro	andavano	avevano	pulivano

13.21. C

Essere (to be) is the most commonly used irregular in the imperfect tense, and is conjugated as follows: *ero, eri, era, eravamo, eravate, erano*. *Dire* (to say) follows a similar pattern: *dicevo, dicevi, diceva, dicevamo, dicevate, dicevano*. Finally, *fare* (to do) is conjugated in the imperfect tense as follows: *facevo, facevi, faceva, facevamo, facevate, facevano*.

Exam Tip: Although it can be difficult to know *when* to use the imperfect tense, it is one of the easier tenses to conjugate as it has very few irregulars. It is important, however, to learn these three well.

13.22. C

Five of the verbs are in the future tense. They include: *guiderà* (he/she/it will drive), *partiremo* (we will leave), *crederai* (you will believe), *ricorderanno* (they will remember), and *spiegherò* (I will explain). Notice how the stem for –ere and –ire verbs is the infinitive (minus the final -e, while with –are verbs, the 'a' is replaced by an 'e', e.g. *guidare* ⇒ *guiderà*.

Also remember the spelling change to verbs ending –gare and –care, e.g. *litigare* (to argue) ⇒ *litigheranno* (they will argue), and *cercare* (to look for) ⇒ *cercherò* (I will look for). The other words in the list do not use the future tense. Instead, some are in the present tense - *scrivi* (you write), *ordino* (I order) and *insegnano* (they teach) - and others in the imperfect - *viaggiavamo* (we used to travel/we were travelling) and *ascoltavo* (I used to listen/I was listening).

Exam Tip: Being able to spot which tense a verb is in is an important skill for getting the most out of comprehension tasks.

13.23. B

The correct conjugation of *giocare* in the first-person singular of the future tense is *giocherò* (I will play). Notice the addition of an 'h' to the stem, in order to maintain the 'ca' sound. The same would apply to verbs ending in –gare. For the future tense endings, see the following table.

Subject	Stem	Future Ending
io	giocher	ò
tu	giocher	ai
lui/lei	giocher	à
noi	giocher	emo
voi	giocher	ete
loro	giocher	anno

13.24. A

The list that contains only verbs with irregular future stems is A: *andare, potere, vivere*. The following table outlines verbs with irregular future stems, e.g. stems that are not their infinitives.

Infinitive	English	Irregular Future Stem
andare	to go	andr-
avere	to have	avr-
bere	to drink	berr-
dovere	to have to	dovr-
essere	to be	sar-
fare	to do	far-
potere	to be able to	potr-
sapere	to know	sapr-
vedere	to see	vedr-
venire	to come	verr-
vivere	to live	vivr-

Remember that verbs ending in –care and –gare become -cher and –gher respectively in their future stems, e.g. *nevicare* (to snow) ⇒ *nevicherà* (it will snow). In a similar vein, verbs ending in –ciare and –giare become –cer and –ger respectively in the future stem, e.g. *mangiare* ⇒ *mangerò*.

13.25. D

The conditional tense is formed with the future stem (see questions 13.22., 13.23., and 13.24.) and the following endings: –ei, -esti, -ebbe, -emmo, -este, -ebbero. For example, if we take the verb *uscire* (to go out), we remove the 'e' at the end of the verb and conjugate the verbs as follows: *io uscirei* (I would go out), *tu usciresti* (you would go out), *lui/lei uscirebbe* (he/she would go out), *noi usciremmo* (we would go out), *voi uscireste* (you would go out), *loro uscirebbero* (they would go out). As you can see from the above example, the conditional tense is equivalent in English to 'would' + verb, e.g. he would find, they would know, etc. It is often used to describe hypothetical situations, e.g. my ideal holiday **would be** in Portugal.

13.26. A

The only verb with an irregular stem from the options is A: *andrei* (I would go). The other sentences use regular verbs in the conditional tense: **dormirei** *bene* (you would sleep well), *mi* **piacerebbe** *un bambino* (I would like a child), and *i suoi genitori* **canterebbero** (his/her parents would sing).

13.27. B

The conditional perfect (*il condizionale passato*) is formed by taking the present conditional of the verb's auxiliary (*avere* or *essere*) and adding a past participle. For example, if we wanted to say, 'he would have done his homework', we need the conditional of *avere* as the verb *fare* (to do) takes this as its auxiliary. We then take the third-person singular of *avere* in the present conditional, *avrebbe*, and add the past participle of fare, *fatto*. Therefore, 'he would have done his homework' is *avrebbe fatto i suoi compiti*. Now let's look at an example with *essere*. To say, 'she would have gone' we now need *essere* as the auxiliary as the main verb is *andare* (to go). The conditional of *essere* in third-person singular is *sarebbe*. Remember that the past participle with *essere* agrees with the subject of the verb, e.g. *andata*. Therefore, 'she would have gone' is *sarebbe andata*.

13.28. A

The correct translation of 'they had found a dog' is *avevano trovato un cane*. The past perfect in Italian is formed by taking the imperfect form of the auxiliary verb (*avere or essere*) and adding the past participle. Remember that the past participle with *essere* agrees with the subject of the verb, e.g. *lei era partita* (she had left). Another example would be 'I had gone', which would require *essere* as the auxiliary e.g. *io ero andato/a*. The other options available in the question were incorrect: *avranno trovato un cane* (they will have found) is the future perfect, *avrebbero trovato un cane* (they would have found a dog) is the conditional perfect, and *hanno trovato un cane* (they found a dog) is the perfect tense.

13.29. D

The first three examples all use the subjunctive: *credo che **sia** un film strano* (I think that it is a strange film), *è necessario che tu **faccia** attenzione* (it is necessary that you take care), and *dubito che lui **compri** i dolci* (I doubt that he buys sweet things). The final example, D, does not need the subjunctive as the subject (*io*) is the same in both clauses: **I** want that **I** go... In this instance, it would be better to say 'I want to go', using the infinitive, e.g. *voglio andare*. If, however, we were to say 'I want you to go', we would need the subjunctive, e.g. v*oglio che **tu vada***.

The following table shows how the subjunctive is formed with regular –are, -ire and –ere verbs (remove the –are, -ire and –ere and add the endings).

	-are	-ere	-ire
io	-i	-a	-a/-isca
tu	-i	-a	-a/-isca
lui/lei	-i	-a	-a/-isca
noi	-iamo	-iamo	-iamo
voi	-iate	-iate	-iate
loro	-ino	-ano	-ano/-iscano

The table below highlights some common irregular verbs in the subjunctive.

	Essere (to be)	Avere (to have)	Andare (to go)	Fare (to do)	Dire (to say)
io	sia	abbia	vada	faccia	dica
tu	sia	abbia	vada	faccia	dica
lui/lei	sia	abbia	vada	faccia	dica
noi	siamo	abbiamo	andiamo	facciamo	diciamo
voi	siate	abbiate	andate	facciate	diciate
loro	siano	abbiano	vadano	facciano	dicano

13.30. B

The three conjugated verbs in list B (*guaderò*, *berrò*, *facevate*) are not in the correct columns because the first two, *guarderò* and *berrò*, are both in the future tense, while *facevate* is in the imperfect tense. See the table below for the meanings of all the verbs in English.

Past (perfect & imperfect)	Present	Future
ho mangiato (I ate) dicevi (you used to say) siamo andati (we went)andavamo (we used to go) **facevate** (you used to do)	ascolto (I listen) iniziano (they start) risparmiamo (we save) spende (he/she spends)	comprerà (he/she will buy) pagheremo (we will pay) parlerai (you will speak) aprirò (I will open) **guarderò** (I will watch) **berrò** (I will drink)

Exam Tip: Demonstrating that you can use more than one tense in the same sentence or paragraph displays a strong grasp of grammatical structures and can make your writing more interesting.

CHAPTER 14

Adjectives and Adverbs

The difficulty rating for each question (Easy [E], Moderate [M] or Hard [H]) can be found in parenthesis next to each question.

14.1. How many adjectives are there in the following sentence? (E)

La piccola ragazza spiritosa può essere timida ma normalmente è sicura di sé.

- A) Two
- B) Three
- C) Four
- D) Five

Extra Challenge: Replace the adjectives in the sentence above with alternatives.

14.2. Where do adjectives generally go in relation to the noun they are describing? (E)

- A) before the noun
- B) after the noun
- C) after the subject of the verb
- D) before the subject of the verb

Extra Challenge: Give five examples of adjectives in Italian.

14.3. Which one of the following lists features adjectives that generally go **before** the noun? (M)

- A) bravo, caro, grande
- B) allegro, debole, arrabbiato
- C) freddo, diverso, sporco
- D) alto, spaventoso, costoso

Extra Challenge: Which other adjectives tend to go **before** the noun in Italian?

14.4. Which of the following adjectives could **not** be used to describe a masculine noun? (E)

A) gentile
B) sano
C) bella
D) nuovo

Extra Challenge: Give three more examples of adjectives that could be used to describe a masculine noun.

14.5. Which of the following adjectives could **not** be used to describe a feminine noun? (E)

A) divertente
B) ordinata
C) stancante
D) comodo

Extra Challenge: Give three more examples of adjectives that could be used to describe a feminine noun.

14.6. Which of the following statements about Italian adjectives is **false**? (M)

A) adjectives ending in -e in the singular generally end in -i in the plural
B) adjectives ending -ica in the singular generally end -iche in the plural
C) adjectives ending in -o in the singular generally end -gli in the plural
D) adjectives ending in -a in the singular generally end -e in the plural

Extra Challenge: Give three examples of how adjectives change from a singular form to a plural form.

14.7. Which of the following adjectives have been given the **incorrect** plural form? (H)

A) il bell'occhio ⇒ i begli occhi
B) lo stesso studio ⇒ gli stesse studi
C) quel libro ⇒ quei libri
D) la donna nubile ⇒ le donne nubili

Extra Challenge: Use different adjectives with the nouns above, both in their singular and plural forms.

14.8. Read the paragraph below about food. (M)

In cucina ci sono poche mele ma tutte sono dolci e gustose. Ci sono anche dei lamponi ma sono un po' amari. Per uno spuntino mangiamo le patatine anche se sono salate e non sono sane. Mi piacciono anche le albicocche; sono squisite in estate.

Which type of adjective is **most common** in the text above?

A) feminine singular
B) feminine plural
C) masculine singular
D) masculine plural

Extra Challenge: Transform the plural adjectives above into their singular forms.

14.9. Read the sentences below. (M)

I negozi vicini a casa mia sono nuovi, ma non sono economici. Secondo me il centro è costoso e pieno di gente, ma è comunque una bella città.

Which of the following statements is **true**?

A) There are more feminine adjectives than masculine adjectives
B) There are more masculine adjectives than feminine adjectives
C) There are more plural adjectives than singular adjectives
D) There are more singular adjectives than plural adjectives

Extra Challenge: Change the meaning of the sentences above by changing all of the adjectives.

14.10. Possessive adjectives describe to whom a noun belongs, e.g. my, your, etc. Which of the following sentences does **not** feature a possessive adjective? (H)

A) La nostra società non cambia mai.
B) Ho visto le sue scarpe.
C) Non ho mai guidato la loro macchina.
D) Mi servono dei piatti puliti.

Extra Challenge: Translate the sentences above into English.

14.11. Which of the following translations using possessive adjectives is **incorrect**? (E)

A) i suoi libri – her/his books
B) le loro biciclette – his bicycles
C) i miei occhiali – my glasses
D) le vostre case – your houses

Extra Challenge: Use the possessive adjectives above with five different nouns.

14.12. Which of the following adjectives does **not** change according to the gender and number of the noun? (M)

A) molto (many)
B) ogni (every)
C) troppo (too many)
D) poco (a few)

Extra Challenge: Create a sentence using each of the adjectives above.

14.13. Which of the following pairs of adjectives would **not** be used to make comparisons in Italian? (E)

A) più / meno
B) minore / maggiore
C) migliore / peggiore
D) fedele / infedele

Extra Challenge: Use the three correct pairings above to make three comparisons.

14.14. Which of the following is the most appropriate translation of the following sentence? (E)

Sport is more interesting than music.

- A) Il sport più interessante della musica.
- B) Lo sport è più interessante della musica.
- C) Lo sport è più interessante che la musica.
- D) Il sport è più interessante che musica.

Extra Challenge: Translate the following sentence into Italian: 'Basketball is more exciting than football'.

14.15. Which of the following is the most appropriate translation of the following sentence? (H)

They sell the best pizzas in the city.

- A) Vendono le migliori pizze in città.
- B) Vendono i migliori pizza della città.
- C) Vendono le meglio pizze in città.
- D) Vendono la pizza migliore della città.

Extra Challenge: Translate the following into Italian: 'this is the worst restaurant in the country'.

14.16. Which of the following sentences has used the **incorrect** form of the adjective 'all'? (M)

- A) Tutti le persone sono stanche.
- B) Ho mangiato tutta la torta.
- C) Non vedo tutte le macchine.
- D) Hanno bevuto tutto il tè.

Extra Challenge: Create four of your own sentences using different variations of *tutto*.

14.17. Demonstrative adjectives refer to the closeness of an object. In English, we would use 'this' or 'these'. In which of the following sentences has the demonstrative adjective been formed **incorrectly**? (M)

A) Questo computer non funziona.
B) Questi fattoria è stata costruita nel 1873.
C) Questi bambini sono viziati.
D) Queste banche sono ricche.

Extra Challenge: Give three of your own examples of sentences with demonstrative adjectives.

14.18. Adverbs describe the verb, indicating how an action is performed. In Italian, adverbs are: (E)

A) invariable
B) dependent on the subject of the verb
C) dependent on the object of the verb
D) dependent on the subject and object of the verb

Extra Challenge: Give three examples of adverbs in Italian.

14.19. Which of the following is **not** an adverb? (E)

A) raramente
B) sempre
C) buono
D) generalmente

Extra Challenge: Use each of the adverbs above in a sentence.

14.20. How many adverbs are there in the following sentence? (H)

Di mattina mi alzo presto e mi vesto rapidamente. Vado a scuola alle otto ma i professori devono parlarmi lentamente perché non sono ancora sveglio.

A) Two
B) Three
C) Four
D) Five

Extra Challenge: Translate the sentences above into English.

14.21. Which one of the following sentences does **not** contain an adverb? (H)

A) Il vento è forte.
B) Canto peggio di te.
C) Ne ho solamente tre.
D) Ero appena arrivata.

Extra Challenge: Translate the sentences above into English.

14.22. What is the most common way to form an adverb in Italian? (E)

A) add the suffix –mente to the feminine form of the adjective
B) add the suffix –mente to the masculine form of the adjective
C) add the suffix –issimo to the masculine form of the adjective
D) add the suffix – issima to the feminine form of the adjective

Extra Challenge: Use three different adverbs in three different sentences in Italian.

14.23. Which of the following translation pairings is **incorrect**? (M)

A) Simona ascolta attentamente – Simona listens carelessly.
B) Giovanni parla rapidamente – Giovanni speaks quickly.
C) Paula lavora diligentemente – Paula works diligently.
D) Dina scrive eloquentemente – Dina writes eloquently.

Extra Challenge: Repeat the sentences above using different adverbs.

14.24. Where do adverbs tend to go in a sentence? (M)

A) before the verb
B) after the verb
C) before the subject of the verb
D) after the subject of the verb

Extra Challenge: Can you think of any exceptions to this rule?

14.25. Which of the following is the most appropriate translation of the sentence below? (H)

They have already decided to run the marathon.

A) Hanno deciso già di correre la maratona.
B) Hanno deciso di correre la maratona già.
C) Già hanno deciso di correre la maratona.
D) Hanno già deciso di correre la maratona.

Extra Challenge: Translate the following into Italian: 'we have already been to the shops this morning'.

14.26. Which of the following lists is chronologically ordered from the most frequent to the least frequent? (M)

A) mai, raramente, a volte, spesso, sempre, ogni tanto
B) ogni tanto, a volte, spesso, mai, sempre, raramente
C) sempre, spesso, a volte, ogni tanto, raramente, mai
D) spesso, ogni tanto, sempre, a volte, mai, raramente

Extra Challenge: Add three other adverbs of frequency to the correct list in the right position.

14.27. Which of the following sentences does **not** use an adverb of time? (H)

A) Ci vediamo presto.
B) Facciamo l'esame domani.
C) Non sto bene oggi.
D) Questo lago è bellissimo.

Extra Challenge: Translate the phrases above into English.

14.28. Which of the following sentences does **not** use an adverb of place? (H)

A) I ragazzi giocano fuori.
B) Forse usciremo subito.
C) Hanno deciso di vivere oltremare.
D) C'erano i mobili dappertutto.

Extra Challenge: Make a list of other adverbs of place.

14.29. Which of the following adverbial phrases has **not** been correctly translated? (H)

A) a poco a poco – little by little
B) senza dubbio – undoubtedly
C) di solito – rarely
D) fino ad ora – until now

Extra Challenge: Use each of the adverbial phrases above in a sentence.

14.30. Read the sentences below. (H)

Non so cantare …….. ma ho voglia di imparare.
Noi litighiamo ………
Lui chiacchiera ……. con il suo amico.

Which of the following should be used to fill in the blanks?

A) adjectives
B) adverbs
C) nouns
D) verbs

Extra Challenge: Fill in the blanks above with words that would make sense in the given context.

Adjectives and Adverbs

Answers and
Detailed Solutions

14.1. C

There are four adjectives in the sentence, which are: *piccola* (small), *spiritosa* (funny), *timida* (shy), and *sicura di sé* (confident). As such, the sentence translates as 'the small, funny girl can be shy but normally she is confident'. Adjectives serve to describe the noun(s) in a sentence, in this case 'the girl'. As the noun is feminine (*la ragazza*) the four adjectives end in –a, given that in Italian adjectives change according to the number and gender of the noun. Notice too that *normalmente* (normally) is not an adjective, but an adverb.

Exam Tip: Using a variety of adjectives in your writing and speaking is very important – and gives you a chance to be creative with your language use.

14.2. B

While in English adjectives tend to go before the noun (e.g. the **blue** hat), in Italian they tend to go after the noun (e.g. *il cappello **blu***). To further practise the position of adjectives in Italian refer to question 14.3. in chapter 14.

14.3. A

Bravo (good), *caro* (dear), and *grande* (big) often go **before** the noun in Italian, e.g. *è una brava ragazza* (she is a good girl), *la mia cara nonna* (my dear grandmother), and *è una grande casa* (it is a big house). Other adjectives that tend to go before the noun include: *bello* (beautiful), *brutto* (ugly), *buono* (good), *cattivo* (bad), *giovane* (young), *nuovo* (new), *piccolo* (small), *stesso* (same), and *vecchio* (old). The other adjectives listed in the question would generally go **after** the noun: *allegro* (happy), *debole* (weak), *arrabbiato* (angry), *freddo* (cold), *diverso* (different), *sporco* (dirty), *alto* (tall), *spaventoso* (frightening), and *costoso* (expensive).

14.4. C

The only adjective that would not be used to describe a masculine noun is *bella* (beautiful), as it ends in –a, and is therefore feminine. The adjective would need to be in its masculine form, e.g. *bello*. Adjectives ending in –o tend to describe masculine nouns, e.g. *sano* (healthy) and *nuovo* (new). However, adjectives ending in –e can describe both masculine and feminine nouns, e.g. *il ragazzo gentile* (the kind boy) and *la ragazza gentile* (the kind girl).

14.5. D

The adjective that could not be used to describe a feminine noun is *comodo* (comfortable) as it ends in an –o rather than an –a. The other three adjectives could be used to describe a feminine noun, as they end in –a like *ordinata* (tidy) and –e, such as *stancante* (tiring) and *divertente* (fun).

14.6. C

The false statement is C: adjectives ending in -o in the singular generally end -gli in the plural. Instead, adjectives ending –o in the singular form generally end in –i in the plural, e.g. *un uomo* **curioso** ⇒ *due uomini* **curiosi**. The other statements are correct. Firstly, adjectives ending in -e in the singular generally end in -i in the plural, e.g. *la domanda è* **difficile** ⇒ *le domande sono* **difficili**. Secondly, adjectives ending –ica in the singular generally end –iche in the plural, e.g. *la fragola è* **fresca** ⇒ *le fragole sono* **fresche**. Thirdly, adjectives ending in -a in the singular generally end -e in the plural, e.g. *la bottiglia è* **vuota** ⇒ *le bottiglie sono* **vuote**.

14.7. B

The incorrect adjective in the plural form is B; *gli stesse studi* should be *gli stessi studi*. Given that *studio* (study) is a masculine noun, the adjective describing it should also be masculine, whether masculine (*stesso*) or plural (**stessi**). Notice the irregular plural forms of *bello* (nice/beautiful) and *quel* (that). See the table below for further details. The final example changes the adjective from *nubile* (single) in the singular to *nubili* in the plural, e.g. *le donne nubili* (single ladies).

	Singular	Plural
Masculine (starting s + consonant/z)	bello/quello	begli/quegli
Masculine (starting with all other consonants)	bel/quel	bei/quei
Feminine	bella/quella	belle/quelle
Before Vowels	bell'/quell'	begli/quegli (m)belle/quelle (f)

Exam Tip: Check your written Italian carefully as mistakes with adjectival agreements (particularly plurals!) are very common.

14.8. B

The majority of the adjectives in the paragraph are feminine plural: *poche* (few), *dolci* (sweet), *gustose* (tasty), *salate* (salty), *sane* (healthy), and *squisite* (delicious). We know they are feminine plural both because they tend to end in –e, and because they are describing feminine nouns. There is also one masculine plural adjective – *amari* (bitter) – but there are no singular adjectives in the text.

14.9. B

Five of the adjectives in the paragraph are masculine (*vicini, nuovi, economici, costoso, pieno*), whereas only one is feminine (*bella*), therefore the true statement is B: there are more masculine adjectives than feminine adjectives. There are the same number of plural adjectives (*vicini, nuovi, economici*) as there are singular (*costoso, pieno, bella*); three of each. The sentences translate as follows: the shops close to my house are new, but they are not cheap. In my opinion the centre is expensive and busy, but it is still a beautiful city (*I negozi **vicini** a casa mia sono **nuovi** ma non sono **economici**. Secondo me il centro è **costoso** e **pieno** di gente, ma è comunque una **bella** città*).

14.10. D

The only sentence that does not feature a possessive adjective is D: *mi servono dei piatti puliti* (I need some clean plates). The other sentences do use a possessive adjective: *La **nostra** società non cambia mai* (our society never changes), *ho visto le **sue** scarpe* (I saw his/her shoes), and *non ho mai guidato la **loro** macchina* (I have never driven their car).

14.11. B

Le loro biciclette means 'their bicycles' rather than 'his bicycles' ('his/her bicycles' would be *le sue biciclette*). The other translations are correct. Notice how *i suoi libri* can be 'his' or 'her' books – it is the gender of the noun that alters the possessive adjective rather than the gender of the subject. For example, *il suo compleanno* (his/her birthday) and *la sua macchina fotografica* (his/her camera).

Exam Tip: It is important to be attentive to the context of possessive adjectives in order to better understand what is being said. For example, *suo/sua/suoi/sue* can mean 'his' or 'her'.

14.12. B

Ogni does not change regardless of the number and gender of the noun it describes, e.g. *andiamo a scuola ogni giorno* (we go to school every day) or *provano un nuovo sport ogni settimana* (they try a new sport every week). The other adjectives do change according to the number and gender of the noun: *lui mostra **molta** gentilezza* (he shows much kindness), *ci sono **troppe** feste* (there are too many parties), and *abbiamo **poche** idee* (we have few ideas).

14.13. D

The only pair of adjectives that would not be needed to make comparisons is *fedele* (faithful) and *infedele* (unfaithful). The other phrases translate as follows: *più* (more) / *meno* (less), *minore* (smaller) / *maggiore* (bigger), and *migliore* (better) / *peggiore* (worse). For further practice with comparisons in Italian refer to questions 11.14. and 14.14. in chapter 11 and 14 respectively.

14.14. B

To make a comparison in Italian you use *più* (more) / *meno* (less) + adjective + *di* when comparing two nouns, e.g. Lo sport è più interessante **della** musica (*sport is more interesting than music*). If you are using two adjectives to compare the same noun, you use *più* (more) / *meno* (less) + adjective + *che*, e.g. *Matteo è più tranquillo che aggressivo* (Matteo is more calm than aggressive).

14.15. A

The most appropriate translation of 'they sell the best pizzas in the city' is *vendono le migliore pizze in città*. To use the superlative in Italian, you need the definite article with *migliore* (singular) / *migliori* (plural) for 'the best' or *peggiore* (singular) / *peggiori* (plural) for 'the worst'. Notice in the translation that *migliori* is plural because it is describing a plural noun (*le pizze*) and it goes **before** the noun. *Meglio* (better) and *peggio* (worse) are adverbs used to describe verbs rather than nouns, e.g. *lei suona la chitarra meglio di me* (she plays the guitar better than me).

14.16. A

The incorrect use of 'all' is in sentence A: it should be *tutte* rather than *tutti*, as the noun being described - *le persone* – is feminine plural. The adjective *tutto* changes according to the number and gender of the noun it describes: *tutto* (masculine singular), *tutta* (feminine singular), *tutti* (masculine plural), and *tutte* (feminine plural).

14.17. B

The sentence which features an incorrect demonstrative adjective is B: as 'this farm' should be feminine singular, rather than masculine plural. It should therefore read **questa fattoria** *è stata costruita nel 1873* (this farm was built in 1873). The other sentences correctly use the demonstrative adjective: *questo computer non funziona* (this computer does not work), *questi bambini sono viziati* (these children are spoilt), and *queste banche sono ricche* (these banks are rich).

14.18. A

Unlike adjectives, adverbs in Italian are invariable, that is to say, they do not change according to the subject or verb. For example, when *molto* is used as an adjective to describe a noun, it changes according to the number and gender of the noun, e.g. *abbiamo molti cani* (we have many dogs). However, when it is used as an adverb to describe the verb, it is invariable, e.g. *ci telefoniamo molto* (we telephone each other a lot).

14.19. C

The only word that is not an adverb is C: *buono*, which means 'good', e.g. *Carla ha una buona famiglia* (Carla has a good family). The other words are adverbs that could describe a verb: *raramente* (rarely), *sempre* (always), and *generalmente* (generally). See question 14.22. for information on how to form adverbs.

14.20. C

There are four adverbs in the sentence: *presto* (early), *rapidamente* (quickly), *lentamente* (slowly), and *ancora* (yet/still). The sentence translates as follows: In the morning, I get up **early** and I get dressed **quickly**. I go to school at 8 o'clock but my teachers have to speak to me **slowly** because I am **still** not awake (*Di mattina mi alzo **presto** e mi vesto **rapidamente**. Vado a scuola alle otto ma i professori devono parlarmi **lentamente** perché non sono **ancora** sveglio*).

Exam Tip: Make sure you use adverbs in your writing and speaking to give further weight to your responses – however, be careful not to use too many!

14.21. A

The sentence *il vento è forte* (the wind is strong) contains an adjective (*forte*) rather than an adverb. The other sentences contain adverbs: *canto **peggio** di te* (I sing worse than you), *ne ho **solamente** tre* (I only have three of them), and *ero **appena** arrivata* (I had just arrived).

14.22. A

The most common way to form an adverb in Italian is to add the suffix –mente to the feminine form of the adjective. For example, if we take the adjective *vero* (true) in its feminine form, *vera*, we add *-mente* to get *veramente* (truly). When an adjective ends in –re or –le, e.g. *regolare* or *gentile*, the final –e is dropped before adding the suffix –mente, e.g. *regolarmente, gentilmente*. If you were to add the suffixes –issimo or –issima to an adjective you would form the absolute superlative, e.g. *noioso* (boring) ⇒ *noiosissimo* (really boring).

14.23. A

The incorrect translation pairing is A because *attentamente* means 'carefully', not 'carelessly'. The other translation pairings are correct: *Giovanni parla rapidamente* (Giovanni speaks quickly), *Paula lavora diligentemente* (Paula works diligently), and *Dina scrive eloquentemente* (Dina writes eloquently).

14.24. B

Adverbs tend to go after the verb, e.g. *lei risponde **intelligentemente*** (she answers intelligently), *parliamo **sempre** di te* (we are always talking about you). However, in compound tenses, *like the passato prossimo*, certain adverbs go in between the auxiliary verb and the past participle. These adverbs include: *mai* (never), *già* (already), *sempre* (always), and *ancora* (still), e.g. *sono **sempre** stata una persona emotiva* (I have always been an emotional person).

14.25. D

The correct translation of 'they have already decided to run the marathon' is D: *hanno già deciso di correre la maratona*. This is because certain adverbs (*già, sempre, ancora,* and *mai*) go in between the auxiliary and the past participle, e.g. *siamo **già** andati ai negozi stamattina* (we have already been to the shops this morning). However, most of the time adverbs go **after** the past participle, e.g. *siamo usciti **tardi*** (we went out late).

14.26. C

The correct chronological order of the adverbs listed from most to least frequent is as follows: *sempre* (always), *spesso* (often), *a volte* (sometimes), *ogni tanto* (from time to time), *raramente* (rarely), *mai* (never).

14.27. D

The sentence that does not contain an adverb of time is D: *questo lago è bellissimo* (this lake is really beautiful). The other sentences all use adverbs of time: *ci vediamo **presto*** (we will see each other soon), *facciamo l'esame **domani*** (we are doing the exam tomorrow), *and non sto bene **oggi*** (I am not well today).

14.28. B

The only sentence that does not include an adverb of place is B: *Forse usciremo subito* (perhaps we will go out straight away). The sentences containing adverbs of place can be translated as follows: *I ragazzi giocano fuori* (the boys play outside), *hanno deciso di vivere oltremare* (they have decided to live overseas), and *c'erano i mobili dappertutto* (there was furniture everywhere). Other adverbs of place include: *dietro* (behind), *contro* (against), *dentro* (inside), *lì/là* (there), and *laggiù* (over there).

14.29. C

The incorrect translation is C, as *di solito* means 'usually', not 'rarely'. The other adverbial phrases have been correctly translated: *a poco a poco* (little by little), *senza dubbio* (undoubtedly), and *fino ad ora* (until now).

Exam Tip: Adverbial phrases such as the ones used in question 14.29. give your writing and speaking further meaning and nuance.

14.30. B

The blanks should be adverbs, rather than adjectives, because they describe the nature or frequency of the verb rather than the noun. The following adverbs would make sense in the context of the sentences: *non so cantare **bene** ma ho voglia di imparare* (I do not know how to sing well, but I want to learn), *noi litighiamo **raramente*** (we rarely argue), and *lui chiacchiera **molto** con il suo amico* (he chats a lot with his friend).

CHAPTER 15

Miscellaneous Grammar

The difficulty rating for each question (Easy [E], Moderate [M] or Hard [H]) can be found in parenthesis next to each question.

15.1. Which of the following would be the **correct** translation of the statement: 'my father's birthday is on the fourteenth May'? (E)

A) Mio padre's compleanno è il quattro Maggio.
B) Il compleanno di mio padre è il quattordicesimo maggio.
C) Il compleanno del mio padre è il quattordicesimo marzo.
D) Il compleanno di mio padre è il quattordici maggio.

Extra Challenge: Write the birthdays of three members of your family, or three friends, in Italian.

15.2. Which of the following pairings of dates is **incorrect**? (E)

A) venerdì il sei marzo – Friday 6th March
B) mercoledì il ventiquattro febbraio – Wednesday 24th February
C) domenica il quindici giugno – Sunday 13th June
D) lunedì il diciannove maggio – Monday 19th May

Extra Challenge: Give five dates in Italian (each in a different month).

15.3. Which of the following is the **correct** translation of 'one thousand, six hundred and twenty-three'? (E)

A) milleseicentoventitré
B) milleseicentotrentatré
C) milleseicentoventisei
D) uno sei vente e tré

Extra Challenge: Translate the following numbers into Italian: 2534, 985, and 231.

15.4. Which of the following is **not** an ordinal number (e.g. third, fourth, fifth etc.)? (E)

A) terzo
B) cento
C) diciassettesimo
D) ottavo

Extra Challenge: Translate the following ordinal numbers into Italian: second, fourth and sixth.

15.5. When telling the time, how do you say, 'it is quarter to five' in Italian? (E)

A) sono cinque e quarto
B) sono le cinque meno un quarto
C) è quarto e cinque
D) è cinque e quarto

Extra Challenge: Translate the following times into Italian: 3:30, 9:15 and 11:20.

15.6. Which of the following sentences does **not** give you the time in Italian? (M)

A) è mezzogiorno
B) sono le undici e cinque
C) sono le tre e mezza
D) è un incubo

Extra Challenge: Translate the following times into Italian: 8:45, 2:10 and 12.25.

15.7. Which statement about *giornata* and *giorno* is **true**? (M)

A) *Giornata* and *giorno* can be used interchangeably.
B) *Giornata* is used to mean the entire/whole day, *giorno* is used more generally.
C) *Giorno* is used to mean the entire/whole day, *giornata* is used more generally.
D) *Giorno* is feminine, *giornata* is masculine.

Extra Challenge: How do you say, 'good day' and 'have a good day' in Italian?

15.8. Which of the following words does **not** mean 'people'? (E)

A) l'età
B) la gente
C) le persone
D) il popolo

Extra Challenge: How are verbs conjugated with the above forms of 'people'?

15.9. Prepositions are short words used to locate the noun, verb or adjective, often in place or time, or connect words and sentences. Which of the following translation pairings is **incorrect**? (E)

A) su – on
B) sotto – underneath
C) a – from
D) con – with

Extra Challenge: Make three sentences with the three correct prepositions.

15.10. Which of the following words does **not** require a preposition directly after it (when referring to a noun or verb)? (H)

A) davanti
B) dietro
C) prima
D) sotto

Extra Challenge: Use each of the words above in a sentence.

15.11. In which of the following examples would you **not** use the preposition *a*? (M)

A) to say you're going home or to bed, e.g. vado **a** casa
B) to say where you live or are going (town or city), e.g. abito **a** Venezia
C) to say where you live or are going (region or country), e.g. vado **a** Spagna
D) to say the time, e.g. gioco a calcio **a** mezzogiorno

Extra Challenge: Give three examples of sentences that use the preposition *a*.

15.12. In which of the following instances would you **not** use the preposition *di*? (M)

A) to indicate possession e.g. Davide's cat (*il gatto di Davide*)
B) to say where you come from with the verb *venire* e.g. I come from Naples (*vengo di Napoli*)
C) to make comparisons e.g. she is wiser than him (*lei è più saggia di lui*)
D) to describe the material of an object e.g. a wooden chair (*una sedia di legno*)

Extra Challenge: Give three example sentences which use the preposition *di*.

15.13. Which of the following does **not** mean 'in the'? (M)

A) negli
B) nello
C) nel
D) nele

Extra Challenge: Translate the following statement into Italian: 'there is a cat in the box'.

15.14. Read the following questions in which the interrogative word is preceded by a preposition. (H)

Which of the answers is **not** logical?

A) A chi stai parlando? Sto parlando a mia mamma.
B) Di chi sono le chiavi? Sono di Mario.
C) Da dove vieni? Vengo da Torino.
D) Con cosa scrivi? Scrivo una lettera.

Extra Challenge: Give three examples of questions that start with a preposition.

15.15. Which of the following sentences does **not** use a negative construction correctly? (E)

A) Non mai uso il computer
B) Non penso più che sia una buona idea
C) Non vedo nessuno
D) Non ho niente di interessante da dire

Extra Challenge: Change the phrases above into the positive.

15.16. Read the following question and answer pairings. Which of the answers uses the **incorrect** negative? (H)

A) Sai già dov'è? Non so nessuno.
B) Vai spesso al cinema? Non ci vado mai.
C) Fai ancora judo? Non lo faccio più.
D) Vedi qualcosa? Non vedo niente.

Extra Challenge: Give three more examples of questions with answers in the negative.

15.17. Which of the following is the most appropriate translation of the sentence below? (H)

I have never been to Germany.

A) Non sono stata mai in Germania.
B) Sono stata mai in Germania.
C) Non sono mai stata in Germania.
D) Sono mai stata in Germania.

Extra Challenge: Translate the following sentence into Italian: 'He never saw the police'.

15.18. Prefixes go at the beginning of words to indicate a particular meaning. Which pair of opposites uses an **incorrect** prefix to change the meaning of the first word? (M)

A) capace ⇒ incapace
B) sensibile ⇒ unsensibile
C) onesto ⇒ disonesto
D) vantaggio ⇒ svantaggio

Extra Challenge: Which other prefixes are often used in Italian?

15.19. A number of prefixes precede the verb *prendere* and therefore follow the same pattern of conjugation as *prendere*. Which of the following prefixes would **not** be used before *prendere* to form another verb? (H)

A) com-
B) sor-
C) ri-
D) inter-

Extra Challenge: What are the past participles of these verbs?

15.20. Suffixes are often used in Italian to give additional meaning to nouns and adjectives. Which of the following translation pairings is **incorrect**? (H)

A) bellissimo – really beautiful
B) librone – a big book
C) tempaccio – awful weather
D) casetta – ugly house

Extra Challenge: Use the suffixes above (-issimo, -one, -accio, and –etta) with five other nouns or adjectives in Italian.

15.21. Which of the following sentences does **not** include a gerund (an –ing word)? (H)

A) Lui beve una limonata mentre legge.
B) Sbagliando, miglioriamo le nostre capacità.
C) Essendo diventato ricco, ha deciso di comprare una casa alle Maldive.
D) Lei scrive ascoltando la radio.

Extra Challenge: Translate the following into Italian: 'having eaten the pasta, she went to bed'.

15.22. Which of the following would be the most appropriate translation of '3 months ago'? (E)

A) Tre anni fa
B) Tre mesi fa
C) Tre mesi da
D) Tre anni va

Extra Challenge: How would you say the following in Italian: 'six years ago'?

15.23. Which of the following expressions with *da* has been **incorrectly** translated? (H)

A) Faccio karate da cinque anni – I have been doing karate for 5 years.
B) Vado da mio fratello – I go to my brother's house.
C) Sto nella sala da pranzo – I am in the dining room.
D) Non mi tratta da amici – He does not treat me like a friend.

Extra Challenge: Give three further examples of sentences that contain the preposition *da*.

15.24. Which of the following question words does **not** elide (the final vowel removed) after the verb *è*? (E)

A) come
B) cosa
C) perché
D) dove

Extra Challenge: Ask a question using each of the question words above and the verb *è*.

15.25. The imperative refers to an instruction or command, e.g. 'listen carefully' or 'run over there'. In Italian, the imperative is generally conjugated in the following subjects: *tu*, *Lei* (formal), *noi*, and *voi*. (M)

Which of the following translation pairings is **incorrect**?

A) Finiamo la pizza – let's finish the pizza!
B) Domanda all'istruttrice – ask the teacher!
C) Andate al bar – go to the bar!
D) Scrivete la lettera – let's write the letter!

Extra Challenge: Conjugate the verb *mangiare* into the four forms of the imperative (tu, Lei [formal], noi, and voi).

15.26. The verbs *essere* and *stare* both mean 'to be' in different contexts. (M)

In which of the following sentences should *stare* be used rather than *essere*?

A) Sono inglese.
B) sii zitto!
C) Suo figlio è giovane.
D) I tuoi capelli sono lunghi.

Extra Challenge: What are the main differences between *essere* and *stare*?

15.27. *Conoscere* and *sapere* both mean 'to know' in different contexts. (M)

In which of the following sentences should *conoscere* be used rather than *sapere*?

A) Non so rispondere alla domanda – I do not know how to answer the question.
B) Sappiamo quando arriverà – We know when she will arrive.
C) Sai mio cugino? - Do you know my sister?
D) Sai che è importante? – Do you know that it is important?

Extra Challenge: Give three of your own examples of sentences with *sapere* and *conoscere*.

15.28. In Italian there are different words that capture the various nuances of the verb 'to leave'. Which of the following words would be most appropriate to fill in the gap in the sentence below? (M)

Mio nonno è .... per la Francia giovedì sera.

A) uscito
B) lasciato
C) andato via
D) partito

Extra Challenge: In which contexts would you use the other verbs above?

15.29. Below are three lists of verbs that are followed by *di* + infinitive. Which list contains verbs that are followed by *a* + infinitive? (H)

A)   cercare, finire, decidere
B)   dimenticare, chiedere, promettere
C)   smettere, tentare, vietare
D)   aiutare, cominciare, continuare

Extra Challenge: Aside from the verbs above, give three further examples of verbs followed by the preposition *a*.

15.30. *Volerci* can be used to express how long something takes. Which of the following is the **correct** translation of the sentence below? (H)

It takes two hours to go to Rome by plane.

A)   Ci vuole due ore per andare a Roma in aereo.
B)   Ci vogliono due ore per andare a Roma in aereo.
C)   Ci vogliamo due ore per andare a Roma in aereo.
D)   Ci voglio due ore per andare a Roma in aereo.

Extra Challenge: Translate the following into Italian: 'it takes one hour to go there by car'.

Miscellaneous Grammar

Answers and
Detailed Solutions

15.1. D

The most appropriate translation of 'my father's birthday is on the fourteenth May' is option D: *il compleanno di mio padre è il quattordici maggio*. Notice how in Italian the cardinal number is used (e.g. *quattordici* [14]), rather than the ordinal number, like in English (e.g. *quattordicesimo* [14th]). Furthermore, remember 'apostrophe + s' in English needs 'noun + di + subject' in Italian, e.g. *il compleanno di mio padre* (the birthday of my dad/my dad's birthday).

15.2. C

The only incorrect translation pairing is option C because *il quindici giugno* means the '15th June' not the '13th June' (*il tredici giugno*). Notice how in Italian months and days of the week do not begin with a capital letter, as they do in English.

15.3. A

1623 in written Italian is *milleseicentoventitré*. Notice how numbers in Italian, no matter how long, are all one word. Remember too that numbers change their form when followed by numbers beginning with a vowel, e.g. *diciotto* (18) unlike *diciassette* (17) and *diciannove* (19).

Exam Tip: When listening to long numbers in Italian, remember to break each part down into manageable chunks.

15.4. B

The ordinal numbers are *terzo* (third), *diciassettesimo* (seventeenth), and *ottavo* (eighth), whereas the only cardinal number in the list is *cento* (one hundred). See the following table for a comparison of cardinal and ordinal numbers.

Cardinal number	Ordinal Number
uno	primo
due	secondo
tre	terzo
quattro	quarto
cinque	quinto
sei	sesto
sette	settimo
otto	ottavo
nove	nono
dieci	decimo
undici	undicesimo
dodici	dodicesimo

15.5. B

The correct translation of 'it is quarter to five' is *sono le cinque meno un quarto*. In Italian, you use *sono* (they are) to describe the time, unless it is one o'clock, in which case you would use *è* because it is singular, e.g. *è l'una* (it is one o'clock), *sono le due* (it is two o'clock). To say a time 'past' the hour use *e* (and), e.g. *sono le tre e dieci* (it is 3:10). To say a time 'to' the hour, use *meno* (minus), e.g. *sono le sette meno cinque* (it is five minutes to seven). 'A quarter' is *un quarto*, 'half past' is *e mezza*, 'midnight' is *mezzanotte*, and 'midday' is *mezzogiorno*.

Exam Tip: When listening to the time in Italian, listen carefully for *meno* to indicate 'to the hour'.

15.6. D

Three of the sentences give the time: *è mezzogiorno* (it is midday), *sono le undici e cinque* (it is 11:05), and *sono le tre e mezza* (it is half past three). Therefore, the only phrase that does not relate to the time is: *è un incubo* (it is a nightmare).

15.7. B

Buongiorno means 'good day' in Italian, whereas *buona giornata* means 'have a good day'. This is because *giornata* is used to refer to the entire/whole day (as one day), while *giorno* is used more generally. *Giorno* is masculine and *giornata* is feminine. When talking about 'the evening', *sera* and *serata* work in the same way as *giorno* and *giornata*.

15.8. A

The only word that does not mean 'people' is *l'età*, which means 'age'. *La gente* is used to mean 'people' in a very generic sense and takes the third-person singular, whereas *le persone* often refers to a more specific group of people and takes the third-person plural. *Il popolo* also means 'people', but tends to refer to the inhabitants of a particular country.

15.9. C

The incorrect pairing is *a* – from. Instead *da* is 'from', and *a* is 'to' or 'in', e.g. *da Londra a Parigi* (from London to Paris), *abito a Bari* (I live in Bari). The other pairings of prepositions are correct: *su* – on, *sotto* – underneath, and *con* – with.

15.10. B

The word that does not require a preposition directly after it is *dietro* (behind), e.g. *la casa è dietro la banca* (the house is behind the bank). See the table below for which prepositions follow other words related to positionality.

Requires a preposition	Does not require a preposition
davanti a (in front of)	dietro (behind)
prima di (before)	dopo (after)
sotto a (underneath)	sopra (above)
fuori da (outside)	nonostante (despite)
vicino a (near)	con (with)
lontano da (far)	

15.11. C

The preposition *a* generally translates as 'to', 'at', or 'in', although careful attention needs to be given to the context of the sentence. For example, *a* is used to say you live or are going, when you are talking about a town or city, e.g. *abito **a** Venezia* (I live in Venice), but the preposition *in* is used when referring to a region or country, e.g. *vado **in** Spagna* (I go to Spain). Note also that *a* changes to *ad* when the following noun begins with a vowel, e.g. *abito **ad** Alghero* (I live in Alghero). Furthermore, although *a* is used for indicating going to bed or going home (*vado a letto/vado a casa*), to talk about going to most places in town you would use *in*, e.g. *Maria va in biblioteca* (Maria goes to the library). Finally, when indicating at what time something happens, use *a* or a compound of *a*, e.g. ***a** mezzogiorno* (at midday), ***alle** due* (at 2 o'clock).

15.12. B

The preposition *di* (often translated as 'of' in English) has many uses. These include: indicating possession, where in English we would use 's, e.g. Davide's cat (*il gatto **di** Davide*) or Benito's book (*il libro **di** Benito*); making comparisons, e.g. she is wiser than him (*lei è più saggia **di** lui*); and describing what an object is made of, e.g. a wooden chair (*una sedia **di** legno*) or a metal table (*un tavolo **di** metallo*). It is not, however, used to describe where someone comes from. Instead the preposition *da* (from) is used, e.g. *vengo da Napoli* (I come from Naples). You would use *di* though when you say, 'I **am** from Naples' (***sono** di Napoli*).

15.13. D

In Italian, the preposition *in* changes when added to the definite article. This is an example of an articulated preposition. As such, there are many different ways of saying 'in the' in Italian, depending on the number and gender of the noun. The table below outlines the different options.

'in' + definite article	= 'in the'
in + il	nel
in + la	nella
in + lo	nello
in + l'	nell'
in + i	nei
in + gli	negli
in + le	nelle

15.14. D

The illogical answer is to question D; the question asks 'what do you write with?/with what do you write?' (*con cosa scrivi?*) so the answer 'I write a letter' (*scrivo una lettera*) does not make sense. It would be more logical to answer, 'I write with a pen/pencil' (*scrivo con una penna/una matita*) or to change the question to *cosa scrivi?* (what are you writing?). The other answers match their respective questions: *a chi stai parlando? Sto parlando a mia mamma* (to whom are you talking? I am talking to my mum); *di chi sono le chiavi? Sono di Mario* (whose keys are they? They are Mario's); and *da dove vieni? Vengo da Torino* (where do you come from? I come from Turin).

15.15. A

In the present tense, negative constructions go around the verb e.g. ***non uso mai*** … (I never use) therefore option A is incorrect. The other phrases in the question are grammatically correct: ***non*** *vedo* ***nessuno*** (I do not see anyone), ***non*** *ho* ***niente***… (I have nothing…), and ***non*** *penso* ***più*** (I no longer think….). Notice that the last one is followed by the subjunctive e.g. *Non penso più che* ***sia*** *una buona idea*. See question 13.29. in chapter 13 for further information about when to use the subjunctive.

15.16. A

The incorrect answer is to question A. The question asks *sai già dov'è?* (do you already know where it is?) to which the answer should be *non so* ***ancora*** (I do not know yet). *Nessuno*, by contrast, means 'no-one' or 'anyone' and should be used with the verb *conoscere*, e.g. ***non*** *conosco* ***nessuno***. The other questions and answers make logical sense: *vai spesso al cinema?* (do you often go to the cinema? ⇒ ***non*** *ci vado* ***mai*** (I never go there), *fai ancora il judo?* (do you still do judo?) ⇒ ***non*** *lo faccio* ***più*** (I no longer do it), and *vedi qualcosa?* (do you see something?) ⇒ ***non*** *vedo* ***niente*** (I see nothing).

15.17. C

When compound tenses (like the *passato prossimo*) are used with negatives, the negative phrase (e.g. *non….mai*) generally goes around the first conjugated verb. As a result, the correct translation of 'I have never been to Germany' is *non sono mai stata in Germania*. We know from the ending of the past participle (*stata*) that this is a female speaking.

15.18. B

The incorrect word is 'unsensibile'; instead *sensibile* (sensitive) uses the prefix *in-* to change the meaning of the word, e.g. *insensibile* (insensitive). Other words that use the prefix *in-* include: *incapace* (uncapable), *intollerante* (intolerant), and *inutile* (useless). *Onesto* (honest) uses the prefix *dis-* to become *disonesto* (dishonest). Other words using this prefix include: *disordinato* (untidy), *dispiacere* (to displease), and *disoccupazione* (unemployment). Finally, the prefix *s-* is often added to the beginning of a word to make it negative, e.g. *svantaggio* (disadvantage), *scorretto* (incorrect), and *sfortuna* (misfortune).

15.19. D

The only prefix that would not be used in front of the verb *prendere* (to take) is 'inter-'. *Comprendere* means 'to understand' or 'to include', *sorprendere* is 'to surprise', and *riprendere* is 'to take back'. These verbs follow the same conjugation patterns as the verb *prendere* (to take), therefore their past participles are *compreso, sorpreso,* and *ripreso* respectively.

15.20. D

The incorrect translation pairing is '*casetta* – ugly house'. *Casetta* means 'little house' as the suffix *-etto/a* generally denotes something small or cute, as does the suffix *ino/a*, e.g. *attimo (moment)* ⇒ *attimino (short moment)*. The absolute superlative is *-issimo* as it tells us that the adjective is in the extreme; it could be translated as 'very', 'extremely', or 'really', e.g. *buonissimo* (extremely good). The augmentative is *–one* because it denotes that something is 'big' or 'large'. Notice how the ending does not change to an -a in the feminine, e.g. *la porta* ⇒ *il portone* (the big/front door). Finally, *-accio* denotes something 'awful' or 'bad', e.g. *parola* (word) ⇒ *parolaccia* (swear word).

15.21. A

The gerund (-ing word) can take two forms: the *gerundio semplice* (simple gerund) or the *gerundio composto* (compound gerund). The *gerundio semplice* is one word and denotes –ing, for example, *sbagliando, miglioriamo le nostre capacità* (by **making** mistakes, we improve our skills) and *lei scrive ascoltando la radio* (she writes, while **listening** to the radio).

For more practice on forming the *gerundio semplice*, see question 13.13. in chapter 13. The *gerundio composto* uses the gerund of the auxiliary verbs *avere* or *essere* and adds a past participle, e.g. **avendo lavorato** *tantissimo tutto il giorno, lei è andata a letto* (having worked hard all day, she went to bed) and **essendo diventato** *ricco, ha deciso di comprare una casa alle Maldive* (having become rich, he decided to buy a house in the Maldives). As such, the only sentence that does not use the gerund is A: *lui beve una limonata mentre legge* (he drinks a lemonade while he reads).

Exam Tip: Using a gerund instead of the regular present tense can be an effective means of demonstrating a variety of grammatical structures.

15.22. B

The correct translation of 'three months ago' in Italian is *tre mesi fa. Fa* is the third-person singular of the verb *fare* and is used after units of time to mean 'ago', e.g. *sei anni fa* (six years ago). 'A long time ago' could therefore be translated as *tanto tempo fa*.

15.23. D

The preposition *da* can be used in a variety of cases. Firstly, it is used to indicate 'since' or 'for + time frame', e.g. *faccio karate da cinque anni* (I have been doing karate for 5 years). Notice that while in English we use the past tense for this construction (I have been doing), in Italian you simply use the present tense (e.g. *faccio*). Secondly, *da* can be used to mean someone's house, e.g. *vado da mio fratello* (I go to my brother's house). This also applies to someone's office, e.g. *sta dall'avvocato* (he is at the lawyer's office). Thirdly, *da* can be used to indicate a purpose, e.g. *sala da pranzo* (dining room) and for set verbs *trattare da amico* (to treat like a friend). Translation D was incorrect, however, as *non mi tratta da amici,* should be *non mi tratta da amic**o***.

15.24. C

The only question word in the list that does not elide when followed by the verb è is *perché* (why), e.g. *perché è così difficile?* (why is it so difficult?). The other question words are elided, e.g. *com'è la pizza?* (how is the pizza?), *cos'è quello rumore?* (what is that noise?), and *dov'è la cucina?* (where is the kitchen?).

15.25. D

The following pairings of translations using the imperative are correct: *finiamo la pizza* (let's finish the pizza!), *domanda all'istruttrice* (ask the teacher!), and *andate al bar* (go to the bar!). When conjugating the imperative, the *tu* and *voi* forms use the indicative form of the present tense, except that –are verbs in the *tu* form take an –a rather than an –i, e.g. *canta* (sing!). The *Lei* form takes the present subjunctive (see question 13.29. in chapter 13) and the *noi* form is identical to the present indicative, e.g. *andiamo* (let's go). The incorrect option is therefore *scrivete la lettera*, which means 'write the letter' because it is in the *voi* form, rather than 'let's write the letter!', in the *noi* form. Remember too that *essere* and *avere* have irregulars in the *tu* form of the imperative: *sii* and *abbi* respectively.

15.26. B

Generally, *essere* means 'to be' or 'to exist', whereas *stare* means 'to stay'. *Essere* is used when describing the features of a noun (e.g. identity, physical attributes, etc). As such, the following sentences correctly use *essere*: *sono inglese* (I am English), *suo figlio è giovane* (her son is young), and *i tuoi capelli sono lunghi* (your hair is long). *Stare*, on the other hand, can be used with idiomatic expressions (e.g. *sto bene/male* [I am fine/not fine]), with the present continuous (e.g. *sto pensando* [I am thinking]), and with precise locations (e.g. *il formaggio sta nel frigorifero* [the cheese is in the fridge]). *Stare* is also used with commands, e.g. *stai zitto* (be quiet), which is why option B should use *stare* rather than *essere*.

15.27. C

The sentence that should use the verb *conoscere* rather than *sapere* is C: *sai mio cugino?* should be *conosci mio cugino?* (do you know my cousin?). This is because the verb *conoscere* (to know) is used to refer to 'being familiar/acquainted with', or 'getting to know'. As such, it is generally followed by people or places, e.g. *conosco quella canzone* (I know that song). *Sapere*, on the other hand, refers to knowledge of facts or specific pieces of information, e.g. *so la risposta* (I know the answer). *Sapere* is also followed by an infinitive, to mean 'to know how to', e.g. *sanno giocare a scacchi* (they know how to play chess).

15.28. D

The missing word is *partito*, as the sentence means 'my grandfather left for France on Thursday evening' (*Mio nonno è partito per la Francia giovedì sera*). *Partire* means 'to leave' in the context of departing from one place to another. By contrast, *lasciare* means 'to leave' in the sense of leaving something or someone behind, e.g. *ho lasciato il mio portafoglio nella cucina* (I left my wallet in the kitchen). *Andare via* means 'to go away' or 'to get going', e.g. *devo andare via* (I have to get going). Finally, *uscire* is often translated as 'to go out', e.g. *mi piace uscire con amici* (I like to go out with friends).

15.29. D

Some verbs are followed by *a* (*aiuto **a** costruire il edificio* – I help to build the building), and others by *di* (*finisco **di** cantare* – I finish singing). Below is a table of verbs that each take the two prepositions.

Verb + a + infinitive	Verb + di + infinitive
aiutare a (to help to)	cercare di (to try to)
cominciare a (to start to)	chiedere di (to ask to)
continuare a (to continue to)	decidere di (to decide to)
imparare a (to learn to)	dimenticare di (to forget to)
incoraggiare a (to encourage to)	finire di (to finish)
insegnare a (to teach to)	promettere di (to promise to)
invitare a (to invite to)	smettere di (to stop)
rinunciare a (to give up in)	tentare di (to try to)
riuscire a (to succeed in)	vietare di (to ban/prohibit)

15.30. B

The correct translation of 'it takes two hours to go to Rome by plane' is *ci vogliono due ore per andare a Roma in aereo*. When referring to how long something takes, *volerci* is only used in the third-person singular with a single unit of time (*ci vuole un'ora*), and the third-person plural with a plural unit or units of time (*ci vogliono cinque anni* [it takes five years]). Of course, like all verbs, *volerci* can also be used in different tenses: *ci è/sono voluto/i* (it took…), *ci vorrà/vorranno* (it will take…), and *ci sarebbe/ro voluto/i* (it would have taken…).

ANSWER KEY

Chapter 1: People and Relationships	
Question	Answer
1.1	**B**
1.2	**D**
1.3	**C**
1.4	**D**
1.5	**D**
1.6	**B**
1.7	**D**
1.8	**A**
1.9	**B**
1.10	**D**
1.11	**B**
1.12	**D**
1.13	**C**
1.14	**A**
1.15	**A**
1.16	**D**
1.17	**D**
1.18	**B**
1.19	**A**
1.20	**D**

Chapter 2: Home	
Question	Answer
2.1	**B**
2.2	**C**
2.3	**B**
2.4	**C**
2.5	**A**
2.6	**C**
2.7	**C**
2.8	**D**
2.9	**C**
2.10	**A**
2.11	**B**
2.12	**D**
2.13	**D**
2.14	**B**
2.15	**D**
2.16	**D**
2.17	**A**
2.18	**C**
2.19	**B**
2.20	**A**

Chapter 3: Education	
Question	Answer
3.1	**A**
3.2	**D**
3.3	**B**
3.4	**D**
3.5	**C**
3.6	**D**
3.7	**B**
3.8	**C**
3.9	**D**
3.10	**C**
3.11	**A**
3.12	**D**
3.13	**B**
3.14	**A**
3.15	**C**
3.16	**C**
3.17	**B**
3.18	**A**
3.19	**A**
3.20	**D**

Chapter 4: Leisure		Chapter 5: Technology		Chapter 6: The World of Work	
Question	Answer	Question	Answer	Question	Answer
4.1	B	5.1	D	6.1	C
4.2	C	5.2	B	6.2	B
4.3	D	5.3	D	6.3	B
4.4	A	5.4	A	6.4	A
4.5	B	5.5	D	6.5	D
4.6	C	5.6	D	6.6	A
4.7	D	5.7	C	6.7	B
4.8	B	5.8	D	6.8	D
4.9	A	5.9	B	6.9	A
4.10	A	5.10	B	6.10	B
4.11	C	5.11	C	6.11	A
4.12	D	5.12	C	6.12	B
4.13	B	5.13	A	6.13	C
4.14	D	5.14	A	6.14	B
4.15	B	5.15	B	6.15	D
4.16	D	5.16	C	6.16	C
4.17	B	5.17	A	6.17	B
4.18	D	5.18	B	6.18	B
4.19	C	5.19	C	6.19	C
4.20	B	5.20	A	6.20	A

Chapter 7: Tourism	
Question	Answer
7.1	D
7.2	D
7.3	B
7.4	A
7.5	A
7.6	D
7.7	A
7.8	C
7.9	D
7.10	D
7.11	D
7.12	A
7.13	B
7.14	B
7.15	C
7.16	B
7.17	A
7.18	A
7.19	A
7.20	B

Chapter 8: Identity, Culture and Festivals	
Question	Answer
8.1	D
8.2	C
8.3	C
8.4	B
8.5	C
8.6	A
8.7	B
8.8	C
8.9	D
8.10	D
8.11	A
8.12	B
8.13	A
8.14	D
8.15	C
8.16	D
8.17	B
8.18	A
8.19	C
8.20	A

Chapter 9: Social Issues	
Question	Answer
9.1	B
9.2	C
9.3	D
9.4	A
9.5	A
9.6	D
9.7	D
9.8	C
9.9	C
9.10	D
9.11	B
9.12	C
9.13	B
9.14	C
9.15	D
9.16	B
9.17	D
9.18	D
9.19	D
9.20	A

Chapter 10: Global Issues

Question	Answer
10.1	C
10.2	A
10.3	D
10.4	D
10.5	B
10.6	B
10.7	C
10.8	C
10.9	B
10.10	B
10.11	A
10.12	C
10.13	A
10.14	C
10.15	A
10.16	B
10.17	C
10.18	B
10.19	D
10.20	A

Chapter 11: Miscellaneous Vocabulary

Question	Answer
11.1	D
11.2	C
11.3	B
11.4	B
11.5	D
11.6	D
11.7	C
11.8	A
11.9	B
11.10	B
11.11	A
11.12	A
11.13	A
11.14	C
11.15	B
11.16	A
11.17	C
11.18	B
11.19	B
11.20	C

Chapter 12: Articles, Nouns and Pronouns		Chapter 13: Verbs and Tenses		Chapter 14: Adjectives and Adverbs		Chapter 15: Miscellaneous Grammar	
Question	Answer	Question	Answer	Question	Answer	Question	Answer
12.1	B	13.1	C	14.1	C	15.1	D
12.2	A	13.2	A	14.2	B	15.2	C
12.3	D	13.3	D	14.3	A	15.3	A
12.4	A	13.4	A	14.4	C	15.4	B
12.5	D	13.5	A	14.5	D	15.5	B
12.6	A	13.6	B	14.6	C	15.6	D
12.7	C	13.7	D	14.7	B	15.7	B
12.8	C	13.8	A	14.8	B	15.8	A
12.9	C	13.9	C	14.9	B	15.9	C
12.10	D	13.10	C	14.10	D	15.10	B
12.11	A	13.11	B	14.11	B	15.11	C
12.12	C	13.12	D	14.12	B	15.12	B
12.13	B	13.13	A	14.13	D	15.13	D
12.14	C	13.14	B	14.14	B	15.14	D
12.15	B	13.15	D	14.15	A	15.15	A
12.16	A	13.16	B	14.16	A	15.16	A
12.17	C	13.17	B	14.17	B	15.17	C
12.18	D	13.18	C	14.18	A	15.18	B
12.19	C	13.19	D	14.19	C	15.19	D
12.20	A	13.20	A	14.20	C	15.20	D
12.21	B	13.21	C	14.21	A	15.21	A
12.22	C	13.22	C	14.22	A	15.22	B
12.23	A	13.23	B	14.23	A	15.23	D
12.24	B	13.24	A	14.24	B	15.24	C
12.25	D	13.25	D	14.25	D	15.25	D
12.26	B	13.26	A	14.26	C	15.26	B
12.27	A	13.27	B	14.27	D	15.27	C
12.28	C	13.28	A	14.28	B	15.28	D
12.29	A	13.29	D	14.29	C	15.29	D
12.30	D	13.30	B	14.30	B	15.30	B

INDEX

Chapter 1: People and Relationships		Chapter 2: Home	
Question	Topic	Question	Topic
1.1	Family Information (M)	2.1	House Descriptions (M)
1.2	Key Questions (E)	2.2	Rooms of the House 1 (M)
1.3	Physical Appearance (E)	2.3	Rooms of the House 2 (M)
1.4	Family Members 1 (H)	2.4	Kitchen and Bedroom (M)
1.5	Family Members 2 (E)	2.5	Home nouns (E)
1.6	Appearance and Character (M)	2.6	Places to Live (H)
1.7	Personality (M)	2.7	What You Can Do (H)
1.8	Family Description (E)	2.8	Places in Town 1 (E)
1.9	Getting on with Family (H)	2.9	Places in Town 2 (E)
1.10	Difficult Relations (H)	2.10	Deciding where to live (E)
1.11	Best Friend (H)	2.11	City Description (H)
1.12	Activities with Friends (H)	2.12	Village Description (H)
1.13	Friendships (E)	2.13	Accommodation Description (E)
1.14	Ideal Friend (M)	2.14	City Life 1 (M)
1.15	Arguments with Friends (H)	2.15	City Life 2 (H)
1.16	Different Generations (M)	2.16	Countryside Living (E)
1.17	Marriage (H)	2.17	Where I Used to Live (H)
1.18	A Wedding (E)	2.18	Directions (M)
1.19	Having Children (H)	2.19	Where I Will Live (H)
1.20	Role Models (M)	2.20	Ideal Place to Live (H)

Chapter 3: Education	
Question	**Topic**
3.1	School Subjects (E)
3.2	Opinions of Subjects 1 (M)
3.3	Opinions of Subjects 2 (E)
3.4	Travel to School (M)
3.5	People and Places in School (H)
3.6	School Description (E)
3.7	School Uniform (H)
3.8	Qualifications (M)
3.9	School Equipment (M)
3.10	Subject-specific Activities (E)
3.11	Opinions of Teachers (M)
3.12	Ideal Teacher (E)
3.13	Homework (H)
3.14	School Trip (M)
3.15	Primary School (H)
3.16	Ideal School (H)
3.17	Exams (H)
3.18	Gap Year (H)
3.19	University (H)
3.20	Studying Abroad (E)

Chapter 4: Leisure	
Question	**Topic**
4.1	Sports (E)
4.2	Sport Verbs (M)
4.3	Sport Opinions 1 (H)
4.4	Sport Opinions 2 (H)
4.5	People, Places and Sport (E)
4.6	Watching TV (M)
4.7	TV Programmes (M)
4.8	TV Opinions (E)
4.9	TV Habits (H)
4.10	Film Preferences (E)
4.11	Film Types (H)
4.12	A Recent Film (H)
4.13	Reading (M)
4.14	Music Preferences (H)
4.15	Music Activities (E)
4.16	Hobbies (E)
4.17	Future Activities (M)
4.18	Free Time (M)
4.19	Last Weekend (H)
4.20	If We Could (H)

Chapter 7: Tourism	
Question	**Topic**
7.1	Holiday Wishes (E)
7.2	Transport (E)
7.3	Plane Travel (M)
7.4	Holiday Types (E)
7.5	Holiday Problems (H)
7.6	Holiday Preferences 1 (H)
7.7	Holiday Preferences 2 (H)
7.8	Holiday Process (M)
7.9	Typical Holiday (E)
7.10	Reasons for Holidays (M)
7.11	Holiday Activities (H)
7.12	For Tourists (E)
7.13	Accommodation Types (M)
7.14	A Recent Holiday (H)
7.15	Countries and Nationalities (H)
7.16	Dream Holiday (M)
7.17	Tourist Guide (E)
7.18	Disastrous Holiday (H)
7.19	Hotel Review (H)
7.20	Future Holiday Plans (M)

Chapter 8: Identity, Culture and Festivals	
Question	**Topic**
8.1	Clothes 1 (E)
8.2	Clothes 2 (E)
8.3	Clothes for Different Occasions (M)
8.4	Fashion (H)
8.5	Mother's Day (E)
8.6	Birthdays (H)
8.7	Birthday Party (H)
8.8	Gifts (H)
8.9	Religion (M)
8.10	Christmas (E)
8.11	Christmas Food (M)
8.12	Christmas Comparison (M)
8.13	Venice Carnival (E)
8.14	Easter (H)
8.15	La Pizza Margherita (E)
8.16	Sporting Events (M)
8.17	New Year (M)
8.18	Churches in Sicily (H)
8.19	International Day (H)
8.20	La Festa Della Repubblica (H)

Chapter 11: Miscellaneous Vocabulary	
Question	**Topic**
11.1	Questions Words 1 (E)
11.2	Questions Words 2 (E)
11.3	Questions and Answers (M)
11.4	Dimensions (E)
11.5	Measurements (M)
11.6	Shapes (H)
11.7	Familiar Phrases (E)
11.8	Apologising (M)
11.9	Colours (M)
11.10	Materials (H)
11.11	Distance (H)
11.12	Location (H)
11.13	Lateness (H)
11.14	Opinions (E)
11.15	Comparatives 1 (H)
11.16	Comparatives 2 (H)
11.17	Time Phrases (E)
11.18	Time of Day (M)
11.19	Connectives (H)
11.20	Synonyms (M)

Chapter 14: Adjectives and Adverbs	
Question	**Topic**
14.1	Identifying Adjectives (E)
14.2	Position of Adjectives 1 (E)
14.3	Position of Adjectives 2 (M)
14.4	Masculine Adjectives (E)
14.5	Feminine Adjectives (E)
14.6	Plural Adjectives 1 (M)
14.7	Plural Adjectives 2 (H)
14.8	Types of Adjectives 1 (M)
14.9	Types of Adjectives 2 (M)
14.10	Possessive Adjectives 1 (H)
14.11	Possessive Adjectives 2 (E)
14.12	Indefinite Adjectives (M)
14.13	Comparative Adjectives 1 (E)
14.14	Comparative Adjectives 2 (E)
14.15	Superlative Adjectives (H)
14.16	All (M)
14.17	Demonstrative Adjectives (M)
14.18	Purpose of Adverbs (E)
14.19	Identifying Adverbs 1 (E)
14.20	Identifying Adverbs 2 (H)
14.21	Identifying Adverbs 3 (H)
14.22	Adverb Formation (E)
14.23	Adverb Translations (M)
14.24	Position of Adverbs 1 (M)
14.25	Position of Adverbs 2 (H)
14.26	Adverbs of Frequency (M)
14.27	Adverbs of Time (H)
14.28	Adverbs of Place (H)
14.29	Adverbial Phrases (H)
14.30	Adjective or Adverb? (H)

Chapter 15: Miscellaneous Grammar	
Question	**Topic**
15.1	Dates 1 (E)
15.2	Dates 2 (E)
15.3	Cardinal Numbers (E)
15.4	Ordinal Numbers (E)
15.5	Telling the Time 1 (E)
15.6	Telling the Time 2 (M)
15.7	*Giornata* vs. *Giorno* (M)
15.8	People (E)
15.9	Prepositions (E)
15.10	Compound Prepositions (H)
15.11	Preposition *a* (M)
15.12	Preposition *di* (M)
15.13	Articulated Prepositions (M)
15.14	Prepositions with Interrogatives (H)
15.15	Negatives (E)
15.16	Negatives Question and Answer (H)
15.17	Negatives in Compound Tenses (H)
15.18	Prefixes (M)
15.19	Prefixes with *Prendere* (H)
15.20	Suffixes (H)
15.21	Gerund (H)
15.22	Ago (E)
15.23	Uses of *Da* (H)
15.24	Elision (E)
15.25	Imperative (M)
15.26	*Essere* vs. *Stare* (M)
15.27	*Conoscere* vs. *Sapare* (M)
15.28	To Leave (M)
15.29	Verbs + *a*/*di* (H)
15.30	*Volerci* (H)

Confirmed Future Titles in the *With Honours* Series

GAMSAT Written Communication: A Practical Guide to Essay Composition

GAMSAT Chemistry: Practice Questions with Detailed Solutions

GAMSAT Physics: Practice Questions with Detailed Solutions

MCAT Biology: Practice Questions with Detailed Solutions

Pre-Clinical Medicine: MCQs and EMQs with Detailed Solutions

GCSE (9-1) French: Practice Questions with Detailed Solutions

For further information about the *With Honours* series and any other enquiries, please visit us at withhonours.co.uk or send us an email at: contact@withhonours.co.uk

 Facebook @WithHonours

 Twitter @With_Honours

 Pinterest with_honours

 Instagram @with_honours

WITH HONOURS

Made in the USA
Coppell, TX
03 June 2021

56754845R00187